TEXAS GARDENING
FOR THE 21ST CENTURY

Planning, Constructing, Planting,
Embellishing, and Maintaining
Your Landscape

bright sky press

2365 Rice Blvd., Suite 202, Houston, Texas 77005
www.brightskypress.com

ISBN 978-1-933979-68-7

10   9   8   7   6   5   4   3   2   1

Library of Congress information on file with publisher.

Book and cover design by Isabel Hernandez and Hina Hussein
Illustrations by Bobbie Beal
Architectural Drawings by Nan Booth Simpson
Cover illustration by Nan Booth Simpson

This book is dedicated to Malcolm Beck, who has been at the forefront of the organic movement in Texas: A farmer in the San Antonio area since 1957, he was considered "faddish, even foolish" for operating without pesticides or chemicals of any sort. He not only made his fruit and vegetable farm a success, but also founded Garden-Ville in 1980 to sell the compost he produced on the property. He influenced a number of people such as John Dromgoole, Howard Garrett and Bob Webster, who have, in turn, reached thousands of gardeners all over the state with their radio programs and publications. Beck's books have been especially inspirational to me. Because we are both getting up in years, the opportunity to spend a couple of hours talking to him about sustainable gardening last year was something I'll always treasure.

— Nan Booth Simpson, April 2009

Table of Contents

Acknowledgements

Many people encouraged me as I wrote this book. I especially want to thank my coauthor, Patricia McHargue, who edited every word and offered innumerable suggestions about making it "reader-friendly" to a non-professional gardening audience. Ed Barger of Landscape Lighting Supply Co. in Richardson proofed the section on landscape lighting and explained new developments in his industry. Esper K. Chandler, an agronomist and soil scientist, who owns Texas Plant and Soil Lab, contributed his considerable expertise to the chapter on soil. Herb specialist Sara Holland provided me with a plant list for a comprehensive Texas culinary herb garden. Thanks also to Austin friends Maydelle and Sam Fason who shared their personal experiences with composting and waste management.

INTRODUCTION

Introduction

As a Texas-registered landscape architect, I have written this book in first person, sharing everything I have learned as a designer of residential gardens for over twenty-five years. Patricia McHargue, my coauthor of *The Texas Garden Resource Book*, served as editor and advisor for this book. We have been friends since childhood, and I designed Pat's first real garden. Pat, an English major at The University of Texas, continues to correct my tendency toward colloquialisms and extravagantly long sentences. If she didn't completely understand something technical I wrote about soil or drainage, it was rewritten until the subject matter was clearly stated for a lay audience!

While most homeowners are eager to immediately leap into planting, this book counsels a much more thoughtful approach. *Texas Gardening for the 21ˢᵗ Century* is arranged in the order in which the work of a landscape architect progresses: designing, constructing, planting, and embellishing the garden with furnishings and art. The last chapter gives instruction for maintaining that perfect garden. The book (and garden design in general) begins with "Finding Your Garden Style." The style should not only be appropriate for the region, but should also fit the architecture of the home and the personality and lifestyle of its owners.

Chapter Two, "Sources of Inspiration and Information," I talk about some of our favorite public gardens (a complete guide to Texas botanical gardens, parks and nature preserves can be found at the beginning of each of the twelve chapters of *The Texas Garden Resource Book*). I have tried to offer enough advice to point gardeners in the right direction and enough horticultural information to assist them in asking the right questions. Rather than including a plant list, I've provided a comprehensive list of Texas garden books on that subject, plus many other great sources of information.

Chapter Three, "Design," asks readers to first envision how they will use their valuable outdoor space. Included is instruction for creating a Master Plan addressing drainage, walkways, terraces, fences, play areas, garden structures, etc. Chapter Four, "Construction," compares hardscape materials and discusses how to prepare for construction and plan for lighting and irrigation systems. Before moving into planting design, Chapter Five provides instruction for soil preparation, the single most important factor in gardening.

Chapters Six and Seven are about planting design. It is not enough to love plants. It is creating a balanced composition of color and texture that transforms a "yard" into a garden. An increasing number of homeowners are no longer satisfied with planting a flat of zinnias and retiring for the summer. For some, gardening has become a competitive sport! For those who crave some rare bulb or a special agave that can only be found in the wild on a remote site in the Trans-Pecos, we have found at least one grower who maintains a fabulous online catalog.

We're fairly certain that the majority of people who will read this book truly enjoy their gardens, but have limited time to spend. They want to spend more of that time relaxing, so Chapter Eight is about a garden's furniture and accessories, the things that make a garden comfortable and inviting. Chapter Nine addresses ongoing maintenance, with labor-saving advice for pest management, water conservation and proper pruning.

Money-saving tips are sprinkled throughout the text to suggest economical ways for readers to improve their gardens. The text is laced with timesaving ideas, and I have carefully researched environmentally friendly products that will make every aspect of gardening easier and more rewarding. This book is meant to encourage gardeners, not to fuel the fires of guilt or send overachievers to a chiropractor's office.

As advocates of sustainable gardening, we both fall into a middle ground. We confess to the occasional use of herbicide when confronted with poison ivy, but we are willing to accept some serendipitous surprises the birds bring in. And, although we advise against it, we are both guilty of impulse buying. (You wouldn't have believed how many plants we piled into the back of my car as we returned to our homes after weeklong research trips!) But, once you have carefully selected a good spot for some gorgeous goodie you couldn't live without and have given the plant reasonable care, don't hesitate to discard it if it doesn't thrive in your garden. It just didn't "belong" there. Part of the fun of gardening is experimentation. Enjoy!

Follow the design process for a Texas Hill Country garden on pages 55, 57, 59, 66, 122, 123, and 161.

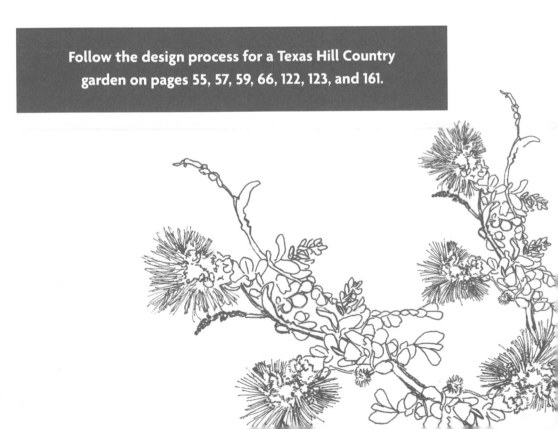

1
Garden Style

Garden Style

We Texans love our state, but we have to admit that Texas is not the easiest place in the world to be a gardener. Locate the center of Texas on a globe and trace with your finger a path around the world at the 32nd parallel. You may be surprised to find that the trip takes you to Morocco, Syria and on around through northern India and central China. While distance from the equator is only one of the factors that affect plant life, in terms of climate Texas has more in common with Egypt than England. For more than a century, however, Texas gardeners patterned their landscape plantings after Northern European gardens. Big mistake!

We can't blame the early settlers. They brought to this vast, virtually vacant land a no-nonsense approach to gardening. On their journey to Texas, homemakers might have stowed a few precious flower seeds and bulbs along with the vegetable seeds, but few ornamental plantings adorned the earliest Texas homes. Houses were sited to catch prevailing breezes, and the gardens were made for feeding the family. The location of the garden would have been based on soil quality and proximity to water rather than any aesthetic consideration. Life on the frontier was not about impressing the neighbors.

A Sense of Place

Well into the 21st century — more than 160 years after Texas became a state — we now are beginning to appreciate our botanical heritage. Lady Bird Johnson once observed, "Texas should look like Texas, and Vermont like Vermont." Within a state as large and diverse as Texas, I would add that the Piney Woods should look like Piney Woods and the Trans-Pecos like Trans-Pecos. As homeowners plan a new landscape or edit their existing gardens to reflect an emphasis on sustainability in the new century, our first design consideration should be regional character, which differs radically from place to place.

The Texas Garden Resource Book discusses in detail the gardening possibilities in each of the state's twelve regions: Cross Timbers & Grand Prairie, Trinity Blacklands, Piney Woods, Coastal Prairies & Marshes, Coastal Bend, Valley, Rio Grande Plains, Central Blacklands & Savannas, Hill Country, Red Rolling Plains, High Plains and Trans-Pecos. In each of these regions, designers are now seeking to develop distinct regional styles that make use of indigenous plants. Before beginning to design (or redesign) your garden, read at least the section on the region where you live in The Texas Garden Resource Book.

The purpose of this book is to provide a road map to a more enlightened way of gardening. Interestingly, the best path may follow the gardening practices of our earliest settlers. I'm cautiously optimistic. I fervently believe that a younger, environmentally educated generation will work (and spend the money necessary) to bring nature back into harmony before it is too late. Already there is widespread interest in the plants that were here when the settlers arrived. There's also new fervor for farming and gardening without the 20th-century commercial fertilizers and pesticides that pollute our rivers and groundwater supplies.

Average Annual Rainfall

1. More than 56 inches
2. 45 to 56 inches
3. 33 to 44 inches
4. 21 to 32 inches
5. Eight to 20 inches
6. Less than eight inches

Most Texans are also coming to terms with the fact that our water demands will soon exceed the capacity of our reservoirs and aquifers. We're beginning to appreciate plants that can survive on scant rainfall. From new water-wise demonstration gardens and nature centers that extol sustainable gardening, we are learning how to choose plants that conserve precious water and offer food and protection to wildlife. But, many homeowners still haven't bought into the program. Some would argue that "sustainable garden" is an oxymoron. Sustainability should not be misinterpreted as a garden that can be kept attractive without maintenance. The later chapters of this book will seek to convince the skeptics that sustainability is achieved by good design, soil restoration, proper plant selection and sensible maintenance. Once you understand the science (climate, soils and "character" of your region), you are halfway toward finding your garden style.

A Sense of Time

Gardening is both art and science. The "art" factor that influences your garden design should begin with the architectural style of your home. Many of the new homes built today refer to architectural styles of other places and times. As never before, landscape architects and designers are drawing on untapped historical models for shaping the space and detailing the walks, walls and structures of both new and existing residential landscapes.

Societies have always tended to adhere to fixed patterns of architecture and garden design that fit their own cultures. Thus, Roman gardens were generally all of one type (ordered) and quite different from typical Chinese gardens of the same period (naturalistic). Not only were the plant materials different, but also the trees, shrubs and perennials were arranged so differently that people of one culture might not have recognized the gardens of the other as "true" gardens! We cannot, *should not* design a garden without understanding something about garden history.

Gardens did not originate as aesthetic enterprises. They were necessary to sustain life. However, the garden has always been a place to express spiritual values while providing food for the family and opportunities for recreation and renewal. Rich in symbolism, gardens reflected the needs and dreams of the cultures within which they were made. Because of the ephemeral nature of gardens, we have few tangible records. What we know of garden design is deduced from the spacing of ancient buildings, from images on walls, vases and carpets and from literature. There can be no doubt, however, that from the beginning, garden design has fluctuated between polar opposites — ordered, intellectual, symmetrical vs. naturalistic, intuitive and asymmetrical.

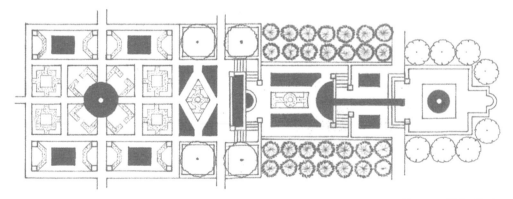

European Water Garden

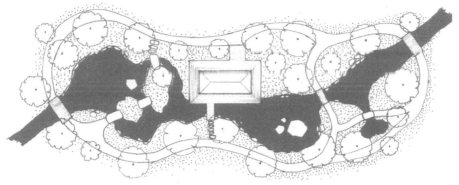

Asian Water Garden

FROM MESOPOTAMIA TO MODERNISM

The Ancient World

Gardening began in Mesopotamia. Archeologists have found evidence of large-scale irrigation projects that flourished as early as 6000 B.C. It may be no accident that the first true gardens documented in Western civilization occurred in hot, dry climates. What could be more primal than the desire for a cool, green oasis in a harsh environment? The Garden of Eden as described in the Old Testament was thought to be in the fertile plain between the Tigris and Euphrates, and sacred texts of ancient Mesopotamian civilizations referred to paradise gardens. The word "paradise" came from Persian to Greek to English; its original meaning was literally "a walled enclosure."

A tomb painting at Thebes (circa 1400 B.C.) depicts the home and garden of an official in the court of Amenhotep III. The property appears to be similar in size to a city lot in Dallas or Houston; it is completely surrounded by high walls, which provided shelter from drying winds. From the entrance gate in the center of the front wall, an arbor-shaded path leads to the house, which is sited at the back edge of the property. The garden's two halves are designed as mirror images: Raised planting beds for herbs, vegetables and flowers adjacent to rectangular ponds filled with fish and water plants flank the central vine-covered arbor. Fruit trees planted around the outer walls provide additional shade and beauty. What is amazing is how pleasant and appropriate this elegantly simple plan drawn 3,400 years ago would be in a Texas landscape today!

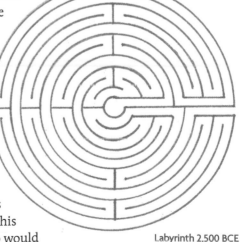

Labyrinth 2,500 BCE

A recurring design theme throughout Western history has been the square divided into four parts, symbolizing the four corners of the earth and the four rivers of heaven. Generally a fountain stands in the center of the square. This straightforward, symmetrical form is depicted on Persian carpets and seen in the atriums of Pompeii. It appears again in the courtyards of Moorish Spain (the meeting place of Islam and Christian cultures) and in the medieval cloisters and Tudor herbal gardens of Northern Europe.

Orderly geometric forms provided a sense of comfort in a disorderly world and fit well within the confines of an enclosure. Throughout most of history, people had good reason to fear the open countryside. Cities, homes and gardens were normally built in a defensive mode. Where large symbolic structures such as Mesopotamian ziggurats or Egyptian tombs were built out in vast open space, the approaches employed long, straight vistas flanked by mirror-image plantings to create a sense of order.

Rigid axial geometry extended even into the large parks in the heart of the Persian Empire, where kings and nobles hunted wild animals imported from the far reaches of their domain. These heavily planted open spaces inspired the Greeks to landscape their agoras. But here, we see a change. Because their country's dramatic topography didn't lend itself to symmetry, the Greeks fit their highly geometric architecture within the natural terrain rather than trying to unduly order nature. While the residential gardens of classical Greece would have been enclosed, Greek literature contains numerous references to sacred springs and groves and vistas of mountains and open seas, implying a reverence for the natural environment.

Roman Gardens

With the Romans came order and planning on a scale never before known. Roman city homes were designed with open interior courtyards where colonnaded covered walkways wrapped around symmetrically arranged planting beds and water features. The country estates, however, represented a new form of residential garden design that took formal, ordered gardens and stretched them out into the open landscape. The ruins of Hadrian's Villa, built in the second century A.D., gives us a glimpse of the long, tree-shaded promenades and parterres (patterned ornamental planting beds meant to be viewed from overlooking windows and terraces) that typified the *villa rustica*. Its 750 acres were organized into architectural "compartments" enclosed with cypress, boxwood and laurel hedges and elegantly ornamented with columns, fountains and statuary.

The Romans may have been the first civilization to design gardens for sheer pleasure. Their villas were replete with pools and bathhouses and outdoor theaters. And, like all people living in hot climates, they enjoyed eating outdoors. Undoubtedly music, dancing and theatricals would have accompanied the meals. Such an embracement of the open countryside was possible only in a society governed by rule of law.

The Asian Aesthetic

While the symbolism and complex philosophical premises of two thousand years of garden-making in Asia may escape a Western viewer, the pure visual impact of a naturalistic Asian garden rarely fails to please even the most casual observer. Chinese landscape design influenced English garden style in the eighteenth century. Japanese garden design inspired American designers in the twentieth century.

The Chinese word for landscape is a combination of the characters for mountain and water. Old Chinese art depicts mountains rising above a misty landscape, water cascading into shimmering lakes, craggy coastlines and wooded hillsides. The ancient Chinese saw the workings of universal forces and laws in their landscape, and their gardens were based on harmony between opposing forces.

Garden art flowed from China to Japan through Korea in the sixth century. While very different styles evolved out of these different cultures, all Asian gardens use rock and water to represent heaven and earth. Unlike Western landscape painters and garden designers, the Asian artist assumes the human is in the landscape, not viewing it from the outside. Asian gardens point out man's insignificance in relation to the majesty of untamed nature.

Chinese gardens remained rich in complexity, but Japanese garden styles became increasingly simplified over time. The earliest Japanese "paradise gardens" were similar to the Chinese, with elaborate adornment and concern for "correct" placement of stones, streams and waterfalls. Even the plant materials were aligned by rules of compass and astronomical instruments. The idea of a garden used for strolling was adopted in Japan during this first period of garden design, but the strolling gardens we find in Americanized Japanese gardens today have more in common with later phases of Japanese garden layout.

Cross Section of a Japanese Garden

After Zen Buddhism flowered in the twelfth century, Japanese gardens increasingly focused on miniature landscapes. Simple compositions of rocks, evergreens and ground covers create intriguing textural contrasts. Layered plant materials conform to the contours of the land, framing little vignettes or disclosing vistas that suggest limitless space. The art of bonsai is part of this trend toward miniaturization and understated elegance.

Drinking tea to prevent drowsiness during meditation was elevated to an art form in the sixteenth century. Tranquil tea gardens were designed to inspire deep contemplation. From these gardens evolved utilitarian features such as stone pathways, wash basins and lanterns to light the way at night. The Japanese also made increasing use of evergreen plants and stones employed as sculpture. Boulders were balanced asymmetrically; for example, three small stones might be played against a large one. Rock was also used to represent flowing water, with different sizes of stones suggesting different sounds and velocities.

Asian gardens are composed of asymmetrically balanced interlocking parts, with materials shaped as mirror images of others nearby. Patterns are repeated to create a jigsaw puzzle effect, yet the transitions between the garden's spaces are smooth. Where Western people most often respond to a straight axis (which allows them to know exactly where they are), the gardens in Japan devise ways to create mystery.

Plants are used to create a feeling of enclosure; walkways are made difficult to negotiate; hidden secrets are revealed behind each bend in the path. There will be great distances hinted-at and the suggestion of things unsaid, all used to draw the visitor irresistibly into the experience.

Medieval European Gardens

After the fall of the Roman Empire, civil disorder became rampant, and gardens once again assumed inwardly oriented forms. Monasteries that flourished during this period were built around interior cloister gardens designed in the form of a cross for walking and meditating. Wrapped around the monastery, but within the compound, were "physick" gardens for growing healing herbs and the vegetable plots and orchards necessary to sustain communal life.

As the general public retreated to the protection of castles and fortified cities, gardens existed primarily for such practical purposes as growing medicinal and edible plants. Drawings from the period depict castle gardens replete with poetic touches in the form of pergolas and fountains. Walled cities were tightly packed, however, so the fabled village fairs and major agricultural pursuits took place in fields outside the walls.

Once the need for fortification diminished, towns spread beyond the walls and people once again began enjoying the luxury of little gardens attached to their houses. By the end of the medieval period, gardens had evolved into something quite fanciful with knot patterns, topiaries, mazes and bowling greens.

Islamic Gardens in Spain

While Christian Europe was still in a period of isolation, Islam (founded in 622 A.D.) had spread by 712 from Persia to the Pyrenees. When Moroccans (Moors) conquered the southern half of Spain, they brought with them a joyful appreciation of the outdoors. Based in part on climatic factors and in part on an Islamic imperative for family privacy, even the smallest house was built around an open-air patio. Characterized by colorful decorative flourishes and fragrant plants, these outdoor rooms were central to daily living.

Typically the spaces were symmetrical in design, like the foursquare Persian gardens that preceded them. A fountain customarily stood in the center of crossing paths, which were constructed of unglazed tiles laid in intricate geometric patterns. Ornate iron gates punctuated the thick white stucco outer walls. Inside walls, fountains and shady niches were richly decorated with polychrome glazed tiles (*azulejos*).

It was in the economical use of water that these Moorish gardens excelled. Based on the ideal of an oasis and always audible, the fountains and pools presented water as life-giving, which indeed it was. In this arid climate, planting beds were kept simple in design. Orange trees and palms provided shade, and flowering plants spilled out of containers. By the time that Islam was expelled from Spain in 1492, the Moorish aesthetic was firmly entrenched. It influenced the renaissance in the rest of Europe, and it was the garden style that the Spaniards brought to the New World.

Moorish Garden

Renaissance Gardens of Italy and France

The Renaissance not only marked a return to civility in Italy, but also a hunger for the civilization of former times. Fourteenth-century Italian pleasure gardens were designed as stage sets, recalling the ancient gods with temple buildings, ruins and grottoes. It was a time for embracing the ancient world. Copies of Greek and Roman statuary appeared in niches or as the focal point of an axis. Urns, balustrades, columns and topiaries punctuated the landscapes, and here the Roman style of arranging plantings into parterre beds became fashionable again.

By terracing hillsides and utilizing natural springs, the Italians created fantastic water gardens with every form of fountain and water cascading down grand staircases. The best known of the Renaissance country estates, Villa d'Este at Tivoli, is a triumph of hydraulic engineering. According to landscape historians, its water organ produced "such unusual sound effects as the booming of a cannon, the song of birds, the bedlam of exploding fireworks and tunes played on organ pipes."

While this villa's fountains are playful in the extreme, its labyrinthine plantings are rigidly geometrical. Were they not deliciously overgrown today, the square, compartmentalized planting beds would appear as monotonous as they did at the time. Other Italian villas more deftly terraced the landscape, using diagonal sight lines to break up the rigid bilateral symmetry and creating complicated routes for visitors to reach the various focal points.

Cross Section of an Italian Villa

The Italians excelled at creating gardens that could withstand their country's dry, hot summers. Floral displays were almost nonexistent. Instead, the sights and sounds in renaissance gardens were contrived to counteract the effects of scorching sun. Playing against cool stonework, the grays and greens of neatly clipped shrubbery soothe the psyche. Crunchy gravel paths, fragrances of sage, cypress and rosemary and the sound of water augment the cooling effects.

A taste for such formality spread from Italy into northern Europe. Rococo fountains, clipped shrubbery and avenues of trees still defined the sight lines, but where the topography was more level, the gardens became progressively less dramatic. In France, the parterres evolved into baroque *parterres de broderies*, planting beds embroidered with flowers. Visually interconnected and totally symmetrical, these beds were organized within crisply defined boxwood edges. French design reached a preposterous apex at Versailles where gardeners changed the color schemes in the planting beds several times a day just for the amusement of the royal family. (No wonder Marie Antoinette was beheaded. Perhaps it was the gardeners who instigated it!)

The English Landscape School

The English countryside as we think of it today was "invented" in the eighteenth century. At the time, most of England's trees had been felled for lumber, and the land had been terraced for strip farming. Grand country homes were surrounded by walled gardens with patterned flowerbeds (pale imitations of Renaissance gardens in Italy and France) to shut out views of mundane agricultural pursuits.

In mid-century, the walls came down. Wealthy landholders opened vistas into vast rolling lawns and serpentine ponds surrounded by great sweeps of deciduous trees. Straight lines disappeared from the landscape. The gardens that Capability Brown and other designers of the era created for their clients were actually no more "natural" than earlier English gardens, but the landscape was made to appear natural. Views from the house became all-important. In bringing grass right up to the doorstep, however, eighteenth-century English landscape designers left the houses looking somewhat austere.

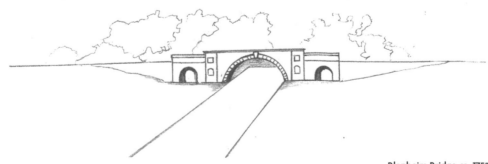

Blenheim Bridge ca. 1752

Blenheim Bridge ca. 1770

"Capability" Brown raised the level of an existing canal and reshaped the land to create a naturalistic lake

Several factors contributed to this notion of co-opting the countryside. French landscape paintings and poetic Chinese woodcuts popular at the time had created a new, romantic vision of nature. But more than just artistic, the naturalistic revolution was a political statement. Strongly antimonarchist, it greatly influenced Thomas Jefferson, whose vast greensward at Monticello was the first in America in the style of the English Landscape Gardening School.

Frederick Law Olmsted, who is remembered chiefly as the designer of New York City's Central Park, was the spiritual successor to this soft, pastoral planting style. It must be remembered, however, that English-influenced landscape designers were working with acres and acres of countryside. Few facilities can support vast expanses of mown grass today. A few large public parks and well-designed golf courses still exemplify the eighteenth-century ideal of naturalistic beauty. In these open, rolling landscapes, we can get a feel for the effect of clipped grass, sparkling ponds, swaths of trees and picturesque background vistas.

One regrettable consequence of English Landscape Style has been the ubiquitous suburban lawn. Grass takes on an entirely different appearance when the rolling acreage of a country estate is reduced to a small urban plot, but, for better or for worse, manicured front lawns remain as the major cultural holdover from the Age of Enlightenment.

Early American Gardens

Elements of medieval walled gardens, seventeenth-century renaissance design and the naturalistic style of eighteenth-century England merged in the gardens of America, especially in the South. George Washington's Mount Vernon remains a model of the early plantation landscape. Here, the front of the house overlooks a sweeping lawn outlined with trees and terminating at the soft bank of the Potomac River. The rear garden is quite formal. It features a vista across an oval turnaround for carriages and a shield-shaped bowling green flanked by symmetrical curving pathways and carefully planted lines of trees. At the far end of the bowling green is centered a low wooden gate that opens into the original approach road and leads the eye through a long, straight vista into the natural woods. Tucked behind the trees beside the bowling green are fenced gardens: a grid-plan kitchen garden on the right side and, on the left, boxwood-edged parterres holding flowers grown for cutting.

The pattern of medieval walled gardens had never disappeared entirely. Even after walls were no longer necessary for security, European farmer's wives continued to grow their herbs, fruits and vegetables behind walls to keep the livestock out. Out of this tradition came the less formal gardens of rural America, which often brimmed with a profusion of fragrant flowers as well as life-sustaining plants enclosed by tidy picket fences.

As the English style was interpreted throughout Virginia, the Carolinas and Georgia and a simplified French style developed in Louisiana, certain features remained constant. Brick gateposts typically marked the approach roads, which were lined with *allées* of magnolia or oak trees. Formal parterres traditionally graced the immediate environs, and park-like grass meadows separated the house from surrounding fields and woods.

A few such gardens might have been found in the antebellum plantations established in East Texas. While it would have been possible to maintain tree-lined entry drives and formal, symmetrical planting beds in the luxuriant Piney Woods, this garden style was clearly out of the question for settlers who moved west into the grassland prairies, where unrelenting sun and summer droughts would have quickly put an end to clipped boxwoods, azaleas and camellias. Even where the growing conditions were right, importing such shrubs was far beyond the means of most of the early immigrants to Texas.

In 1854, Frederick Law Olmsted, conservationist and social reformer, followed the Old San Antonio Road (now Texas Highway 21) through the hardscrabble countryside of northeast Texas to San Antonio. He saw no evidence of any ornamental gardening until he reached New Braunfels, where he encountered little homesteads lovingly tended by their German owners. Botanist Ferdinand Jacob Lindheimer, who built his home there in 1852, was one of several influential naturalists who studied and appreciated native Texas flora. More than 20 species, including the now-popular perennial, *Gaura lindheimeri*, bear his name. Regrettably, few people saw the beauty in our native vegetation.

Garden historian Dr. William C. Welch noted, "Today as you travel the state you can explore these relatively intact German communities, with their tidy well-planned gardens and family-oriented parks. Take note of the historic plants in cemeteries, the ornate fences, and the orchards and tree-lined streets. Public and private gardens alike have been influenced by this group of settlers."

Victorian Sensibilities

The Civil War and Victorian taste combined to put an end to the formal garden style of the Old South plantations. With the coming of the railroads, American communities began growing rapidly. Town gardens quickly evolved into something far more ornamental than rural landscapes. The advent of dependable water supplies and such "modern conveniences" as lawn mowers and canvas hoses made lawn grasses and elaborate flowerbeds more feasible. With the abandonment of the labor-intensive parterres, which had served as a transition between the house and the landscape, gardeners began banking plants around the foundations of even the most modest houses built in the late 19th century. As affluence and leisure time increased, the garden began to be seen as a healthful retreat from the vexations of everyday life.

The national press touted "correct taste," and people who built fashionable new homes in San Antonio's King William area, on Galveston's Broadway Street and in other prosperous enclaves were not to be outdone. They surrounded their residences with tight corsets of shrubbery and dotted the lawns with sentimental statues, pergolas, dovecotes, rose arbors, fountains and fishponds. Flowerbeds cut into the lawns in the shapes of hearts, circles and fans and brimming with showstopping "bedding plants" became increasingly popular. Plants came to be prized as "specimens" rather than part of a soothing overall mass.

It was a time of great energy in the field of horticulture in Texas. A now-thriving nursery industry began introducing a wide variety of plant materials for Texas gardens. Unfortunately, the plants native to Texas were forsaken in the effort to be fashionable. Fascination with "exotic" plants reached a zenith as the twentieth century began. City gardens were often designed by nurserymen who imported ornamental shrubs and trees from all over the world. In this environment, no one was propagating our own native plants. It's interesting to note that many of the plants we consider as Southern as "grits and gravy," were introductions from China and Japan — gardenias, mimosas, boxwoods, daylilies, althaeas, and flowering quince!

Victorian Terraium

Vestiges of nineteenth-century design ideas remain to this day. Intensively pruned foundation plantings still surround many houses, long after the high foundations of Victorian-era homes have given way to slab construction. And most of our gardens are still brimming with imported, nonnative plants that generally require inordinate quantities of water to survive the summer.

However gaudily their displays of petunias, marigolds and zinnias were executed, the Victorians pursued city beautification with a passion. In public parks throughout Texas today we still see happy holdovers from the era's design ideas. Maintenance costs have diminished the exuberance of former times, but brightly colored flowers are still used to create a sense of place, as evidenced by the much-photographed Flower Clock at the intersection of State Highway 114 and O'Connor Boulevard in Las Colinas (Irving) and at hundreds of entries to new subdivisions across the state.

Devoting a separate section of the garden to roses and planting them in a formal arrangement appears to have been another late-nineteenth-century phenomenon. The American Rose Society, formed in 1899, is responsible for most of the rose displays and test sites we enjoy in parks throughout Texas, most notably in Tyler, but also in towns from Victoria to El Paso. Enthusiasm for single-species gardens has inspired other plant societies (chrysanthemum, iris, daylily, canna, etc.) to display their prize-winning blooms in numerous Texas public parks and gardens. Greenhouses allowed homeowners to indulge their enthusiasm for palms, bromeliads, cacti, orchids and assorted tropical exotics from all over the world.

Cottage Garden Style

In the late 1800s, English painter-turned-garden designer Gertrude Jekyll led a revolt against imported plants and Victorian garden styles. Her work revived the strong architectural forms of Elizabethan walled gardens, but she softened the walls with unpruned shrubs and profuse perennials. She made the transitions between house and garden in rhythmic stages, connecting different areas of the garden with grassy paths flanked by double flower borders. Her soft, harmonic hues could not have been more different from the bold color contrasts that typified urban Victorian style in this country.

Contemporaneously with the arts and crafts movement, which stressed quality of workmanship, she accented her gardens with simple, classical garden furniture, elaborate pergolas and handsome containers. The English country homes that Ms. Jekyll embellished are mansions by today's standards, but the beguiling charm of the cottage garden lives on at a different scale today. The designs of her successors — 20th-century English designers Penelope Hobhouse, Rosemary Verey and Graham Stuart Thomas — continue to inspire gardeners on both sides of the Atlantic. At the heart of this garden tradition is a love of such old-fashioned plant materials as shrub roses, flowering vines and billowing perennials chosen for texture, color and fragrance.

Beaux-Arts Classicism

After the turn of the twentieth century, classical architecture supplanted fanciful Victorian residential styles throughout the United States as architects, trained at the Ecole des Beaux-Arts in Paris, promoted a new sense of restraint. With this change came a returning taste for a more formal approach to the landscape. The discovery of oil allowed Texas' newly affluent citizens to begin building suburban villas in the fashionable new developments of our growing cities.

City residences were now sited farther back from the street, surrounded by manicured grass and punctuated with symmetrical arrangements of clipped hedges and obligatory rose gardens. Where the prairie landscape offered neither dramatic topography nor venerable trees, neoclassical garden style in Texas amounted to little more than a "suitable setting." Several notable landscape architects set up practices in Texas during the era, however, and a few Texas gardens compared favorably with any estate garden produced in the country at the time.

In The Golden Age of American Gardens: Proud Owners, Private Estates, 1890–1940, Mac Griswold and Eleanor Weller provide details on the development of Bayou Bend in Houston's River Oaks where Miss Ima Hogg carved a magnificent fourteen-acre garden out of dense woods. The book also commends the DeGolyer Estate, which is incorporated into The Dallas Arboretum, where its formal side gardens have been restored to reflect the prevailing style of the late 1930s, complete with a quatrefoil parterre and a magnolia allée with a large fountain as its focal point.

Modernist American Gardens

The modernist movement of the 1920s in architecture brought changes in landscape design as well, although the changes were not felt on the residential level until after the Second World War. As families resumed their lives, land developers could still afford to be generous. In front of the ranchburger houses in the seamless front yards in the endless suburbs that sprang up around our cities, homeowners happily linedup little shrubs like soldiers on guard duty. Now everyman had his own half-acre of grass to mow.

In the late 1940s, California landscape architect Thomas Church had discovered in the gardens of Japan a source of inspiration compatible with contemporary horizontal house forms. In 1955 he published Gardens Are for People. Church's melding of the home's interior and exterior was nothing short of revolutionary. His designs incorporated new materials and addressed new economic realities. With fewer people trained to do garden maintenance (or few people willing to pay garden laborers a living wage), Church and the residential designers that followed him began designing for lower levels of maintenance. To replace lawns and elaborate planting beds, Church used flowing swaths of pavement surrounded by loose, informal plantings.

Modern American Garden

National magazines hailed his "outdoor living rooms." Never mind that the magazine photos usually included an ocean view (and presumably ocean breezes), Texans had recognized a style of outdoor living more in keeping with our notions of hospitality. By the 1960s this new garden style had firmly entered the Texas design vocabulary. As we look at Thomas Church's book today, some of his work is a bit dated (think kidney-shaped swimming pools surrounded by large aggregate concrete patios), but his ideas were truly ahead of their time. As he noted in the second edition, "Art Moderne strangled in the mesh of its own steel tubing... 'Modern' can be revived as an honest word when we realize that modernism is not a goal, but a broad highway."

Modern Asian-inspired Gardens

Unlike gardens in Japan, which are generally the creation of a garden master working in a period style, Asian gardens in America and Europe appropriate freely from the several schools of garden art. For contemporary houses and somewhat featureless ranch-style houses, there are many aspects of naturalistic Asian gardens that work well. Texas gardeners with small lots can borrow optical "tricks" that have been practiced for hundreds of years in Asian gardens. Streams and paths narrow as they get farther away. In the foreground, trees are kept small so they will not disrupt the view; the middle ground is fully developed to create an illusion of distance. Smaller elements and small-leafed plants are placed in the rear to appear diminished. The background (which can simply be treetops "borrowed" from the landscape beyond) is used to suggest unlimited space.

An Asian garden is above all a display of nature's handiwork, but it is no less man-made than Versailles. Structures, lanterns and bridges are used here, in fact, to represent human presence amid the symbols of heaven and earth. Louis XVI would not have understood it at all. For modern mankind, Asian-inspired gardens include a lesson in humility. Perhaps, after the environmental disruption created by the industrial revolution is analyzed, we may realize what Asian garden-makers have known all along — humans are not the center of the universe.

OLD SOLUTIONS FOR NEW PROBLEMS

Architects are recognizing that the early settlers had the right idea when they built their homes to capture breezes. Returning to favor are the large windows that provided cross-ventilation, French doors that opened into courtyard gardens, and shady screened porches with ceiling fans. Because popular building styles for most new homes evoke elements of French, English, Italian, Spanish Colonial, Early American or Victorian architecture, some knowledge of garden history is imperative. Landscape design should, first and foremost, complement the architecture of a house. *A Field Guide to American Houses* by Virginia and Lee McAlester is an excellent resource for identifying the features that distinguish the prevalent architectural styles of our country's past.

Today, Texas garden design professionals are borrowing freely from every era of garden design. By exploring old ideas to create new, more appropriate garden styles, designers are rediscovering such basics of European Renaissance and Early American traditions as doorways flanked by mirror image plantings, terraces enclosed with attractive balustrades, geometrical garden beds and allées of trees to tie the landscape into the symmetry of formal architecture. Entry courtyards in the Spanish style or English cottage gardens surrounded by tidy clipped hedges or low iron fences have returned to favor as a means of creating a sense of privacy for small front gardens.

Garden designers are also putting new emphasis on sustainability and comfort, and in the process are making outdoor living areas easier to maintain. While flowing curves and free-growing shapes remain suitable for asymmetrical and low, horizontal structures such as the mid-20ᵗʰ-century ranch houses, designers are taking cues from the 18ᵗʰ-century English Landscape School and from modern Asian ideas to provide more "character" in naturalistic landscapes. Architectural design, in short, should always inspire the lines and forms that comprise a compatible, visually interesting garden.

Greek Revival House
Traditional Formal Garden

'60s Shed-style House
Formalistic (architectural) Garden

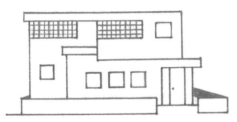

'30s International Style House
Formalistic Garden with Naturalistic elements

Victorian or Neo-Victorian House
Formalistic Garden with Naturalistic elements

Neo-Gothic Eclectic House
Naturalistic Garden with Formalistic elements

'50s Ranch House
Naturalistic Garden

Just as there is no one plant palette for the entire state, neither can there be one Texas garden style. Each new 21st-century Texas garden can be as colorful and individual as its owner. There will continue to be strong connections between outdoor and indoor living spaces. There will be trees, shade structures and water features to counter the hot summer sun and sufficient shelter from the cold winter winds. In place of expansive lawns, there will be planting beds filled with easy-care shrubs and ground covers, wildflower meadows and inviting surfaces built for entertaining and relaxing. Seating areas will be as carefully furnished as any living room and accessorized with cheerful plants spilling out of containers. One can see these solutions in all the best magazines today. Funny thing is, the ancient Egyptians thought of them first...

2

Inspiration and Information

Inspiration and Information

Sources of Inspiration

The 12 chapters of the *Texas Garden Resource Book* begin with general descriptions of each of the state's 12 gardening regions, followed by listings of the public places we think gardeners will want to visit for design inspiration. In seeking a personal "design style," you don't need to limit yourself to the landscapes of your own region. A San Antonio homeowner interested in creating an Asian garden would certainly want to see Fort Worth's exquisite Japanese Garden and the Chinese-based Chandor Gardens in Weatherford. A Dallas gardener whose property lends itself to formalism will find a beautiful example in the gardens of Bayou Bend in Houston. An art collector from anywhere in the state will appreciate the deft way that sculpture blends into the landscape at the naturalistic Umlauf Garden in Austin or is showcased at the elegant new Nasher Sculpture Garden in Dallas.

When it comes to plants, however, every region of the state is distinct. For inspiration, Mother Nature remains the best teacher. Native vegetation in your area is the best indicator of which plants will thrive in your garden. It's imperative that you select trees, shrubs and flowering perennials well adapted to the specifics of your own soil, climate and landforms. As you visit public gardens, parks and nature preserves, notice the color harmonies, the forms and textures of the plants. Look closely at the way a stream bends. Study the way the rocks occur (or note the absence thereof). Tuck a copy of *The Texas Garden Resource Book* into the glove compartment of your car when you travel around Texas. There are many hidden treasures to be discovered in our great outdoors!

THE STATE'S GREAT PUBLIC GARDENS

As a landscape architect, I have taken ideas from gardens all over the world and translated them into designs for Texas gardens. When I speak to garden clubs and other groups about the history of gardens, I'm often asked which Texas public garden is my favorite. That's a great question with an impossible answer. I begin by explaining that our public gardens are relatively new compared to Kew Royal Botanic Garden (founded in 1730), the Boston Public Garden (1837), Longwood Gardens in Pennsylvania (which dates back to an arboretum planted on the site in 1798 and expanded to its present-day grandeur by Pierre du Pont in the early 20th century), New York Botanical Garden (1891) or San Francisco's Japanese Tea Garden (1894).

The Fort Worth Botanic Garden, established in 1933, was this state's first (and for many years only) public garden. It is still wonderful. When one considers that gardening is more difficult in Texas than on the East or West coasts and that until the oil boom of the early 20th century, there were few people of significant wealth in the state, it is not surprising that public gardens were "late bloomers" here. Much of the credit for our newly established botanical gardens belongs to the ladies of 20th century garden clubs. Their complete history can be found on the website, www.texasgardenclubs.org. It notes, "Women, no longer confined to the home and a tight community, had acquired the vote in 1920 and were eagerly looking for ways to demonstrate their newfound place in the world. Social consciousness developed when Henry Ford's newfangled contraption carried the homebound out onto rutted mud roads that would gradually be replaced by macadam and concrete. Sharp eyes and keen minds envisioned beauty, found needs to champion and ways to exert their exciting freedom." My grandmothers and aunts were among these women, and I hope that my granddaughters, whose world is very different, will follow in their footsteps.

Certainly the public gardens in Fort Worth, Austin (established in 1955), Dallas and San Antonio (both of which opened in the 1980s) are our most comprehensive botanical gardens. In the past twenty years many of the smaller cities (Amarillo, Beaumont, College Station, Corpus Christi, El Paso, Lubbock, Nacogdoches, Orange and Weatherford) have also begun developing extensive public gardens and arboretums to showcase the gardening possibilities of their respective regions. Zoos in Brownsville, Abilene and Victoria, new nature centers in every corner of the state, and water-wise display gardens at several AgriLife Extension Centers are also contributing to the state's collective botanical education. There are some Texas public gardens that I think are so special they should be on every gardener's list of places to visit, even if they have already seen Europe and America's older, more famous gardens.

First on my list would be Houston's **Bayou Bend Collection and Gardens**. It was developed in the early years of the 20th century by Ima Hogg in wild woodlands on the bank of Buffalo Bayou. Over the years, as several prominent Texas landscape architects contributed ideas and elements to this landscape, it became widely known as the finest private garden in Texas. What sets Bayou Bend apart, even today, is its exceptionally strong overall design. It draws from several centuries of European garden art. Handsome statuary, formal fountains and colorful plantings keep your eye moving from place to place. A broad terraced lawn behind the house leads to a pool and arching fountain designed to frame a white marble statue of Diana, goddess of the hunt. Here, the sculpture plays dramatically against a backdrop of dark, columnar clipped hedges. Directly west of the Diana Garden is a parterre where Clio, the muse of history, presides on a central pedestal, encircled by brick walks and beds filled with clipped azaleas and boxwoods. Its formality dissolves into luxuriant naturalism at the property's outer edges. Members of the River Oaks Garden Club lovingly (and organically) maintain Bayou Bend.

Two of my favorite gardens were designed specifically to display private sculpture collections. In downtown Dallas, nationally known landscape architect Peter Walker transformed a two-acre parking lot into a "peaceful retreat for reflection of art and nature" at the **Nasher Sculpture Center**. Walker devised an asymmetrical layout within the rectangular walled garden, which employs deceptively simple lines of trees and planes of grass through which walkways terminate in water features and raised planters at the garden's terminus. In Austin's **Umlauf Sculpture Garden**, a steep slope accommodated the rock-lined recirculating stream and waterfalls that provide a gorgeous backdrop for Charles Umlauf's lyrical sculpture. A teacher at The University of Texas for forty years, he produced works in bronze, stone, wood and terra cotta that come together under a heavy canopy of trees below the artist's home.

The Fort Worth Botanic Garden still offers a world of design ideas to gardeners from all parts of the state. It holds an impressive collection of 23 specialty gardens in a heavily wooded 110-acre site, including the architectural Fuller Garden, extensive formal rose gardens, which take inspiration from Italy's renowned Villa Lante, numerous water features and an extensive naturalistic perennial garden.

Prominent garden club members first conceived the idea of a major botanical garden for San Antonio as early as the 1940s. They developed a master plan in the late 1960s. Funding began in 1970, groundbreaking was held in '76 and, finally, their dream was realized for **San Antonio Botanical Gardens** in 1980. Similarly, after many years of planning, The **Dallas Arboretum and Botanical Society** opened its gates in 1984 on the site of two elegant '30s-era residences that backed up to White Rock Lake. The designers of this magnificent 66-acre garden took full advantage of the homes' mature trees and shrubs as the basics for creating what I consider to be the state's most sophisticated botanical garden in terms of hardscape. Its plantings are almost too perfect.

There is something about Asian gardens that particularly touches my soul, so time and again the **Japanese Garden** has drawn me back to the Fort Worth Botanic Garden. I love to stroll its mellow maze of paths that crisscross interconnected ponds. Designed in 1968 by landscape architect Kingsley Wu, a graduate of the University of Tokyo, this Edo-period garden in an abandoned gravel quarry explores water in all its forms — cascading down a bluff, gurgling over rapids, shimmering in large reflecting pools and swirling symbolically in raked gravel. At the water's edge, mature native plants grow alongside familiar species from Japan. Every hardscape detail is exquisite. In terms of how to plant a pond edge, frame a view, punctuate with sculpture or create a delicious sense of mystery in your garden, modern designers should look for enlightenment here.

At about the same time the Ft. Worth garden was under construction, Isamu Taniguchi began carving out of a caliche cliff his own **Japanese Garden** at Austin's **Zilker Botanical Gardens**. For the next 23 years he worked with no salary and no restrictions, personally maintaining the garden until his death in 1992. Two other examples of authentic Asian gardens have followed. Tucked behind the National Museum of the Pacific War in Fredericksburg is the serene **Japanese Garden of Peace** designed in Japan and constructed by seven Japanese craftsmen working in Texas for two months in 1976, and the lovely **Houston Japanese Garden** in Hermann Park designed in 1992 by Japanese landscape architect Ken Nakajima, who used crepe myrtles in lieu of traditional cherry trees to create breathtaking vistas, especially when viewed through the opened screens of the teahouse. Strolls through these serene gardens reveal vignettes presented as landscape paintings, much as we might translate into our own gardens the scenes we remember from nature walks in the parks and wildlife refuges in the various regions of Texas.

The courtyard of the **McNay Art Museum** in San Antonio gives us a splendid model for garden architecture of the Spanish Colonial period. The cottage garden of the **Schultz House** preserved in San Antonio's Hemisfair Plaza or the **Steves Homestead** in the upscale King William Historic District demonstrates the garden style and range of plants favored by 19th-century German gardeners. Such contemporary glass houses as the **Lucile Halsell Conservatory** at the San Antonio Botanical Garden, Moody Garden's **Rainforest Pyramid** in Galveston, the **Conservatory of the Fort Worth Botanic Garden**, **Ruby N. Priddy Butterfly Conservatory** in Wichita Falls and the **Cockrell Butterfly Center** in the Houston Museum of Natural Science continue the Victorian tradition of exhibiting horticultural rarities.

Rediscovering the beauty of Texas as it existed in the early 19th century motivated the development of several public gardens and nature preserves in the 1980s. Most prominent is **Lady Bird Johnson Wildflower Center** where the plantings and water features illustrate just how rich and varied Texas landscapes can be! Now part of The University of Texas at Austin, its new Master Plan calls for enlarging the gardens and establishing a Texas Arboretum. This is truly a garden for the 21st century, and it's a place I regularly visit to relax and learn!

In Nacogdoches, the **Mast Arboretum** occupies a twenty-four-acre site on the campus of Stephen F. Austin State University. This impressive endeavor began as a humble planting area beside the Agriculture Building in 1985. With over 8,600 plants arranged into a series of theme gardens, it has quickly risen to national stature under the direction of Dr. David Creech.

I'm also enthusiastic about **Shangri La Botanical Gardens and Nature Center** in Orange, which opened a mere two years ago. Its striking contemporary buildings, gardens and large nature preserve are built in an ecosystem originally developed by H. J. Lutcher Stark more than 60 years ago. Outdoor classrooms are located deep in the cypress swamp, and adjacent to the botanical gardens is a bird blind that allows visitors to observe nesting birds in the garden's heronry. This is the first project in Texas and the 50th project in the world to earn the U.S. Green Building Council's Platinum certification for LEED®-NC, which verifies the design and construction reached the highest green building and performance measures.

I first visited **Peckerwood Garden** in Hempstead when I was a student at Texas A&M. John G. Fairey, a teacher in the Department of Architecture, began this remarkable project in 1971. It now qualifies as one of America's most important collections of rare plants native to a wide region of the southern United States and Mexico. This exquisite private garden is open to the public only a few days each year, but a nonprofit foundation has been formed, with guidance from the Garden Conservancy, to ensure its preservation and continued development.

A newly reopened garden in Weatherford took my breath away when I first saw it last year! Chinese and English garden styles are interwoven at **Chandor Gardens** where English portrait artist Douglas Chandor sculpted his private paradise out of four rocky acres of a former cow pasture. Prominent visitors from all over the world traveled to Weatherford in the '40s and '50s for elegant parties in his work of "living art." It deteriorated for four decades and was largely forgotten. In 2002, the city purchased and restored this splendid garden for all to enjoy its ponds, bridges, Chinese decorative art, moon gate, grottos and completely believable 30-foot-high rock waterfall. Nearby, between Weatherford and Mineral Wells, is another little-known treasure, **Clark Gardens Botanical Park**, which, like Chandor, began as a private garden and opened in 2000 as a 35-acre botanical park maintained as a non-profit organization. The garden's paths wind through wisteria-covered pergolas and arbors laden with cascading Lady Banks' roses to a series of color gardens, three lakes graced by trumpeter swans and a natural woodland.

These are but a few of my favorite places to visit for inspiration. Dozens more appear (along with addresses, hours of operation and admission prices) in *The Texas Garden Resource Book*. These gardens are repositories of information. Many offer classes, plant sales, volunteer opportunities for hands-on learning and the sharing of ideas with fellow gardeners.

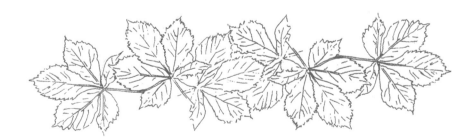

Sources of Information

GARDEN BOOKS AND PERIODICALS

My favorite way to spend a winter evening is pouring over a good garden book. From my armchair, I've visited all of the world's great gardens. Long before I was able to spend three weeks crisscrossing the British Isles, Graham Stuart Thomas's *Great Gardens of Britain* transported me there. Griswold and Weller's *The Golden Age of American Gardens* introduced me to hundreds of private gardens in this country that I'd d never be able to see; some are not open to the public, others no longer exist.

My viewpoint was greatly enriched by *The Landscape of Man*, a wonderful history by Geoffrey and Susan Jellicoe that describes the climatic, topographical, historical, social, economic and philosophical factors that shaped gardens from prehistory to modern times. (This is the same Geoffrey Jellicoe who designed the master plan for The Moody Gardens in Galveston.) From Anthony Huxley's *An Illustrated History of Gardening*, I've gained new appreciation for people who created uncommon beauty without the mechanization we employ today.

In terms of design, I was influenced by Thomas D. Church's *Gardens Are for People*. I also recommend John Brookes' *The Book of Garden Design*, which details the basics of landscape design in simple language and reinforces the text with excellent illustrations. I also love *Bold Romantic Gardens: The New World Landscapes of Oehme and van Sweden*. Their book illustrates a new, naturalistic way of planting that incorporates grasses and great drifts of hardy wildflowers. When you look at the pictures, however, substitute in your mind Mexican bush sage (*Salvia leucantha*) for their pink loosestrife (*Lythrum salicaria*) and imagine planting caladiums where they use hostas. Many of the plants they use are drought-tolerant and very acceptable choices for Texas landscapes.

The problem is that none of these books feature plants that are suitable for Texas landscapes. Design is design, but where plant materials are concerned, we must turn to books written by Texans for Texans. Our hot-summer climate does not lend itself to the lush woodland species you'll see pictured in the books published in New York or Great Britain. Even such excellent sources as the *Southern Living Garden Book* features some plants that are ill-suited to the long periods of drought we routinely experience in our southwestern climate.

Several years ago in an Austin bookstore I observed a couple mulling over the choices in the gardening section. From the conversation I was overhearing, I could tell they were new to the state, so I stepped in and literally snatched from the woman's hand a book published in New England. I directed the couple, instead, to Neil Sperry's *Complete Guide to Texas Gardening*. It pictures the plants most often used in Texas landscapes and contains a great deal of general information on soil types, fertilization needs, pests and diseases common to Texas. For the best ways to deal with these problems, I also recommended Howard Garrett's *Texas Organic Gardening Book*, which explains in its preface, "Organics is not just a switch of products, but a completely new way of life. It's about understanding and enjoying nature."

I introduced them to *Native Texas Plants, Landscaping Region by Region* by Sally Wasowski and Andy Wasowski, which illustrates with beautiful photographs how to identify and save what already may be on your property and how to build upon it with plants indigenous to your area. I also pointed out another "must have" book for anyone gardening in limestone, alkaline clay and/or caliche (which describes Austin and more than half of Texas): *Gardening Success with Difficult Soils* by Scott Ogden.

If you're interested in old gardening traditions of Texas, you'll love *The Southern Heirloom Garden* by William C. Welch and Greg Grant. Another book, one that belongs in every hiker's backpack, is Geyata Ajilvsgi's *Wildflowers of Texas*, which is color-coded and very user-friendly. Texas also has its own bird book, *Field Guide to the Birds of Texas*, by the late Roger Tory Peterson, who called this "the #1 bird state."

If you are about to undertake garden construction, you'll want to look at the familiar Sunset paperback series on outdoor living published by Oxmoor House. Other publishers, including Creative Homeowner and Taunton Press, offer other highly informative books, which usually can be found in a rack at the big home improvement stores. Home Depot now has its own series. These books are full of practical advice for do-it-yourself garden designers. Even if you're turning your garden over to a professional, I highly recommend these and other good garden design books as tools for helping you communicate your ideas and personal preferences.

Recommended Books for Texas Gardeners

General Gardening Encyclopedias

> ***Howard Garrett's Plants for Texas***, J. Howard Garrett
> ***The Lone Star Gardener's Book of Lists***, William D. Adams and
> Lois Trigg Chaplin
> ***Neil Sperry's Complete Guide to Texas Gardening***, Neil Sperry
> ***The Southern Living Garden Book***, Steve Bender

Garden Design

> ***Bold Romantic Gardens***, Wolfgang Oehme & James van Sweden
> ***The Essentials of Garden Design***, John Brookes
> ***Landscape Design...Texas Style***, J. Howard Garrett
> ***Planting Design***, Theodore D. Walker
> ***The Southern Heirloom Garden***, William C. Welch and Greg Grant
> ***Southern Home Landscaping***, Ken Smith
> ***Southern Living Landscape Book***, Southern Living

Garden Construction

Garden Stone, by Barbara Pleasant
The Landscape Lighting Book, Janet Lennox Moyer
Making Garden Floors, by Paige Gilchrist
Pergolas, Arbors, Gazebos, Follies, David Stevens
Stonescaping, Jan Kowalczski Whitner
Trellising, Rhonda M. Hart

Garden Conservation

Complete Guide to Texas Lawn Care, Dr. Bill Knoop
Doug Welsh's Texas Garden Almanac, Doug Welsh
The Garden-Ville Method: Lessons in Nature, Malcolm Beck
How To Become an Organic Gardener in Seven Easy Steps, Judy Barrett
Howard Garrett's Texas Organic Gardening Book, J. Howard Garrett
Month-by-Month Gardening in Texas, Dale Groom and Dan Gill
The Pruner's Handbook, John Malins
Soil Science Simplified, Helmut Kohnke and D.P. Franzmeier
The Texas Bug Book, Malcolm Beck and J. Howard Garrett
1001 Most Asked Texas Gardening Questions, Neil Sperry

Naturescaping

Attracting Birds, Neal Oldenwald
Butterfly Gardening for the South, Geyata Ajilvsgi
Field Guide to Butterflies of Texas, Raymond W. Neck
How to Grow Native Plants of Texas and the Southwest, Jill Nokes
How to Grow Wildflowers, Eric A. Johnson and Scott Miller
Landscaping with Native Plants of Texas and the Southwest, George
  Oxford Miller
Landscaping with Native Texas Plants, Sally Wasowski and Julie Ryan
Landscaping with Native Trees, Guy Sternberg and Jim Wilson
Native Gardens for Dry Climates, Sally Wasowski
Native Plants for Southwestern Landscapes, Judy Mielke
Native Texas Gardens: Maximum Beauty, Minimum Upkeep, Sally Wasowski
  and Andy Wasowski
Native Texas Plants: Landscaping Region by Region, Sally Wasowski and
  Andy Wasowski
Texas Monthly Field Guide to Wildflowers, Trees and Shrubs of Texas,
  Delena Tull and George Oxford Miller
Texas Wild: The Land, Plants, and Animals of the Lone Star State,
  Richard Phelan
Wildflowers of Texas, Geyata Ajilvsgi

Trees, Shrubs & Grasses

A Field Guide to Texas Trees, Benny J. Simpson
Encyclopedia of Ornamental Grasses, John Greenlee

Gardening Success with Difficult Soils, Scott Ogden
Grasses, by Nancy Ondra
Manual of Woody Landscape Plants, Michael Dirr
Texas Gardener's Guide, Dale Groom
Texas Trees: A Friendly Guide, Paul Cox and Patty Leslie
Trees, Shrubs and Woody Vines of the Southwest, Robert Vines

The Flower Garden

Antique Roses for the South, William C. Welch
Garden Bulbs for the South, Scott Ogden
The Complete Guide to Using Color in Your Garden, David Squires
The Organic Rose Garden, Liz Druitt
Perennial Garden Color, William C. Welch
Perennial Gardening for Texas, Julie Ryan
Southern Living Big Book of Flower Gardening
The Texas Flower Garden, Kathy Huber

The Edible Landscape

Designing and Maintaining your Edible Landscape Naturally, Robert Kourik
Growing Fruits, Berries and Nuts Southwest Southeast, Dr. George McEachern
Herbs for Texas, J. Howard Garrett
The Herb Garden Cookbook, Lucinda Hutson
Herb Gardening in Texas, Sol Meltzer
How to Grow More Vegetables, John Jeavons
Landscaping with Herbs, Jim Wilson
Mother Nature's Herbal, Judy Griffin
Southern Herb Growing, Madalene Hill and Gwen Barclay
The Southern Kitchen Garden, William D. Adams and Thomas R. LeRoy
Texas Gardener's Guide to Growing and Using Herbs, Diane Morey Sitton
Texas Organic Vegetable Gardening, Malcolm Beck and J. Howard Garrett
The Vegetable Book: A Texan's Guide To Gardening, Dr. Sam Cotner
What Can I Do with My Herbs?, Judy Barrett

Water Gardens

Complete Guide to Water Gardens, Kathleen Fisher
Encyclopedia of Water Plants, Ann Lovejoy
Water Gardens: Simple Projects, Contemporary Designs, Hazel White

Houseplants

The Indoor Garden Book, John Brookes
The New Houseplant Expert, D. G. Hessayon

Container Gardening

The Book of Container Gardening, Malcolm Hillier
The Contained Garden, David Stevens & Kenneth Beckett
Landscaping with Container Plants, Jim Wilson

Pots in the Garden: Expert Design and Planting, Ray Rogers
The Practical Guide to Container Gardening, by Susan Berry and Steve Bradley

Garden Furniture & Accessories

Decorating Eden, Elizabeth Wilkinson and Marjorie Henderson

Regional Books

Austin:
Guide to Gardening in Austin, Travis County Master Gardeners
Native and Adapted Landscape Plants, City of Austin Watershed Protection

Dallas:
Dallas Planting Manual, Dallas Garden Club
Plants for the Metroplex, J. Howard Garrett

Houston:
A Garden Book for Houston and the Texas Gulf Coast, River Oaks Garden Club

San Antonio & South Texas:
Gardening in San Antonio and South Texas, H. R. Newcomer and Roy C. Bates
South Texas Garden Book, Bob Webster

I can't walk into a bookstore without adding a few more gardening books to my collection. But even for a landscape professional it's hard to choose from the plethora of titles out there. Over 700 new garden books are published each year, and thousands of older books remain in print because many of the garden "secrets" our grandparents knew are still valid. Only the library stands between me and credit card overload! In most public libraries, however, the gardening collections are limited by lack of funding. The good news is that all libraries have borrowing privileges from other public libraries in the country.

Moneysaving Tip: Ask your local public library about "inter-library loans," through which you can obtain almost any book in print.

Magazines that Celebrate the Texas Landscape

Libraries also offer an economical way to keep up with garden-related magazines. I take advantage of the library's copies of *Horticulture, Garden Design, Fine Gardening* and *Organic Gardening*, to name a few. There are six Texas magazines filled with information specific to gardening and naturescaping in Texas that I heartily recommend:

Homegrown
P.O. Box 524
Taylor, Texas 76574
512.365.5154
www.homegrowntexas.com

Neil Sperry's GARDENS
P.O. Box 864
McKinney, Texas 75070
972.562.5050 or 800.752.4769
www.neilsperry.com

Texas Highways
P.O. Box 141009
Austin, Texas 78714
512.486.5823 or 800.839.4997
www.texashighways.com

Texas Gardener
P.O. Box 9005
Waco, Texas 76712
254.848.9393 or 800.727.9020
www.texasgardener.com

Texas Parks and Wildlife
4200 Smith School Road
Austin, Texas 78744
800.937.9393
www.tpwmagazine.com

Wildflower
Lady Bird Johnson Wildflower Center
4801 La Crosse Avenue
Austin, Texas 78739
512.292.4100
www.wildflower.org

PERSONALIZED SOURCES OF INFORMATION

Gardeners learn by seeing, reading and questioning. I've always heard that a green thumb is equal parts knowledge, intuition and luck, but knowledge is the only thing that works for me. Luck I've never trusted, and the kind of intuition that allows a gardener to differentiate between weeds and precious seedlings is built on first-hand experience! Happily, Texas is replete with people trained to answer your gardening questions.

"Green Industry" Professionals

Professionals in the fields of landscape design, horticulture and arboriculture can provide you with expertise that may save you hundreds or thousands of dollars in the long term. If you are building a new home or planning a major landscape renovation, by all means consult a professional. While you own your home, you'll enjoy the benefits of a well-designed, healthy, easy-to-maintain garden. When you sell the house, a beautiful landscape will pay another dividend. You can expect to speed up the sale by five to six weeks and recover your investment by as much as 200 percent. Before hiring someone to help with your garden, however, you should know that different types of professionals are trained in different, specific fields. The "green industry" is regulated to an extent by professional organizations, but not all landscape services are regulated. **Moneysaving Tip: Within each area of "expertise," there are people who don't know what they are doing. No matter what kind of landscape service you employ, ask about credentials, check references, and look at examples of their work.**

Selecting a Designer

Among design professionals, landscape architects are the most highly trained. To be able to use the title "landscape architect," one must have graduated from an accredited university program, practiced for a number of years and passed a rigorous national exam that covers design, construction techniques, plant materials, history and professional ethics. Most are members of the American Society of Landscape Architects (ASLA).

He or she will be trained to help you maximize the use of your property, which includes planning circulation patterns, designing outdoor living areas and selecting the best plant materials in terms of energy efficiency and environmental sensitivity. Not only is a landscape architect qualified to provide help with aesthetic issues, but also with such matters as building codes, structural details and drainage considerations. Landscape architects can help you prevent such costly mistakes as planting trees too close to the house or creating future maintenance problems.

A number of people who call themselves "landscape designers" may be graduates of university programs in landscape architecture who have not yet taken the registration exam. Other designers are self-taught individuals who may have years of practical experience and a real flair for aesthetics. Some have passed exams to become members of the Association of Professional Landscape Designers (APLD). Their emphasis is usually slanted more toward plant materials than hardscape (the garden's walks, walls, drainage and irrigation systems, outdoor lighting, etc.).

Unfortunately, the yellow pages include under the listing, "landscape designers," anyone who can afford to have business cards printed and pay for an ad. If there is major structural work to be done, a difficult site with slopes that will require retaining walls, serious drainage problems or a landscape in need of ecological restoration, you should consult a landscape architect or degreed designer. Most landscape architectural firms do not specialize in residential design, but landscape architects enjoy garden design in addition to their work with larger-scale public and commercial projects.

Some landscape architects and professional landscape designers operate "design/build" firms, which include both design and construction services. Some firms virtually give away their design services to get the more profitable construction contract. My best advice to homeowners is not to lock yourself into a construction contract that doesn't allow for the process of competitive bids unless you personally know the individual with whom you are dealing and highly respect the company's work. (See section on Landscape Contractors on page ____?.)

Consulting a Nursery or Landscape Professional

The Texas Nursery and Landscape Association (TNLA) is composed of the state's wholesale nursery-stock growers, garden center retailers, landscape contractors and designers, maintenance contractors and allied suppliers. The Association certifies nursery personnel through training programs, apprenticeships and examinations. To become a Texas Certified Nursery Professional a person must pass a four-part examination that covers basic principles of plant identification, plant growth, plant disease and insect control, weed control, fertilization and proper use of chemicals. To become a Texas Master Certified Nursery Professional, one must attend classroom training and pass an examination that requires an advanced level of knowledge in these subjects. Landscape contractor supervisors, owners, and managers qualify for the designation of Texas Certified Landscape Professional by way of a self-study course followed by an exam. The exam covers 20 topics including management, landscape and irrigation design, resource efficiency, building materials, botany, turf, and pruning.

The TNLA website (www.txnla.org) makes available to the public a list of certified professionals for every region of Texas. Most large garden centers employ Certified Nursery Professionals to give advice on plant selection and answer gardening questions. Some also provide design and landscape installation services. In the plant source chapters of this book, you'll find a number of nurseries that offer free classes and send out newsletters not only to promote products, but also to keep their customers informed about new developments in the field of horticulture. Ask to be added to the mailing list of every nursery where you trade.

When to Call an Arborist

Trust your valuable trees to an insured, licensed arborist. Maintaining the health and form of your trees may be the best money you invest in your garden. Competent arborists are certified by the International Society of Arboriculture (ISA), and many are also members of the Society of American Foresters and the National Arborist Association. Not only should you expect professional affiliations, but also you should demand that the people to whom you entrust your trees be educated in forestry, horticulture or a related field. Your local extension service may be able to provide you with a list of certified arborists in your area.

Unfortunately, Texas does not have a licensing program, so anyone who can afford a pickup truck and chain saw can call himself a "tree trimmer." No matter how desperate you are to get tree work done (like, immediately after a storm), do not even consider hiring some "trimmer" who rings your doorbell or select someone out of the newspaper want ads. The work of untrained tree-care people can be seen all over Texas in trees that have been topped or otherwise mangled, misshapen and ultimately ruined. At a seminar I attended recently, someone asked how to find a reputable tree company. An experienced arborist answered, "Call a company and ask if they top trees. If they say 'yes,' hang up!"

Taking down a tree that must be removed doesn't require the services of a certified arborist, but it is a dangerous job that is best left to a pro. The International Society of Arboriculture recommends that you negotiate a written contract that specifies how the tree is to be removed, where the wood will be taken and who is liable in case of damage. If you want the stump removed as well, provision for this service should be spelled out in the contract.

Moneysaving Tip: Because you probably don't have the proper tools and ladders to safely prune your own large trees, a professional arborist will not only prolong the life of your valuable trees, but may also save you from a stay in the hospital.

AgriLife Extension Services

Cooperative Extension Services (so named because they are joint ventures between the United States Department of Agriculture, county governments and land-grant universities) were begun in 1914 for the benefit of farmers. As the population became more urban, the agencies widened their focus to include consumer affairs, food and water quality, home and family issues and gardening. In rural areas the extension agents still concentrate on the needs of farming and ranching families, but urban extension agents are responsible for answering the multitude of horticultural questions asked by homeowners, park departments, schools and city governments. Now named AgriLife Extension, it operates with a vast network of 250 county Extension offices, 616 Extension agents, and 343 subject-matter specialists; the expertise they provide is available to every resident in every Texas county. These services are either free or modestly priced.

Moneysaving Tip: AgriLife Extension Services are funded by your tax dollars. Tap into this gold mine at http://texasextension.tamu.edu!

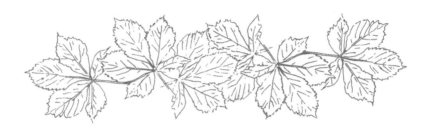

The Master Gardener Program

The task of dispensing information in the large urban counties has become impossible for one agent to handle. The Master Gardener Program was begun to train enthusiastic laymen to share the work of overburdened county agents. It has worked beautifully. Master Gardeners now answer garden questions, set up demonstrations, diagnose plant problems and make recommendations for the control of plant diseases, insect infestation and cultural problems. Thousands of Master Gardeners in the U.S. and Canada take part in this program today.

If accepted into the Master Gardener program in your county, you will attend a Master Gardener training course. Classes are taught by AgriLife Extension specialists, agents, and local experts. The program offers a minimum of 50 hours of instruction that covers such topics as lawn care, pest management, soils, vegetable gardening, fruit production and water conservation. Check with your County Extension office for specifics or go to: http://aggie-horticulture.tamu.edu/MASTERGD/mg.html/.

In exchange for training, participants are asked to volunteer at least 50 hours of service within one year following the training. The type of service varies according to the community's needs and the abilities and interests of the Master Gardeners. Some answer telephone requests for information related to gardening. Others staff plant clinics or displays in shopping malls or community centers. Master Gardeners may speak to local groups and conduct workshops. They may help establish community garden projects, work with 4-H youth or assist their agent with news or radio releases related to gardening. The Master Gardener Coordinator in the AgriLife Extension office decides how volunteer time can be best utilized.

Texas Master Naturalists

This partnership, which is funded by AgriLife Extension and the Texas Parks and Wildlife Department, has already certified almost 3,000 Texas Master Naturalist™ volunteers in 39 local chapters across the state. An individual gains the designation of Texas Master Naturalist after a training program with a minimum of 40 hours of combined field and classroom instruction, obtaining eight hours of approved advanced training, and completing 40 hours of volunteer service. To retain the title, volunteers must complete eight additional hours of advanced training and provide an additional 40 hours of volunteer service during each subsequent year, so it's not for the casually committed. These citizen volunteers may implement youth education programs, operate parks, nature centers and preserves, and provide leadership in local natural resource conservation efforts.

According to the website, since its establishment in 1998 Texas Master Naturalist volunteer efforts have provided over 450,000 hours of service valued at more than $8 million. They have enhanced 75,000 acres of wildlife and native plant habitats. One member discovered a new plant species! The program has gained international recognition. For more information, go to http://masternaturalist.tamu.edu/.

Organizations Working to Keep Texas Clean and Green

Audubon Texas
2904 Swiss Avenue
Dallas, Texas 75204
214.370.9735
www.tx.audubon.org

Audubon Texas is the state program of the National Audubon Society. Its mission is to conserve and restore natural ecosystems, focusing on birds, other wildlife, and their habitats for the benefit of humanity and the earth's biological diversity. The state organization works with local chapters, cities, state agencies, and public and private landowners to restore habitat, manage preserves and bird sanctuaries, and educate 50,000 students and adults each year. Interested in volunteering? There are 21 local chapters in Texas. Much more than bird watching, participation provides a wonderful way to meet new people, learn new things and work on projects that really matter.

Lady Bird Johnson Wildflower Center
4801 La Crosse Avenue
Austin, Texas 78739
512.292.4100
www.wildflower.org

This special place is an organization that leads by example. Beyond introducing people to the beauty and diversity of wildflowers and other native plants, it directs internationally influential research. In 2006, the Center became an organized Research Unit of The University of Texas at Austin. It could not exist, however, without the support of volunteers who serve as docents, work in the gardens, assist researchers, teach others the importance of environmental awareness and serve as special volunteers for restoration and sustainable development in other parts of the state.

Native Plant Society of Texas
320 West San Antonio Street
P.O. Box 3017
Fredericksburg, Texas 78624
830.997.9272
www.npsot.org

Founded in 1980 to protect the state's botanical legacy, this organization has grown to a network of more than 30 local chapters. Education-based, it promotes the preservation of natural habitats and the use of appropriate native plants in landscaping. Individual chapters hold regularly scheduled meetings, lectures and plant exchanges. Activities include field trips and community work projects, habitat restoration and plant surveys. The statewide annual meetings alternate between the state's different vegetational regions. An informative quarterly newsletter keeps members current on local and regional events and publishes feature articles and book reviews. Annual membership is only $25 (individuals), $15 (students) and $40 (families).

Sierra Club
1202 San Antonio Street
P.O. Box 1931
Austin, Texas 78767
512.477.1729
www.texas.sierraclub.org

For over 40 years this environmental advocacy organization has been influencing policy matters in Texas. In the summer of 2008, it was fighting the Border Wall, which threatens the migratory pathways of several animals and will close off access to public recreation and wildlife viewing. It was also addressing recommendations for the General Management Plan for Guadalupe Mountains National Park. The hot-button issues may change, but the critical need for environmental support will only increase in years to come. With membership comes the privilege of attending events and outings, as well as a sense of accomplishment.

Texas Nature Conservancy
P.O. Box 1440
San Antonio, Texas 78295
210.224.8774
www.tnc.org/texas

The Nature Conservancy maintains 23 preserves throughout the state and two in Northeast Mexico. Most of these fragile and endangered landscapes are not open to the public, but member volunteers are invited to take part in workdays, botanical inventories, field trips and other events. The organization now protects more than 750,000 acres of land and water in cooperation with private owners and partnerships with businesses, environmental groups and several governmental agencies. Among the varied ecosystems the Conservancy is safeguarding in Texas are a beech-magnolia forest, tallgrass/blackland prairie, estuarial marshes, Chihuahuan high desert and Tamaulipan shrubland. There are several regional chapters. To learn more about the Conservancy and its properties that are open to the public, contact the state organization. You can sign up on the Great Places Network to get monthly e-mails about conservation in Texas and around the world.

Texas Wildscapes
Texas Parks and Wildlife Department
4200 Smith School Road
Austin, Texas 78744
800.792.1112
www.tpwd.state.tx.us/wildscapes

This excellent statewide program enables Texans to contribute to the cause of conservation by developing wildlife habitats where they live, work and play. Texas Wildscapes provides a roadmap for habitat restoration and conservation of both rural and urban areas. It can be as simple as providing food, water and shelter in a small area of your own backyard or as elaborate as restoring native vegetation on a family farm or ranch.

There are two certification options available for the Texas gardener through Texas Parks and Wildlife Department — the traditional Texas Wildscapes certification and the more challenging Best of Texas Backyard Habitats program. Texas Wildscapes requires that the person be providing food, shelter and water for wildlife using a majority of native plants. Best of Texas certification not only requires that the site is a native plant habitat, but also that the applicant is taking active measures to control nonnative threats and be involved in a number of conservation stewardship activities. A new edition of the book, *Texas Wildscapes: Gardening for Wildlife* from Texas A&M Press will be in bookstores November 2009, garden centers and on the TPWD website. You can get an application for certification as a Texas Wildscape online. Once certified, you can buy a metal backyard habitat sign.

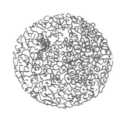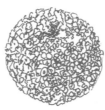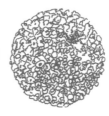

CONTINUE YOUR EDUCATION

Join a garden club! For over 75 years, Texas Garden Clubs, Inc. has been a force for environmental awareness and change. During WWII, garden clubs helped people start Victory Gardens at their own homes and sponsored gardens in rural areas to feed the poor. In the '50s Texas Garden Clubs lobbied the Texas legislature to provide a horticulture center at Fair Park in Dallas (now named **Texas Discovery Gardens**) and an arboretum in Austin (now **Zilker Botanical Gardens**). TGC persuaded the Department of Transportation to begin preserving and planting wildflowers along Texas highways. It also started the first Texas anti-litter campaign. (Remember the "Don't Be a Litterbug" slogan?)

The organization has led the way in restoration projects involving many old homes and gardens, and it has supported such organizations as **Wild Basin Wilderness** in the Hill Country. Garden clubs host hundreds of lecture series and gardening classes throughout the state. It sponsors courses in Landscape Design, Garden Study, Environmental Study and Floral Design. Its members are eager to share information, and may even find mentors for enthusiastic novices. Watch local newspapers and regional magazines for times and dates of special gardening events.

Go to **www.texasgardenclubs.org** and click on "Find a Club" or Texas Garden Clubs, Inc. will help you form a new club. Through the years garden clubs have evolved beyond the stereotypical ladies club that meets on a Wednesday morning every month. "Our clubs come in many different forms and sizes just like Texans. Clubs can meet at any time and design programs to meet the varying needs of the group," says the website. Today there are Mothers' Night Out groups for young working moms, Couples' Garden Clubs, Men's Garden Clubs, Family Garden Clubs, Church Garden Clubs for helping church members care for the plants in and around the church. "You can form a group to meet your needs in the gardening world. We stand ready to help you set up the structure of your club and connect with other clubs and gardening specialists."

If you prefer to learn on your own, many community colleges offer horticultural classes. Every major newspaper features garden columns, and almost every "talk-radio" station and TV channel offers a gardening program that allows you to call in with questions. Almost all of the public gardens and nature preserves mentioned in this chapter and listed at the beginning of each chapter in *The Texas Garden Resource Book* have educational components featuring classes, lectures and informative signage. Many of the nurseries featured in the book also offer seminars and printed information.

EXPERIENCE THE GREAT OUTDOORS

There's also no substitute for experiencing the natural landscapes of Texas. One of the least expensive ways to do that is by visiting state and national parks. A Texas State Parks Pass at $60 per year opens the gate to all of the system's parks to everyone in your car. A National Parks Passport offers a world of wonders in Texas, as well. This Pass is $50 per year (call 888.GO.PARKS.)

Texas Parks and Wildlife Department
4200 Smith School Road
Austin, Texas 78744
800.792.1112 (general information), 512.389.8900 (customer service center for reservations and passes)
www.tpwd.state.tx.us

Our State Parks play host to over 25 million visitors each year! A Parks Pass offers many benefits. Besides unlimited visits to more than 100 state parks, pass holders receive "members only" discounts on camping (restrictions apply), park store merchandise and recreational equipment rentals and are eligible for special promotions like waived activity fees, free programs, and a special subscription rate for Texas Parks & Wildlife magazine. You can sign up for e-mail updates and the State Parks Getaways e-newsletter, which will have the latest information on events and great parks to visit.

The Parks Pass is available at most state parks and, by phone, from the customer service center in Austin. Persons 65 and over and individuals who are permanently disabled as a result of a mental or physical impairment who are currently receiving benefits under the Social Security Act can get a free Bluebonnet Pass, which entitles them to a 50 percent reduced entry fee (rounded up to the next dollar). All fees will be waived for veterans of the U.S. Armed Services holding a 60% or more service-connected disability (as determined by the U.S. Veterans Administration). In order to receive a Bluebonnet Pass (a.k.a. Texas Parklands Passport) you must apply in person, with proof of eligibility, at any Texas State Park site.

MAKE GOOD USE OF THE INTERNET

As a landscape professional I use my computer frequently. For example, I have found that I can type into my server the common or botanical name of any plant and pull up a wealth of information about it. (Sometimes there may be several species with the same common name, so go with the botanical, if possible.) When I visit nurseries I often come across a plant that does not have a complete informational label attached. I jot down the name of the plant, and the cultivar name if applicable, then I go home and look it up on the internet before purchasing it. More than once I've been disappointed to learn that the beautiful little plant I coveted is not appropriate for my planting zone.

Lots of people I know have gotten interested in garden blogs. One that appeals to Texas gardeners is **http://forums,gardenweb.com/forums/txgard/**, where registered members post questions and get answers from experts and fellow garden enthusiasts. Computers are great learning tools, but the internet can also be a source of serious misinformation. Be aware that most of the sites in cyberspace are not applicable to the Texas climate. Here are the two I've found most helpful:

http://aggie-horticulture.tamu.edu

The information server of the Texas A&M Horticulture Program contains Master Gardener information, links to botanic gardens and arboreta all over the world and images of numerous ornamental plants. There are archives of articles written by Extension Agents on a wide variety of gardening issues and Publications & Fact Sheets on such topics as starting seeds, autumn leaf management and landscape water conservation.

There are links to such sites as "Composting Information" and "Plant Propagation." Need the answer to a question? Dr. Jerry Parsons and a team of horticultural experts address the most commonly asked home gardening questions. Looking for a plant? The plantSEARCH database allows you to find the best plants for your area or landscape situation. Want to learn what Earth-Kind™ gardening is all about? Get information on environmentally friendly cultural practices for the home garden.

www.wildflower.org

Use the Lady Bird Johnson Wildflower Center's Native Plant Database to search nearly 7,000 native plant records by traits or names and use the Image Gallery to browse through a collection of almost 23,000 photographs of native plants. Print out a list of plants that deer tend to avoid or the natives that work well in water gardens or plants that work well in cut-flower arrangements. Have a question? Ask Mr. Smarty Plants. Read the many "How To" articles.

One could easily spend an entire day just exploring the contents of those two websites. There is more to learn about gardening than any one person can absorb. It's what I love most about my chosen profession. I just wish for a few more hours in every day!

3
Design

Design

Before You Begin

You've read about the history of gardens and become inspired by the public gardens and nature centers of your region. From books, magazines, lectures and online sources you've armed yourself with information. Right? Now it's time to choose your garden style and begin the design process. Whether you're establishing a new landscape or simply improving an existing one, take a hard look at what you've got before spending a penny! Good design is the difference between a yard and a garden. A garden is prime living space, worthy of as much attention as you've given to the arrangement of the rooms within your house. To achieve a coherent design, you may want to hire a professional garden designer, or you may prefer to create your own plan. The process is the same either way.

Moneysaving Tip: (a.k.a. Rule #1): Plan before you plant!

THINK ABOUT FUNCTION

Professional designers begin by examining how the existing landscape works. Is there adequate space for parking, gardening and outdoor entertaining? A place for children to play? Good circulation? Adequate storage? Sufficient privacy? Night lighting? Are there drainage problems? Problems with soil erosion?

While visiting the homes of prospective clients, I've observed people who would never tolerate a clumsy kitchen or cluttered closet enduring all sorts of inconveniences in the landscape. Sometimes there's no way for guests to get to the rear garden without encountering garbage cans or stepping into a mud puddle. Often the concrete patio poured by the contractor as a "selling feature" is too small for entertaining. There's no place in the garden to store rakes, hoses, bone meal or barbecue grills. The list goes on.

MAKE A "WISH LIST"

Family members should discuss how they would like to use their outdoor space — *He has always wanted a greenhouse and a vegetable garden, she dreams of a shady spot to curl up and read, the teenage daughter demands a sunning deck, and the ten-year-old son wants a basketball goal and a tree house. The dog needs a place to run.* Everyone will perceive the property in different ways. Often this is where a professional designer is able to serve as family "therapist," asking the right questions and listening carefully. As the various members of the family start expressing their dreams for the property, ideas will begin falling into place.

Money-saving Tip. Think about function first.

A Client's Hill Country Home

Notes from Meeting with Homeowners

New contemporary addition planned for back of house

Have eclectic furnishings and contemporary art

Like to entertain outdoors

Want outdoor kitchen

Want to incorporate their contemporary
  sculpture in rear garden

Want a water feature

Need a dog run

Minimize grass (front and back)

Want a "welcoming" front yard

Minimize dominance of front-entry garage

CONSIDER THE CLIMATE

Another advantage a professional designer can bring you is familiarity with the region where he or she practices — average dates of first and last frost, average annual rainfall, humidity levels, wind patterns, sun angles through the season, etc. Anyone new to gardening in Texas will have a lot to learn about the climate. Native Texans know that spring and fall are the most pleasant times for open-air entertaining. And, no matter how cold the winter months may become, you can always expect some sunny, seventy-degree days, perfect for enjoying your garden. Summer days are for taking cover from the brutal sun.

While outdoor living is possible throughout the year, good regional design accommodates our variable winters and sustained summer heat. For example, an open west-facing deck that would have been delightful for supper on an August night in Seattle would be unbearable in San Antonio. Shade structures will be a vital component of any Texas landscape. A terrace with a fireplace to mitigate the winter chill may allow you to enjoy your garden in January.

SURVEY YOUR SITE

The garden's Master Plan starts with a Site Plan (a drawing of what exists). The tools you'll use include graph paper, an architect's scale and a 50-foot tape for measuring the property. You may have a property survey in your files or be able to obtain one from the city. It will probably be drawn at an engineer's scale (1 inch = 20 feet), but you can have it photomechanically enlarged to ⅛-scale. Or, you can take measurements and draw the house and grounds on a large sheet of ⅛-inch graph paper, with each square representing one foot. If your lot is too large for the paper, divide the Site Plan into sections (usually front and rear).

Locate the home's windows and doors, and note all wall dimensions on the plan. Draw a north-pointing arrow on the plan and observe which direction each side of the house faces. Locate existing trees and shrubs. Pay particular attention to what you see from inside the house...*Nice view to the south, unsightly view of the neighbor's boat from the dining room window, patio baking in the afternoon sun, gorgeous tree beside the garage, wasted space on the side...*Observe the garden's vistas from every direction, and write notes on the Site Plan.

In planning outdoor living areas, keep in mind that each side of the house has its own microclimate. At our latitude, in summer the sun rises a little to the north of true east and sets slightly north of true west. Throughout the day it will appear to be directly overhead. In winter, of course, the angle of the sun drops, which can be used to great advantage if you design for it. Also consider wind patterns. Winter winds are generally blowing from the north and west. In summer prevailing breezes (if there are any) are from the south and east. In the coastal areas of South Texas, winds are almost always directly off the Gulf of Mexico. Winters are less predictable. "Northers" sweep down rapidly. As the old West Texas farmer observed, "There ain't nothin' between Texas and the North Pole but barbed-wire fences."

You'll want to look at the landscape's effect on household energy consumption. Evergreen trees and shrubs planted on the north can serve as a windbreak to reduce heat loss in winter. Deciduous trees planted on the south and west sides of the property can help cool your house in summer. In winter, they will lose their leaves, allowing the sunshine in to warm patios and other seating areas.

Next consider the slope of your land. You can use a string level to determine the slope of a simple site. Assume the elevation of the ground floor of the house to be 100 and set the property elevations on your Site Plan accordingly. For example, an elevation of 98 would be two feet below the level of the floor of the house. If the lot is so steeply sloped that you have problems with erosion or so flat that you have potential drainage problems, call a surveyor to map your property.

Note any utility easements shown on your plat. If you don't know exactly where the buried lines run, call the various service companies (gas, electric, telephone and cable) to come and mark them. You may need a plumber to trace your water and sewer lines. Draw all lines onto the Site Plan. Draw the aboveground telephone and power lines in, as well. If you have an irrigation system, locate those lines.

Moneysaving Tip: Locate all utility lines before even thinking about building anything in the landscape.

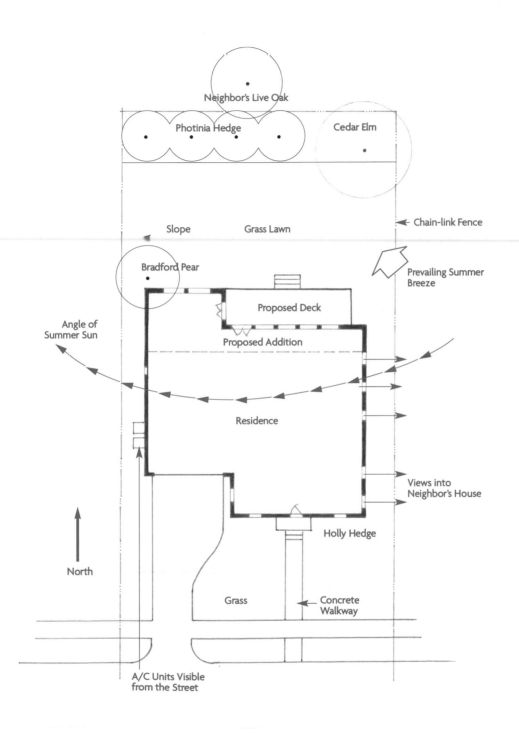

Neighbor's Live Oak

Photinia Hedge

Cedar Elm

Slope

Grass Lawn

Chain-link Fence

Bradford Pear

Prevailing Summer Breeze

Proposed Deck

Angle of Summer Sun

Proposed Addition

Residence

Views into Neighbor's House

North

Holly Hedge

Grass

Concrete Walkway

A/C Units Visible from the Street

SITE ANALYSIS

Schematic Designs

After you have a drawing of what exists and you've analyzed how the house is sited on the lot, it's time to start matching your wish list with the property's potential. Designers call this the "schematic." Think of it as brainstorming. Place a piece of tracing paper over the site plan and sketch in the various amenities your family members have proposed. (Try lots of different arrangements; tracing paper is cheap!) Every corner of the garden has a personality waiting to be developed, and even the tiniest lot will yield myriad solutions.

LOOK AT YOUR OPTIONS

In an unused side yard, you may discover the potential for a kitchen garden, a "secret garden" off a bedroom or a safe place for children to play. You'll want to select the most comfortable spots in the garden for the outdoor living areas, even if that means appropriating part of the front yard. There's no rule that says a patio must open off the back door. An entry courtyard might be an ideal place for dining outdoors or reading the Sunday paper. Perhaps an open spot in the rear garden has potential for a sunning deck. Just for visual pleasure, you might decide to break up an expanse of lawn with a gazebo or a fishpond. You may decide to build a rose arbor over a gate.

Moneysaving Tip: It's a lot easier to erase pencil marks on a plan than it is to tear out a misplaced wall or walk!

Before simply slapping an off-the-shelf fence around the perimeter of your property, consider investing in a decorative fence. You might also want to coordinate your fences with other garden structures. Here, you might save money *and* achieve a more pleasing effect. For example, fence posts can double as supports for an arbor or become part of a covered deck. An enclosed gazebo at the rear corner of a property may serve in lieu of a section of fence. A combination of evergreen shrubs and a lattice summerhouse might be used instead of a fence to screen off an unpleasant view while providing a shady spot to enjoy the outdoors.

You may even consider alterations to the house itself, such as French doors to link the house and garden or floor-to-ceiling windows that frame a section of the garden and visually expand the interior living space. You might build a solarium addition out into the garden or extend the roofline to create a covered outdoor seating area.

Moneysaving Tip: Be sure to check your local building codes before designing any landscape construction project.

CREATE "COMFORT ZONES"

As people rediscover the joy of entertaining and vacationing at home, outdoor living areas have become the most essential elements in the landscape. In selecting a site for a patio or other seating area, consider the comfort of all who will be using the space. You'll want privacy and protection from the wind, sun and rain. You'll also need to consider proximity to running water and electricity, and you may want to provide for a CAT5e connection and, if you enjoy music, an outdoor sound system. Covered terraces with ceiling fans are especially nice in this climate, and an

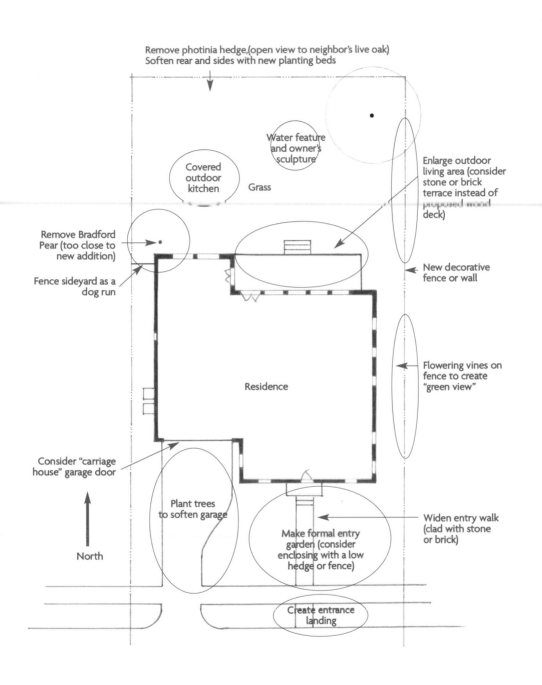

Remove photinia hedge,(open view to neighbor's live oak)
Soften rear and sides with new planting beds

Water feature and owner's sculpture

Covered outdoor kitchen

Grass

Enlarge outdoor living area (consider stone or brick terrace instead of proposed wood deck)

Remove Bradford Pear (too close to new addition)

Fence sideyard as a dog run

New decorative fence or wall

Flowering vines on fence to create "green view"

Residence

Consider "carriage house" garage door

Plant trees to soften garage

North

Make formal entry garden (consider enclosing with a low hedge or fence)

Widen entry walk (clad with stone or brick)

Create entrance landing

SCHEMATIC PLAN

outdoor fireplace to warm your living space on chilly nights can extend the season throughout the year. (If you install an outdoor fireplace, be sure to consider prevailing breezes to avoid a back draft of smoke, and be careful of overhanging limbs that could pose a fire hazard.)

The mistake most people make is providing too little outdoor living space. It's a pity to go to all the trouble and expense of constructing a deck, for example, only to discover that a few more feet would have made the area far more functional. When you're designing a deck or patio, plan the sitting areas as carefully as you would plan the seating arrangement of your family room. You will want the sitting area to face a pleasant view and ample room for a sofa and as many chairs as you'll need to accommodate the kind of entertaining your family enjoys.

In addition to the space required for a seating arrangement, allow ample room for walking around and through the outdoor sitting room. If you're designing an outdoor dining room, you'll need a minimum of eight by eight feet for the eating area, plus a place for a barbecue grill and a service bar. Outdoor kitchens are very sophisticated these days and may require as much space as your indoor kitchen! You'll want a minimum of four feet as a transition area between the cooking and eating areas. You might want to consider built-in benches to define and separate the various spaces.

Moneysaving Tip: Make outdoor living spaces large enough to meet all your needs.

REDISCOVER GARDEN "FOLLIES"

Modern gardeners have fallen in love with romantic garden structures. Arbors, belvederes, bowers, gazebos, grottos, hermitages, kiosks, lathhouses, pagodas, pavilions, pergolas, summerhouses, temples and trellises have played important roles in the landscapes of every culture. These structures remain popular because they are practical! Wonderful vine-covered arbors still provide cooling shade in summer. Pavilions continue to make lovely places to escape for al fresco dining, relaxing or sleeping. Beyond mere shelter, garden "follies" are important focal points.

Today's garden structures can be traditional or contemporary in design. An old-fashioned gazebo might incorporate a spa with benches that double as storage compartments. A summerhouse may include a built-in barbecue grill, a wet bar and under-the-counter refrigerator. A fanciful pergola might be used to camouflage the side of a garage as well as support a flowering vine. Lattice lath houses can be designed to screen off a dog run while providing a place for potting and propagating plants. You'll find small garden structures such as trellises and rose arbors in all the home improvement stores and large garden centers. See the resources for furniture and garden accessories in your region in *The Texas Garden Resource Book*. At the end of this chapter there are listings of Texas companies that ship gazebos and other garden structures throughout the state.

MAKE ROOM FOR A GREENHOUSE

While the primary appeal of a greenhouse may be to indulge an interest in orchids or cacti, it also allows you to get a head start on spring or store your patio plants in winter. It may simply be a quiet retreat where rain-or-shine greenery offers solace for the soul. Greenhouses have often been used as visual features in the garden, but tool shed and storage buildings have rarely served any use other than function. Well-designed storage structures may serve as attractive focal points in the garden while addressing more practical functions.

Greenhouses range from small window units to pricey solariums elegant enough to serve as a breakfast room, a spa enclosure or even an entrance hall. There are so many options today! If it's to be attached to your house, you may want a unit with glass glazing and nicely detailed framing. If it will be screened off from the living areas of the house and garden, one of the less expensive, more utilitarian fiberglass or plastic lean-to greenhouses may work well for you. A third option is a well-detailed freestanding greenhouse that functions as focal point in the garden.

One of the best I've ever seen was designed by the coauthor of The Texas Garden Resource Book. At her previous home, Patricia built a handsome freestanding greenhouse that also housed a small exercise pool and a comfortable sitting area. It provided a cozy place for plants and people in winter, and with its multiple French doors open, the space functioned as part of the garden in summer. Designed to replicate the colonial style of her home, the building was linked to the house by a covered breezeway.

Attached greenhouses are generally less expensive to heat than freestanding models because they share a wall with the house, and they are easier to hook up to utilities. By placing an attached greenhouse on the south side of the house and selecting energy-efficient high-performance materials, the structure may actually be used to collect solar energy for the house. Before you attach a working greenhouse, however, consider the moisture factor and the heat-load on your home furnace. **Moneysaving Tip: Be sure to check local building codes before ordering any greenhouse or garden building.**

PLAN FOR PLAY

In the past forty years, there has been a revolution in manufactured play equipment. It began with wonderful wood structures developed for city parks and has now reached the realm of backyard play. Having designed numerous "creative" playgrounds in Dallas and other Texas cities and participated in hearings at the Consumer Product Safety Commission in the 1970s, I'm personally gratified to see all this new, safer equipment. My interest in playgrounds was sparked because my own kids got hurt on the slides, seesaws, monkey bars and merry-go-rounds at school and in the local parks. Especially dreadful were the swings, which came equipped with wooden seats guaranteed to knock out teeth. Beneath all the equipment was a layer of potentially deadly asphalt. Things had to change.

I've always thought my father was lucky to have grown up in the country, where he had access to creeks, trees, hills, rocks and animals. He realized that urban dwellers need to create settings where kids can build strong bodies and develop imagination, so as a child I was allowed to make playhouses out of cardboard boxes, drag the garden hose to a sandbox to build castles, skate on sidewalks and play hide — and — seek in the garden shrubbery.

When my three children were small, I turned our entire backyard into a playground. I surrounded the lawn with a curving concrete pathway for tricycles, built a huge sandbox and bought the sturdiest swing set on the market. As they grew older, we built a playhouse with a marvelous "lookout" platform tucked into the branches of an old tree. When they became teenagers, the playhouse became my garden storage shed and the tricycle-path served as an edging for flowerbeds. Finally sandbox and swings gave way to a swimming pool. A beautiful garden is one of the few rewards of old age, but I'll never regret having provided a special place for my children and their friends to indulge in imaginative play.

Backyard play areas have a great advantage over parks and schoolyards. At home you can not only provide space for climbing and playing games, but also encourage the messy activities that stimulate creativity. You should include sandboxes (double the fun with a garden hose nearby), outdoor art easels, workbenches with scrap lumber, small garden plots and a section of driveway that's available for chalk drawings and racing toy trucks.

If you are going to install a play structure in your landscape, you'll want to ensure that it is as safe as the structures mandated for public property. Remember that children grow quickly, and the little plastic slides and playhouses that work for a two-year-old will not support the weight of a couple of rowdy eight-year-olds. To prevent eye injury and abrasions, any equipment you buy or build must be constructed with recessed bolts. Structures should never be nailed together!

The most important factor in playground safety is the surface that's under the play structure. Children *will* fall! All equipment, including plastic structures for toddlers, should be installed over a soft cushion of sand, pea gravel or bark chips. Grass (which is pictured in all the catalogs) will not stand up to the foot traffic of children, so the surface around a play structure will quickly turn into hard-packed earth, which can be as lethal as concrete. The safety surfacing under and around any piece of climbing equipment should be at least ten inches deep. It should extend a minimum of six feet beyond the edge of the equipment or the arc of a swinging device.

Regular maintenance will be critical. You'll need to check the depth and cleanliness of the surfacing material and replenish it as needed to maintain a yielding surface that will absorb the impact of a fall. Keep sandboxes covered when not in use. Check the bolts every few weeks to make sure they remain tight. Keep a close watch for wood splinters, frayed rope or open S-hooks.

At the end of this chapter you'll find listings for sources of well-designed play structures that incorporate climbing, sliding and swinging activities. If you cannot afford a sturdily constructed play structure or don't have time to keep it well-maintained, perhaps it would be better to take your children to a public park. For older children, and their parents, we have a source for game courts. (See page 72 and 73)

PROVIDE ADEQUATE UTILITY AREAS

You'll need to accommodate the "business" end of the garden, and for many homeowners a garden shed is indispensable. Inside this structure, you may want to provide built-in benches and worktables as well as designated space for lawn mowers, wheelbarrows and other tools of the trade. Ideally the shed will have a water source and ample space to organize items by the season in which they will be used. A freestanding structure can also be strategically positioned to screen off unsightly compost piles, cold frames, trash containers and such garden debris as old pots and garden stakes.

Such utility buildings as sheds and greenhouses take up a considerable amount of space on a small lot, so here's where you may want to get creative. With a bit of imaginative design, a homeowner might extend the eaves of a tool shed to create an arbor-like covered sitting area. The structure's roof could even be designed as a play fort for your children. Or, a greenhouse and garden shed could be combined into a single, handsome structure. Whatever its size, shape and function, a garden building should be incorporated into the landscape as part of an overall plan, and if possible it should be designed to complement the style of the garden and the architecture of the house.

CONNECT THE GARDEN WITH PATHS

Walkways are to a garden what hallways are to the house. I like to think of the entry walk as the home's first foyer. It sets the tone and character of the landscape. A plain, straight concrete walk between the street and front door, although quite functional, doesn't hold the same welcoming appeal as a meandering pathway constructed of stone or brick. For formal, symmetrical houses, however, I usually prefer a straight approach. The width of the walkway should be dictated by the width of the porch opening. Leading to an 18ᵗʰ-century-style Georgian home in Dallas, for example, I designed a six-foot-wide walk made of cut Pennsylvania bluestone and lined with brick that matches the house. At a 19ᵗʰ-century country cottage I suggested a 10-foot-wide gravel path leading to equally wide wood steps up to the large front porch.

More often I've designed pathways that gently curve or make geometric jogs as they approach the house. These walks have been constructed of cut stone or irregular flagstone, crushed granite lined with stone, concrete pavers, exposed aggregate concrete, brick in herringbone, basket-weave and pinwheel patterns, and even wood used as a bridge over a ravine. The advantage of a pathway that turns is that visitors are encouraged to slow down and enjoy the garden that surrounds it. A walk does not even have to be solid; it can be broken up into square or rectangular blocks or huge irregular slabs of stone separated with bands of ground cover.

A wide landing at the street not only makes it easier for guests to get out of their cars, but also makes the walkway appear more welcoming. A pair of handsome pots can be used to define the landing. I prefer walks that link the house to the street, but since the late 1950s the combination of smaller lots and subdivisions without alleys forced builders to put garages on the front of houses. To save money it became acceptable to run a concrete entry walk from the driveway to the front door. I've often suggested replacing it with a new walkway that traverses the middle of the lawn and used plantings to minimize the view of the garage.

The walkways and the edges of planting beds create line in the garden. To complement formal, symmetrical architecture or sleek contemporary houses, the gardens that surround straight walkways generally feature geometric shapes such as semicircles, squares and rectangles. Informal free-form shapes work best for cottages, ranch houses and historically based homes with asymmetrical facades. A meandering pathway through a narrow garden can be used to make the space appear wider or to create changes of perspective.

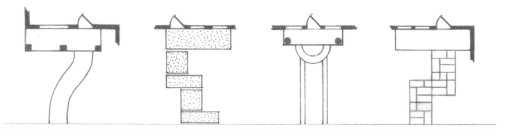

Walkways not only serve as connectors between the house and street, but also lead from space to space within the garden. They may delineate between different sections of the landscape or be used to separate the lawn from the planting beds. They should be large enough for two people to walk abreast or for a gardener to maneuver the wheelbarrow or lawn mower. Three and a half feet is considered a minimum width for the garden's major connecting links. For reasons of comfort and practicality, the main passageways should be paved. Pathways that lead to seldom-used portions of the garden or simply allow access within a large planting bed can be constructed of stepping-stones, bark, gravel or crushed granite.

Steps require very special attention. The proportions of garden steps should be different from indoor stairs. In the landscape, steps are more comfortable with deep treads and low risers (I like them no more than six inches high and 14 to16 inches deep). It's important to keep the riser heights constant throughout the landscape because unanticipated variations in height can cause people to trip and fall. A single step down also presents a danger in that it may not be immediately obvious. It's better to ramp the grade change if you need only one step down. And, if more than five steps are required, break up the staircase with a landing. All steps should be lighted at night.

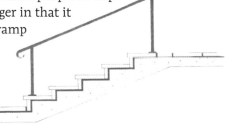

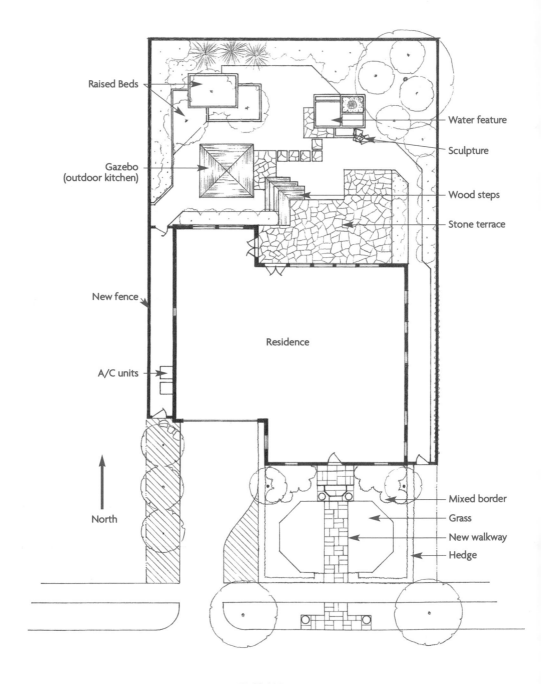

Raised Beds

Gazebo
(outdoor kitchen)

Water feature

Sculpture

Wood steps

Stone terrace

New fence

A/C units

Residence

North

Mixed border

Grass

New walkway

Hedge

MASTER PLAN

The Master Plan

Once you are sure you've included every amenity you'll ever want in your Schematic Plan, take it to a copy shop and have it enlarged to ¼-scale for the Master Plan and for the Planting Plans you'll design in detail later. As a landscape architect, I prefer to work on the final designs at this larger scale because it is easier to be precise with the width of walls, the exact size of the structures the client wishes to build, etc. Generally, I'll split the drawings into two parts, one for the front and another for the rear garden.

SHAPE THE LAWN AND PLANTING BEDS

Every square inch of ground not covered by hardscape elements (walks, walls, terraces, decks, water features, gazebos, sheds, playscapes and swimming pool) will need to be planted. Here's where you'll want to decide just how much grass you really need. Grass is the least expensive plant material to install, which is the main reason new houses come with such big lawns. (The builder had to cover the bare ground with something!) Unfortunately, lawns are the most expensive and time-consuming part of the landscape to maintain: fertilize, water, mow, edge, water, mow, edge, and before long, it's time to fertilize again. You know the drill.

Chapter Six deals with Planting Plans, which will not be necessary to complete in detail until after the construction and soil preparation are finished. But for the Master Plan, you'll need to consider the shape of the lawn areas and future beds, the location of existing trees, where you'll need new trees and screening shrubs, locations for seasonal color and possibly a place for fruits and vegetables. In the garden renovation projects I do, I'm usually asked to help homeowners eliminate great expanses of grass. Larger decks and terraces, swaths of ground cover under the tree canopy and wildflower meadows for sunny areas are usually part of the plan. My advice to young families who want a grassy play area is to place it where they might later want a pool.

DO FENCE ME IN

The last piece of the design puzzle is where to fence the property. Fences not only serve the functions of privacy and security, but also make an architectural statement. Often the fence is the strongest visual element in a new landscape. Constructed along the rear perimeter, a handsome fence provides a nice backdrop for an interesting planting scheme. Sections of fencing within the property can be used to create intimate spaces, separate the garden's functions or allow you to utilize an unused portion of the landscape. For example, you might convert part of an open front yard into an entry court or reclaim a side yard as a secure play area. It must be remembered, however, that a high, tight fence built as a visual screen will also act as a windbreak, which may be an asset or a liability.

The architectural style of your home should dictate the style and material for your fence(s). For a traditional cottage, I might select a wood fence topped with lattice, a picket fence or ornamental iron. I might punctuate this fence with a rose-covered trellis arching over the garden gate. A diagonally patterned wood fence would better serve a contemporary residence, and here I might incorporate an arbor with strong diagonal bracing. I would probably surround a formal garden with a brick wall or a beautifully detailed painted wood fence. For an Oriental effect, I might prefer a stone wall, a bamboo fence or an intricate design in wood set off with a handsome roofed gate.

Wood is by far the most commonly used material for fences. Don't settle for a plain, off-the-shelf fence until you've looked at the many textural patterns possible with wood fencing — vertical, horizontal, diagonal, basket weave, lattice and louvered. Attention to detail is what makes each fence special. Numerous home improvement books include pictures that inspire creative thinking. I hire a freelance carpenter to build wood fences for my most discriminating clients, but many of the fencing companies listed in the yellow pages are willing to do custom-quality work.

In my professional opinion, a chain-link fence devalues a residential landscape unless it is completely hidden by evergreen shrubs or vines. New vinyl-clad chain-link fencing, which is available in black, brown or green, tends to "disappear" within a leafy background. To economically surround a large backyard, I've used brick walls or ornamental iron on the side facing the street and vinyl-coated chain-link (screened with plantings) along the sides and back of the property. Vinyl chain-link fencing compares favorably to a wood fence, with the added advantage of increased durability.

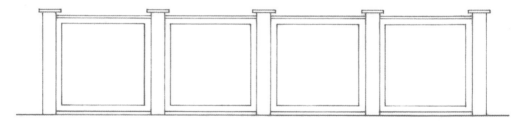

Ornamental iron fencing, which was widely used around Victorian homes in Texas, is making a strong comeback in garden design today. An airy iron fence is especially nice where you have a view. Because even the simplest ornamental iron fences run about three times more per linear foot installed than ordinary wood fences, most people choose iron only for highly visible portions of the fence, especially to separate the front from the rear gardens. Sections of antique iron fencing can also be used as attractive focal points within the garden.

Another increasingly viable option is vinyl fencing. I've used vinyl lattice extensively for fencing and trellis work because it never needs painting and doesn't rot. The lattice is available in a multitude of colors, various thicknesses, several patterns and different panel widths. It is as attractive as wood lattice and far more durable (albeit more expensive) than the thin wood lattice sold in sheets at building supply stores. Vinyl lattice used atop wood slats "dresses up" a fence, allows greater air circulation in the garden and provides a place for lacy vines to twine.

Whatever your fence material, the garden gate should make a good first impression. It should stand out from the pattern of the fence, yet harmonize with the fence design. Often, I'll pick up an architectural detail from the house and repeat it in the gate design. To make the gate even more distinctive, I like to set off the gateposts with finials or lights. It's up to homeowners to know what they want and to demand the highest quality possible within their budget. In fencing, like most other things, you'll get what you pay for.

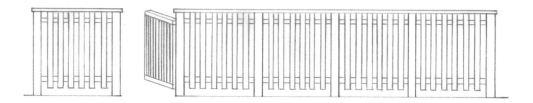

Once you've considered several possible Schematic Designs, it's time to draw a final Master Plan. This plan is usually a culmination of weeks or months of exploration. There will have been compromises along the way. As the final blueprint for the garden's future, however, the Master Plan should show every deck, patio, walkway, fence, gazebo, etc., you someday hope to include in the garden. It should reflect the character of the house and its occupants, the family's needs and the capabilities of the site. If you, like most people, cannot immediately afford every improvement, divide the plan into sections (Phase 1, Phase 2, etc.) and build the garden at a pace and price you can manage.

Moneysaving Tip: Don't be afraid to invest in your landscape. According to MONEY magazine, landscaping has a 100 to 200 percent recovery value.

Online Resources for Garden Structures in Texas

Sheds & Decorative Wood Materials

Affordable Portable Structures
www.affordableportable.com

10500 North IH-35
Austin, Texas 78753
512.251.5757 or 800.926.5657

5510 Hwy 290 West
Austin, Texas 78735
512.892.0797

6046 Williams Drive
Georgetown, Texas 78628
512.930.1488

This company carries gazebos constructed by Amish craftsmen in Lancaster County, Pennsylvania. These structures are made of #1 treated, kiln-dried pine with shake cedar roofs and handcrafted cupolas. Optional seats and screening complete

(LISTING CONTINUED ON THE NEXT PAGE)

(CONTINUED)

each of the six styles. They can be ordered as kits or built on your site anywhere in Texas. The company also makes its own handsome, durable portable buildings, but these are available only to customers within 50 miles of the Austin area.

The Gazebo Factory
148 Main Street
Farmersville, Texas 75442
214.603.9013
www.discountgazebos.com

"In the twenty-something years we have been in business, we have produced and installed thousands of gazebos, pergolas and other structures for homeowners throughout the country," says Jim Klein, owner. "Why buy a gazebo or pergola kit, pay to have it shipped, pay for labor to do the foundation/site work, then assemble the structure and possibly have to paint or stain it yourself? Let us do all the work, make your life easier and save you money at the same time." Begun in 1985, Klein spent eleven years exhibiting his gazebos at the State Fair of Texas. Now his company has added porch swings, patio covers, pergolas and pavilions in a variety of sizes. The products can be ordered in pressure-treated pine or cedar. And if you don't find what you want in the online catalog, he'll do custom work.

Vintage Woodworks
Hwy. 34S – P. O. Box 39
Quinlan, Texas 75474-0039
903.356.2158
www.vintagewoodworks.com

"We're still 100 years behind the times...still handcrafting from solid wood... still more concerned about service than about making a 'quick buck'...still shipping promptly...and still absolutely guaranteeing your happiness," say the folks at Vintage Woodworks. Their products are particularly applicable for traditional-style houses, but there are ideas for everyone here. For decks, they have newel posts, balusters and railings. For porches and other garden "follies," there are decorative posts, brackets, and gable decorations. You can even order *The Porch Book*, which is filled with design ideas and construction information. They offer bead board made of AZEK® for porch ceilings, as well as AZEK® deck materials. They've got real cedar shingles (plain and fancy) and a wonderful selection of screen doors in their comprehensive online catalog.

The Wood Factory
111 Railroad Street
Navasota, Texas 77868
936.825.7233

Remodeling contractor Dean Arnold found an old machine and began making fine copies of Victorian millwork. Thirty years later, his company has expanded into a custom woodworking shop noted for distinctive gingerbread details, entry doors, screen doors and gazebo parts. Among the product lines you'll find beautifully crafted posts, finials, and pickets for traditional wood fences, prefabricated from redwood and pre-sanded for painting. The company offers reprints of several old millwork catalogs. "We couldn't possibly include all the designs that were original to the Victorian period in our catalog. We pride ourselves on our reputation for matching existing porch parts or creating a new look for your individual needs," says Dean. He and his wife Shelly are available to help you achieve that custom look. Call for more information or write. You can send samples to help the Arnolds envision what you need.

Greenhouses

The Greenhouse Mall
9900 Ranch Road 620 North
Austin, Texas 78726-2203
512.250.0000
www.greenhousemall.com

Whether you want a beautiful tropical environment for a year-round hobby, get a head start on seedlings for your garden or simply a place to keep outdoor container plants during the winter, this is a complete source for hobby-size greenhouses and accessories. In business since 1977, it offers a variety of styles in many different sizes, as well as such accessories as heaters, ventilation systems, shade cloth and other greenhouse items. The Greenhouse Mall installs (anywhere in Texas) about 98% of the several lean-to and freestanding greenhouses it sells. Paul Parker oversees the manufacturing and installation, and he'll be able to answer any questions you may have.

Rounhouse
18488 Highway 105
Cleveland, Texas 77328
800.238.7289
www.rounhous.com

A manufacturer of steel-frame, Quonset-style greenhouses for almost 40 years, Rounhouse now also makes an A-frame unit. The company sells fans, heaters, cooling systems, oversize shade cloth, polycarbonate sheeting and ground cloth, as well. These utilitarian structures are available in a wide variety of sizes suitable for growers and serious hobbyists.

Texas Greenhouse Company, Inc.
812 East Northside Drive
Fort Worth, Texas 76102
800.227.5447
www.texasgreenhouse.com

In business since 1948, Texas Greenhouse has long been considered a leader in the design and manufacture of graceful curved-glass greenhouses. The company's "American Classic" series is constructed of powder-coated aluminum glazing bars

(LISTING CONTINUED ON THE NEXT PAGE)

suspended on a galvanized substructure. Online photos show the units on handsome brick and stone bases, as well. All are made with double-strength glass and adjustable roof ventilators. Several sizes are available in the freestanding units, ranging from a 9' x 12' model designed for small gardens to very spacious structures. Smaller units are available with a choice of glass or twin-wall polycarbonate panels. Texas Greenhouse also makes good-looking lean-to structures that can be attached to your house and a wall-hung unit that serves as a bay window. The catalog includes benches, heating and cooling equipment, roll-up shades and other garden amenities such as fog systems. If you are on a tight budget, there are do-it-yourself kits.

Play Structures

Backyard Adventures
14201 I-27
Amarillo, Texas 79119
806.622.1220 or 800.345-1491
www.backyardadventures.com

A father of six, Charles Sammann of Amarillo invented this line of play equipment because he was keenly aware of children's need for safe, creative, physically stimulating play. "We encourage you to compare our design, function and value," he told us. It's sold throughout the country now. The company builds its structures with kiln-dried cedar or redwood, and it uses patented compression clamps to join accessories to platforms. All of its steel components are powder-coated for durability, just like the best park equipment. The most popular models are in the "Treehouse Series," wood-roofed platforms with several optional configurations and such accessories as swings, chain ladders, rock wall mountain, and spiral, straight and wave slides (even hammocks and picnic tables), all pictured in the colorful online catalog. Thirteen dealers operate showrooms throughout Texas.

Rainbow Play Systems
800.724.6269
www.rainbowplay.com

This manufacturer is out of South Dakota, but it sells through an extensive network of dealers in Texas. Over the last 23 years it has grown from a small custom job shop to a high-tech manufacturing facility. "Our focus remains on continuing to produce the safest, most durable and highest-quality play systems." The decking is redwood, cedar or cumminghamia finished with a 10-step sealing process, and the company also offers products in plastic-encapsulated lumber. There are over 100 accessories listed in the online catalog. All the attachment hardware is recessed, and all of the units are expandable as your children grow.

Sport Court of Texas
www.sportcourt-texas.com

Austin Courts and Floors
10208 Highway 620 North
Austin, Texas 78726
512.335.9779

NexCourt
609 Stadium Drive
Arlington, Texas 76011
817.265.4141

AllPro Courts
5829 W. Sam Houston Pkwy. North
Houston, Texas 77041
832.467.4909

Grand Slam Courts
16002 Wolf Creek
San Antonio, Texas 78232
210.496.3399
800.880.0234 (central office for Texas)

Sport Court® makes courts for 15 different sports and games, and all are surfaced with a modular resilient material that quickly sheds water. They make great play areas for children of all ages. Tots even use them for tricycles. The interactive website allows you to participate in the design of your game courts, basketball and tennis courts, and putting greens. There are rebounders for soccer, tennis and softball, plus new skateboard products, as well. The company has been in business in Texas for 30 years. Its products are meticulously installed, and it guarantees the surfacing tiles for ten years. "Investing in a Sport Court® does more than add value to your home. You're investing in a place for families to bond and friendships to blossom," says Greg Dettman, CEO. "Our high-performance game courts help reduce injuries and can be custom-built to fit your own backyard. They keep your children there, and the rest of the neighborhood back there with them." One toll-free call to the 800-880-0234 will put you in touch with the dealer that serves your area.

4
Construction

Construction

Implementing your Master Plan

After the Master Plan is drawn, the homeowner selects the materials that will be used in the garden. Once the material choices have been made, the landscape architect will prepare a Grading Plan for drainage and get down to detail with Construction Drawings.

SELECT APPROPRIATE MATERIALS

Your choice of materials for walls, pathways and fences should be selected to complement both the architectural style of the house and the garden you envision. Brick, stone, tile, concrete and wood are the basic materials you'll be considering, but these materials are available in many forms and colors, and they can be used to create an almost infinite number of patterns and textures in the landscape.

Materials can be combined to create interest, but too many materials become distracting. Never use more than three. If you want to make a small garden seem larger, select a single material for all of the walls, walks and patios. Consider your options carefully, because the cost of garden construction depends not only upon the material you choose, but also the labor involved for installation.

Walls present special design challenges. Freestanding walls require footings that will stand up to wind loads, and retaining walls are subject to tremendous forces of water. Walls of any significant height require reinforced concrete footings, and provision must be made for weep holes to ensure proper drainage. Get professional advice before building any walls over three feet in height.

Poured Concrete

Concrete is the single most overused landscape material. Yes, it's durable, relatively inexpensive and easily molded into intricate forms. It may be the only feasible choice if you're dealing with large areas and/or curving shapes. However, large expanses of concrete can appear cold and monotonous. Exposed aggregate concrete is warmer than brush-finished concrete, and if the concrete is combined with a brick border or stone insets, it takes on an even more friendly feeling.

I'm enthusiastic about the effects that can be achieved with colored, stamped concrete that simulates the feel of cobblestone, slate or brick. It "dresses up" the garden, yet it costs less than half as much as professionally installed natural stone or brickwork. The process is tricky, so it's not a job for amateurs. Ask to see completed examples of the work of companies that pour and form stamped concrete. They operate through trained, local licensed contractors, who serve large geographical areas. (Look in your local yellow pages under Concrete Decorative and Stamped)

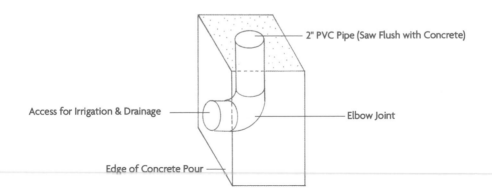

2" PVC Pipe (Saw Flush with Concrete)

Access for Irrigation & Drainage

Elbow Joint

Edge of Concrete Pour

If you are pouring a new concrete porch, patio or landing, cast an L-shaped section of 2" pvc pipe for drainage and drip irrigation everywhere you plan to place pots

Tile, Brick & Concrete Pavers

Tile is a great choice for covering an unattractive old entry porch or small concrete terrace, but it's the most expensive material you can choose for large-scale new construction. It runs two to four times more per square foot than brick or concrete pavers, and it must be set on a concrete base. To be suitable for landscape use, the product must be non-skid and frost-proof. Included among the wealth of handsome tile paving materials readily available for Texas gardens are terra-cotta clay tiles and quarried stone cut in the form of tiles.

Pavers are attractive and versatile, but labor-intensive to install. Given a choice between natural (fired-clay) brick and concrete pavers, I have generally preferred the look of brick. However, concrete pavers have become increasingly sophisticated in recent years, and the variety of colors and shapes available have made it possible to create remarkably interesting patterns in the landscape. (Sometimes contractors get carried away and create color combinations that are too "busy" for my taste.)

Mortared brick walkways and patios usually require the skills of a mason. The average homeowner can lay a relatively durable walk or patio by placing the brick on a bed of compacted crushed stone or crushed concrete. To hold the loose bricks

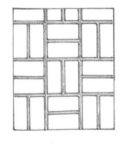

Basketweave

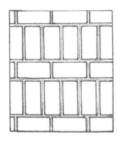

Alternating Running Bond and Soldier courses

45° Flanders Weave

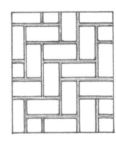

Classic Herringbone

in place, however, you'll need to install a solid edging, such as mortared brick, treated wood or one of the new plastic or steel edging materials made for the purpose. After the brick is in place, sweep a dry sand mix mortar between the joints, and moisten with a hose to activate the mortar.

Clay brick generally costs slightly more than concrete pavers. But if your house is brick and you find a brick that matches, that would be your best choice. Other than cost, there's no real advantage to using concrete pavers for walkways and patios. However, clay brick cannot be used for a driveway unless it has a reinforced concrete base, while interlocking concrete pavers need only a highly compacted crushed stone base. So, if you want to match the driveway and walkways, concrete pavers would certainly be the more cost-effective choice.

Several companies make handsome modular block for retaining walls, which enables homeowners to build mortarless walls that do not require concrete footings. The retaining walls may be straight, concave, convex or laid as serpentine curves. Made of high-strength concrete, these walls are virtually maintenance-free. Attractive capstones made to top the walls also make nice material for steps. Retaining wall blocks vary in size and weight; some may be up to 114 pounds. You'll need a licensed civil engineer to design any wall over four feet in height. For simple raised beds or a retaining wall less than two feet high, several companies make a lightweight block, which can be easily installed by homeowners. These products are available from home improvement stores. Be sure to ask for design and installation guides, which should be available from the manufacturer.

Natural Stone

Ironically, the biggest difficulty with natural stone is making it appear natural. You'll be more pleased with the results if you choose a stone that harmonizes with the color of the local soil. Limestone "belongs" in the Hill Country, while red sandstone blends better into the landscapes of East Texas and the Red Rolling Plains. Stonework can appear very arbitrary in the Blackland Prairies and coastal regions where there is no native stone.

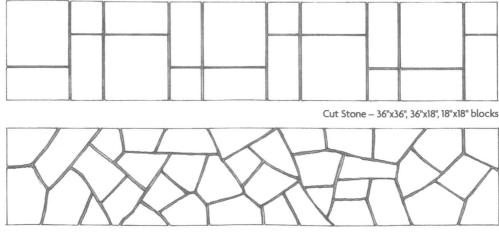

Cut Stone – 36"x36", 36"x18", 18"x18" blocks

Random Flagstone

There's artistry involved in setting stone, but a non-professional can lay it if the pieces are small enough to lift by hand. There are numerous books on stonescaping, and I'd suggest looking at several before selecting stone for your garden. For ideas on the use of rock in the landscape and beautifully detailed walkways, look at books on Japanese garden design. The Japanese are masters of the art; some of their secrets include paying attention to the grain of the rock and partially burying boulders, just as they are found in nature.

"Weathered" stone is generally more attractive and almost always more expensive than freshly cut stone. When I built an extensive limestone patio at my home in Austin, I used an affordable mix of weathered and new stones. The contractor mixed lampblack into the mortar, which unified the surface and created the overall effect of old stonework.

Texas native stone of every description is readily available throughout the state. Stone companies carry a dizzying array of local and imported limestone, sandstone from various regions in the country, slate, schist and granite, including Texas pink and other varieties. The larger dealers will also offer specialty aggregates from different parts of the United States, including Texas "rainbow rock" and black Mexican beach pebbles. Crushed granite should not be overlooked as a handsome material for walks and driveways. It's particularly attractive when contained within bold landscape timbers or bordered with mortared stone edging. It can also be used as filler between stepping-stones.

New polymeric sands, which can be found wherever masonry products are sold, are good for filling between closely set stones, pavers and bricks. The products are water-soluble (or activated by water) to hold paving materials in place and prevent weeds from growing and ants from colonizing between the pavers. You can also mix the products with crushed granite to make a more solid surface. The price will vary from dealer to dealer, but in general you can expect to pay three times more for polymeric sand than you would for an ordinary bag of silica sand or torpedo sand. The cost should weighed against future maintenance expenses.

Stone and gravel are expensive to ship, so whether you are looking for flagstones or landscape boulders, begin your search with local dealers. If there is more than one source for decorative rocks and paving stones in your area, visit several before deciding which material to choose. You may be surprised to find great differences in prices and selections. There are several companies in Texas that provide cut stone for special uses such as formally patterned walkways, pool coping and architectural detailing. You'll find them listed on page 88-90.

Wood

The appeal of wood is that it blends comfortably with the natural environment and achieves warmth that no other material can match. Wood decking is comparable to mortared brick or stonework in terms of cost, but it is, of course, not as durable. If you overlook a steep slope, wood decking allows you to build out over part of the landscape, in some cases doubling your gardening space, with container gardening on the deck and a shade garden beneath.

However, if you're building an outdoor living area close to ground-level and do not have sufficient space between the ground and decking for good air circulation, choose another material. You'll see decking and wood walks built right on the ground in some of the national magazines, but it's never an advisable practice.

If you want to use wood, I'd recommend cedar, redwood or one of the newly available South American hardwoods such as *ipe*. I'm leery of treated wood. The old CCA (chromated copper arsenate) was very toxic, and was discontinued a few years ago for most building construction. There are newer formulations for treating wood, but they remain to be proven safe over time. I'd certainly not specify treated wood of any kind for building raised planting beds where there will be edible crops. There is, however, new recycled plastic made to resemble wood that is increasingly popular. It is more expensive but longer-lasting than wood, and doesn't require sanding, staining and other routine maintenance.

A wood fence, if it is properly designed and built, should last without repair for twenty years. Its posts are the critical element for ensuring durability. I specify metal posts. There is nothing pretty about metal posts, but they can be clad in a wood surround or hidden inside a double-faced fence.

Getting Started on the Project

Once you have selected materials and your designer has completed the Construction drawings, it's time to select a General Contractor or decide if you can complete the project yourself with the help of specialized contractors and your own two hands.

FINDING A QUALIFIED CONTRACTOR

Once the design work is complete, most homeowners decide to seek the services of a general contractor who will hire and supervise the work of such specialists as irrigation contractors, lighting contractors, paving and fencing contractors. Landscape architects and designers normally prepare plans and written specifications that allow you to get bids from several different contractors. Often they will recommend several landscape contractors with whom they have worked in the past. If you are seeking a contractor or subcontractor on your own, avoid anyone who calls himself/herself a "landscaper." I wince when I hear this term. Qualified people in the industry refer to themselves as landscape contractors. Most good general contractors are members of the Texas Nursery and Landscape Association (TNLA).

Make sure that the person you are dealing with is licensed and bonded. Ask for his/her registration number and confirmation of liability insurance. The best landscape contractors take great pride in their profession and back up their work with years of experience and training. They should be happy to give you references. Take time to call the references and study every detail of any contract before signing it.

Moneysaving Tip: Obtain recommendations and interview several firms. The lowest bid is not necessarily the best bid.

DOING IT YOURSELF

With all the helpful do-it-yourself books on the market, some homeowners prefer to construct hardscape elements themselves. Home improvement stores usually have racks of books, classes on topics from tile-setting to deck-building, and, if you are lucky, personnel to give you advice. Other homeowners supplement their own efforts with the help of subcontractors who provide the expertise and labor for such portions of the job as pouring concrete or building stone walls. Many garden centers offer basic building services in addition to plant installation services or can recommend qualified people to do the work.

Be aware that specific technical requirements govern such site amenities as driveways, freestanding masonry walls and retaining walls over three feet in height. The factors that must be considered in the design of a driveway, for example, include angle of slope, turning radius and the weight of the vehicles that will be using it. Walls must be designed to withstand the forces of wind and water.

Moneysaving Tip: Seek professional help with the design and construction of hardscape elements that require complicated calculations and special engineering techniques.

A number of people I know really enjoy working with wood and are quite capable of building a wood fence or deck. There are a number of paperback books on fences and decks with color photographs to spark your imagination. Most will include information on ways to maintain the wood deck, which will help protect your investment.

Once you're ready to tackle the project, your local lumberyard or home improvement store will be a good source for landscape materials. Every city in Texas has listings in the Yellow Pages for retail suppliers of specialty materials for landscape construction and contractors who can help you implement your plan. See page 70 for sources of decorative balusters and hand-turned woodwork to complement the porches and decks of Victorian and other period houses.

Be sure the depth and width of the posthole is sufficient to accommodate a stout concrete footing. Depth of burial should equal one-third of the height of the metal post above ground (i.e., the post for a six-foot-high fence could be no less than eight feet long). The width of the footing should be at least three times greater than the diameter of the post. Set the bottom of the post in four or five inches of gravel so that the metal does not stand in water or come in contact with earth. The concrete is then poured around the posts on top of the gravel. The top of the concrete footer should be rounded to shed water. I also specify that the tops of the posts be capped or beveled to shed water, as well.

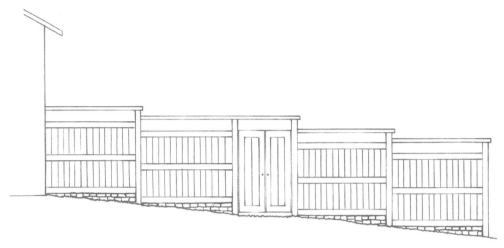

Build a stepped fence on a slope

Beware of mass-market companies that assemble fences with staples rather than ring-shank galvanized nails. If you're building down a slope, insist that the fence be designed to step down in increments, with the top of each section horizontal. (The cheap and easy way is to saw off the tops at an angle.) Be sure that gates are to be constructed with extra-sturdy posts and diagonal bracing; otherwise, they will begin to sag within a few months.

Moneysaving Tip: Before signing a contract for fence installation, ask to see samples of a company's work and closely inspect their construction methods.

Setting the posts is the really backbreaking part of the job. I know a homeowner who found a fence company willing to dig the holes and set the posts. He then completed a decorative double-sided fence in a day with boards purchased pre-cut from a lumberyard. So, if you are handy with a hammer, this could save you both time and money.

Preparing for Construction

Before any soil preparation or planting begins, complete your construction projects. Construction is *always* messy! Don't even think about new plants at this time. The final steps in the design process will be the Specifications for Soil Preparation, which we will discuss in Chapter Five, and the Planting Plan, which we'll get to in Chapter Six. In the meantime, just take good care of the plants you have.

Site preparation is the most time-consuming part of many landscape projects. If you are building a walk, driveway, patio or garden structure over an existing lawn, you may need to remove old concrete or get rid of existing grass. Killing grass, especially Bermuda grass, is infinitely more difficult than getting it to grow. You can smother it for a couple of months under black plastic or use herbicide to dispatch it quickly. In either case, it's prudent to remove the dead grass and its tenacious root system with a sod cutter before construction begins. If you're laying brick on crushed stone, you'll need to place a barrier beneath the sand to reduce the chance of vegetation growing up between the cracks. A layer of polyethylene will suffice, but a brand-name product designed specifically for the job will be more effective.

Then you'll need to ensure proper drainage, so some earth-moving will probably be involved as well. On level ground, walkways should be poured or laid with a slight "crown" along the center to shed water. On a slope, walkways should drain downhill, following the contour of the slope. Where walkways adjoin planting beds, raise the level of the walkway so that soil and mulches won't wash out onto the path every time it rains. All driveways and patios should be sloped away from the house, if possible.

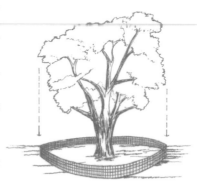

Expect construction damage. I've seen leftover concrete dumped on tree roots, paint splattered all over hedges, and plants trampled to a pulp. If you have valuable trees on your lot and there's going to be any construction, keep all men, machines, materials and portable potties out from under the drip line of the trees at all times. Build a temporary fence around the trees and rope off planting areas that are to be protected.

Tree Protection should extend to the outer edge of the canopy

Do not allow any cut or fill around your trees. If it appears that cutting or filling around tree roots or cutting the roots will be essential to the completion of your building project, there are ways to minimize the damage. Consult an arborist.

Moneysaving Tip: Protect existing plants from construction damage by writing in a dollar amount that will cover the cost of replacement if the contractor does not follow the rules!

DEAL WITH DRAINAGE PROBLEMS

Proper grading is vital because Texas weather alternates between frog-choking rain and dust-bowl drought. Finding a way to rapidly carry rainwater away from the house can be a nettlesome problem. If standing water is severe and continual, you'll probably need professional help.

The average homeowner can usually correct minor, recurring puddles in lawn areas or planting beds with the addition of soil or a simple subsurface drainage system (often called a "French drain"). It's made by digging a trench 12 inches deep and 12 inches wide, with the bottom of the trench sloping away from the problem area toward a slope or storm drain. Line the trench with a layer of gravel, lay four-inch-diameter perforated PVC pipe wrapped in filter fabric and back-fill with coarse gravel. To drain effectively, the slope of the drain should descend at a minimum of one foot per 100 feet.

City regulations may require you to retain rainwater on your site rather than discharge it into the storm sewer system. One attractive solution is to construct a dry creek that leads excess water toward a small depression in the lawn that serves as a holding pond. When it isn't carrying water, a rock-lined creek bed can be an attractive landscape feature. Perhaps you'll want to run a flagstone walk beside it, line it with iris and design a bridge to cross it. The "stream bed" can terminate in a "bog garden" filled with plants that can withstand both wet and dry conditions. Artificial berms can be constructed to direct both rainfall and excess irrigation water into these wet/dry planting areas.

French drains are used to channel
water away from a house.

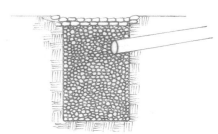

A Dry Well can be used to collect
water from a downspout

If, on the other hand, you are dealing with a steep slope and rapid runoff, you may want to construct a series of steppes or retaining walls. (Farmers in dry climates have used terracing to maximize rainwater for centuries.) Rather than let water rush down a slope, terraces conserve the precious water that falls on your site, releasing it more slowly, allowing it to penetrate the soil and preventing erosion. A French drain behind each retaining wall can prevent the soil from becoming waterlogged during periods of heavy rainfall. For more moderate slopes, erosion-control fabric is useful for covering newly-tilled soil until plants are established to hold the dirt.

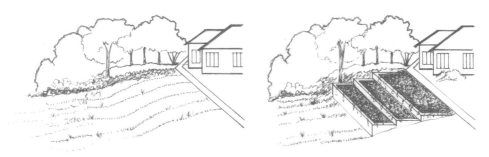

Terrace a steep slope to prevent erosion and retain irrigation water.

PLAN FOR IRRIGATION AND LIGHTING SYSTEMS

If you've ever had to tear out a section of driveway to install an irrigation line, you'll appreciate how nice it would have been if someone had thought to cast a piece of open pipe into the concrete form *before* the concrete was poured. Called "sleeves" in the industry, pipes set at intervals under new pavement allow you to decide later where you want to run electrical or irrigation lines. Place at least two sections of 2-inch schedule 40 PVC pipe underneath all new walkways and driveways for future use.

Moneysaving Tip: Pennies spent on pipe sleeves can literally save hundreds of dollars.

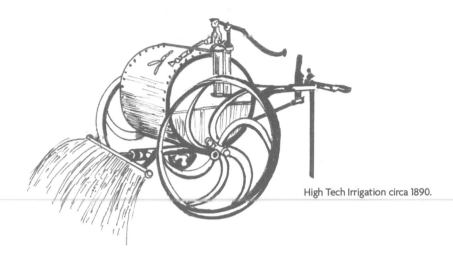

High Tech Irrigation circa 1890.

Irrigation

The time to explore a new irrigation system is before the start of construction. I always advise my clients to invest in an automatic irrigation system if they can possibly afford it. I also advise renovating an existing system along with any major garden renovation. Most old irrigation systems put out more water than the soil can absorb, resulting in big losses due to runoff and evaporation. In the past decade, there has been a lot of improvement in automated irrigation systems. Fabricated of new high-quality plastics and designed to throw as little water in the air as possible, today's irrigation systems cut down on evaporation. They feature computerized controls that precisely regulate the amount of water that goes to each zone, and solenoid electric valves that adjust flow and prevent valves from getting stuck open.

If you're putting in a new automatic irrigation system, insist on separate zones for lawn and planting beds, and be sure that the system can be adjusted for seasonal differences. Consider investing a few extra dollars for rain and freeze sensors, two items that will save considerable grief and water. Once the Master Plan is complete, the hardscape is built and the land is approximately graded properly, the irrigation contractor can run lines for the system. The types of heads can then be determined once the Planting Plan is designed. Immediately after the plants are installed, there is always some "tweaking" needed to make sure coverage is correct. (Find more about irrigation in Chapter Nine.)

Lighting

Many homeowners think of outdoor lighting as something reserved for the wealthy, but in fact, you can make a big impact for as little as $250. With a budget of $1,500 you can achieve a truly sophisticated lighting system in an average-size garden. If you consider that lighting adds refinement and value to the house, enhances safety, and extends your hours of enjoyment in the garden, it's a bargain. A few well-placed fixtures allow you to reveal the garden's best features while hiding others. Lighting can make a large garden seem intimate or create an illusion of depth in a small space. The design should be in the planning stages before construction begins.

Moneysaving Tip: Light only the areas you use at night.

Painting the landscape with light can create magical effects. Use soft uplighting to display a sculptural plant in silhouette against a wall or to define the trunk and branching pattern of a graceful tree. Employ downlighting to create a dance of shadows on lawn and terraces beneath the tree canopy. Tuck a string of low-voltage lights into ground covers to illuminate pathways and define the edges of planting beds. Mark the entrance to a driveway or frame a garden gate with handsome post lights.

Good lighting design involves controlling not only the direction but also the color and intensity of the light. It's best done by a professional who is trained to place the right fixtures and the right lamps in the right spot. Twice as many of the wrong fixtures may give half the impact, so assistance from a lighting designer can save you money in the long run. Many retail lighting stores and outdoor lighting contractors offer moderately priced design services when you buy fixtures from them.

As a "picture book" source of ideas for how different lighting effects appear at night, *The Landscape Lighting Book* by Janet Lennox Moyer is top-notch. Even if you're bringing in a professional lighting designer or planning to work with a lighting dealer, the book's color photographs will enable you to visualize and communicate what you want. If you're installing a system yourself, the book contains a wealth of information on planning, installation techniques and maintenance.

For large properties, you may want to consider a commercial-grade line-voltage system that runs on household current. Note, however, that such a system must be laid in metal conduit, which is more expensive to buy and install than plastic. (With plastic conduit there is a dangerous potential for cutting through the conduit with a shovel or spading fork.)

Low-voltage systems eliminate the need for conduit altogether. These systems offer a wide choice of small, unobtrusive fixtures, and the fixtures are easily moved as the garden grows and changes. Until recently, low-voltage systems could not be strung more than 50 feet without losing candlepower at the end of the line. New multi-tap transformers no longer restrict the length of the line. Low-voltage systems are less expensive to operate than a line-voltage system because they put out twice the lumens per watt as a 120-volt system. (It's the lumens that count.)

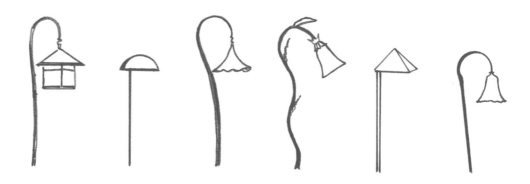

Twelve-volt systems currently available at local hardware and home improvement stores are safe, easy to install and inexpensive. I recently found a kit of four plastic low-voltage pathway lights for $34.99. The same store had attractive shell-shaped cast-metal lights for under $25 apiece and all of the wiring and transformers necessary to devise your own twelve-volt system. Inexpensive kit-form fixtures are better than no lighting at all, but not very durable. I always suggest to my clients that they buy the highest quality fixtures they can afford and add lighting in phases if necessary.

The lamps in packaged lighting kits typically put out very low levels of light, so you need to space them very close together. Better-quality fixtures that use MR16, MR11 and MR8 lamps (MR means multifaceted reflector) can be placed 15 to 18 feet apart, so you actually need fewer of them. The life expectancy of MR lamps is now up to 10,000 hours. You won't have to change the "bulb" but every three to four years. Line-voltage lamps remain at 1,000 to 2,000 hours, requiring more frequent maintenance.

The newest development in low-voltage lighting is LEDs (light-emitting diodes). The lighting industry is working to perfect this energy-efficient solid-state technology. Several factors make these innovative products very exciting. More lights can be run on one wire. There's no voltage drop at the end of the line. In addition to saving money on electricity bills, the best news for the consumer may be that the "light bulbs" last up to 50,000 hours. Lighting professionals are telling me that in the next few years, LEDs will revolutionize outdoor lighting.

Be sure any lighting equipment you buy bears a label that indicates approval by Underwriters Laboratory (UL). In terms of durability, copper and burnished brass rank highest. Powder-coated aluminum is also very durable, but the aluminum will deteriorate over time in alkaline soil, which includes most of Texas. So while coated aluminum works well for above-ground fixtures, it's better not to use aluminum fixtures as buried bullets in the caliche soils of Austin, for example. Many good quality in-ground fixtures are now molded of a fiberglass-reinforced composite material, which is proving to be durable in every type of soil. With any fixture you want to look for silicone gaskets. If vandalism might be a problem, consider buying a fixture with Lexan™ lenses rather than glass.

By day, you want fixtures that complement the architectural style of your house. At night, the most important visual aspect is the color effect created by the lamp inside the fixture. For natural-looking color in the landscape, fluorescent or halogen lamps (such as MR16 or PAR 36) are much closer to daylight (warmer in color) than mercury vapor lights, which are used for tree lighting to create a "moonlight" effect. Some designers love the cool bluish color-rendering characteristics of mercury vapor lights. My personal opinion is that they are more appropriate out in the distance in estate-size landscapes than in a small intimate garden.

There are a number of "bells and whistles" you can add to a lighting system, including photocells that turn the light on at dusk. You can also get motion detectors that sense intruders or turn lights on as you come in late at night. Many systems come with timers that turn off certain lights at a specified time. For example, you may want the security lighting left on, but choose not to burn decorative lighting all night. Remote controls allow you to turn on security lights from inside.

If you seek professional help, and I highly recommend that you do, ask to see several of the firm's completed projects and talk to homeowners who have used their services. Don't be afraid to request a demonstration in your own garden. If you're into doing-it-yourself, take flashlights out in your garden and see what uplighting will do for trees or how a wash of light might enliven a wall. There is an excellent online lighting source listed on page 91.

Moneysaving Tip: Try various fixture arrangements before you decide on permanent placement. Get it right the first time!

Online Resources for Hardscape Materials in Texas

Cut or Carved Stone

Arte en Cantera
2900 North McColl Road
McAllen, Texas 78501
956.682-1623
www.arteencantera.com

This company's in-house manufacturing facility has allowed owner Ricardo Azubell "to meet our customers' demands quickly and efficiently." Arte en Cantera designs, hand-carves and installs products made from cantera stone (in 12 colors), limestone (in six colors) and travertine. These handsome pieces include columns, fireplaces, balustrades, fountains, moldings, flooring, pool coping and signs and entries. In business for 15 years, Arte en Cantera produces quality products and offers a warranty on all pieces.

Materials Marketing
www.mstoneandtile.com

120 West Josephine Street (home office)
San Antonio, Texas 78212
210.731.8453

1626 Hi Line Drive, Suite A
Dallas, Texas 75207
214.752.4226

806 Foch Street
Fort Worth, Texas 76107
817.348.8579
115 Wild Basin Road, Suite 105
Austin, Texas 78746
512.328.682

3433 West Alabama
Houston, Texas 77027
713.960.8601

Materials Marketing can supply you with every imaginable architectural embellishment for the exterior of upscale homes — balusters, columns, fireplaces, door and window surrounds and handsome fountains from its quarries in Mexico. It's a wonderful source for ceramic, Saltillo and Cantera stone pavers and decorative tile to be used on walls, pools, fountains and outdoor countertops, as well. The website will link you to other manufacturers and artisans this company represents, and its portfolio will inspire your creativity.

Custom Stone Supply
www.customstone.com

2627 Joe Field Rd.
Dallas Texas 75229
972.243.1144

9850 John W. Elliott
Frisco, Texas
972.335.4122

2725 Prestige Road
Keller, Texas 76248
817.337.4408

4523 Brittmoore
Houston, Texas 77041
713.937.3966
3434 Fountain View
Houston, Texas 77057
713.974.1911

225 Highway 146 South
Texas City, Texas 77590
409.945.6000

4433 Terry-O Lane
Austin, Texas 78745
512.462.3363

1581 Highway 195
Georgetown, Texas 78626
512.864.9601

1409 Royston Lane
Round Rock, Texas 78664
512.990.7335

23754 Highway 281 North
San Antonio, Texas 78258
830.980.7697

Custom Stone supplies Texas customers in the four largest metropolitan areas with huge stocks of local and imported limestone, granite, including Texas pink and sandstone from various regions of the country. The stone yards have every imaginable variety of flagstones and ledge rock, as well as "Big Block" suitable for walls. There is a wealth of gravel and pebbles, including black Mexican pebbles for lining streambeds, and beautiful boulders. The company offers custom milling for architectural and paving purposes, plus pre-cut pool coping that can also be used for wall caps, fireplace mantles and hearthstones. Delivery is available throughout the state.

Texas Quarries
1800 West Whitestone Blvd.
Cedar Park, Texas 78613
512.258.1474
www.texasquarries.com

Since 1929 Texas Quarries has fabricated limestone in a variety of finishes for both interior and exterior applications. All of the stone is indigenous to Texas (Cordova Cream and Cordova Shell from the Hill Country, and 270 million-year-old Lueders from the Abilene area). "We can make just about anything — turned columns, coping, balusters, etc.," says manager Robert Copeland. "Ornate carving is our specialty." The company offers matching pavers in 1¼ and 2¼-inch-thick patio stone that is finished top and bottom to provide a level walking surface.

Irrigation Equipment

Submatic Irrigation Systems
3002 Upland Avenue
Lubbock, Texas 79407
800.692.4100
www.submatic.co

A pioneer in drip irrigation for more than 30 years, this company is a leader in do-it-yourself systems for the home gardener. There are many kits available; one is designed especially for pot plants and hanging baskets. Some of the drip lines are designed to work with your automatic sprinkler system. If your soil and grass type is right for it, drip applications can even serve for turf areas. Timers and valves allow you to fully automate the system. A siphon mixer makes it possible to inject fertilizer through the lines. Most of the company's trade is through the website, which has photos and drawings. The company offers technical and design support.

Weathermatic
www.weathermatic.com
3301 West Kingsley Road
Garland, Texas 75041
972.278.6131 or 888.484.3776

For the homeowner who wants a top-quality, professionally designed and installed irrigation system, Weathermatic is an excellent choice. Established in 1945, Weathermatic is a Dallas-based worldwide manufacturer of water-efficient irrigation products. Its products have been installed in over 70 countries at such prominent sites as the U.S. Capitol Building, Buckingham Palace and Biltmore Estate. Weathermatic's SmartLine series of weather-based controllers won "Best New Product of the Year" awards from several professional associations. While the company does not sell directly to the public, its products are made in Texas and sold through numerous distributors throughout the state. Visit the website for a distributor near you and read the FAQs to learn more about the company.

Lighting Fixtures

Brandon Industries, Inc.
1601 West Wildreth Road
McKinney, Texas 75069
972.542.3000
www.brandonindustries.com

Here's a company that manufactures new lights with an historic flavor. Rustproof, durable and reasonably priced, the company's products are shipped by UPS within two weeks. The lines include eight mailbox designs and courtyard lighting in five different styles of base and a variety of luminaires. There are also wall sconces and deck lights units in the online catalog. For the energy-conscious, there are LED and metal halide options available.

Landscape Lighting Supply Co.
780 South Floyd Road
Richardson, Texas 75080
972.480.9700 or 800.238.0346
Hours: Mon–Fri 8–5, Sat 10–4
www.landscapelight.com

As far as we know, this is the state's only lighting store devoted exclusively to outdoor lighting. Well-known brands the company carries include: *Greenlee*, a Texas company, plus *FX*, *Hevilite*, *Hadco*, *Kichler*, *Kim*, *Lumiere* and *Unique*. The fixtures are constructed of solid copper, burnished brass, powder-coated cast aluminum or a high-grade composite material. You can order from the company's excellent website where you'll find all of the components involved in an outdoor lighting system. The website features a photo gallery of lighting techniques and helpful installation tips, and the company has experts to assist you with the design and wiring plan for your lighting system. "We know landscape lighting!" says owner Ed Barger. "If you aren't

(LISTING CONTINUED ON THE NEXT PAGE)

(CONTINUED)

the 'do-it-yourself' type, we would be more than happy to recommend reputable lighting contractors in the major cities of Texas."

Luminarios Ceramic Design Incorporated
2403 Boardwalk Street
San Antonio, Texas 78217
210.824.5572

This company's ceramic and punched tin lighting fixtures are works of art. The ceramic fixtures are available in unglazed or colored, glazed finishes. The metal ones can be crafted of copper, brass or galvanized metal. Available for wall mounting or hanging, the handsome fixtures are ideal for porches and entryways where they can be enjoyed up-close. Most have a southwestern flavor, but some are well-suited to contemporary architecture, and others draw upon early Texas or seaside motifs. Owner Rusty Konitz is willing to work directly with a client who wants something distinctive. The Lady Bird Johnson Wildflower Center is among the places where you can see this company's product. Luminarios will refer you to the nearest dealer or sell directly to customers in areas where there is no dealer. Call for a free catalog.

Mel Northey Company
303 Gulf Bank
Houston, Texas 77037
800.828.0302
www.melnorthey.com

This company advertises the handsome fluted street lamps and wall sconces it manufactures in trade magazines throughout the country. Graceful posts support a variety of traditional lamp shapes. These cast aluminum fixtures are available in black, dark green and white. The new Dark Sky options decrease the amount of night sky pollution, while reducing the electrical energy usage by as much as 42%. Among the large line of mailboxes designed to complement the fixtures, the Williamsburg box is especially attractive.

Two Hills Studio, Inc.
www.twohillsstudio.com
2706 South Lamar
Austin, Texas 78704
800.239.5530 or 512.707.7571

Two Hills Studio produces an array of handsome handcrafted sconces, lanterns and hanging fixtures. Copper, brass, tin, zinc, glass, mica, and mirrors are the craftsmen's media here. The company has developed innovative techniques to enhance the play of light and shadow in its fixtures. Custom commissions are welcome. The website offers numerous examples of this company's work.

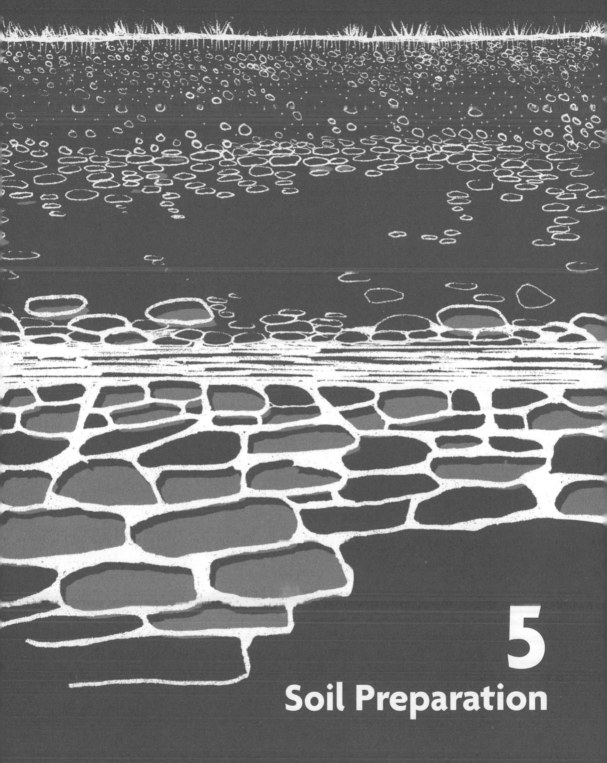

5

Soil Preparation

Soil Preparation

Whether you are starting a new landscape or renovating an existing one, you should improve your soil before even thinking about planting. Good soil is the garden's key ingredient. In this chapter I'm attempting to share everything I've learned about enhancing soil because I *promise* it will make lighter work of all your garden tasks.

All About Soil

Soil is a combination of weathered rock, air, water, decaying organic matter (humus) and living creatures (mostly microorganisms). Texas soils range from remarkably rich river valley loams to thin, rocky caliche. Most could stand improvement. We are generally dealing with soil that was depleted of nutrients and compacted by farming and ranching long before our home was built on the site. As gardeners we need to be concerned about the soil's depth, texture, chemistry and, finally, its fertility.

Moneysaving Tip: It's a total waste to put good plants in poor soil!

In our eagerness for lush, green gardens, our instincts, fueled by TV commercials, tell us to dash to the garden center and pick up a bag of 16-16-16. STOP! Any experienced gardener can attest to the effectiveness of a "quick-fix," but we're setting up a vicious cycle when we rely on synthetic fertilizers to keep plants healthy.

Microorganisms and earthworms are essential for "stirring" the soil and helping to make nutrients available to plants. Their digestion of organic materials actually binds soil particles into a crumb-like structure that increases the soil's water-holding capacity. The problem with chemical fertilizer is that microorganisms can't convert it to a usable form without humus. They take their nutrition from the existing humus in the soil. As the organic matter is depleted, microorganisms begin to disappear. Without humus, water-soluble nitrogen leaches into the water table and salt residues tend to build up in the soil. The poorer the soil becomes, the more fertilizer it takes to keep the plants green.

We should treat our topsoil with the respect we would accord any living thing, for that is what it is. Within a handful of healthy soil are millions of living, breathing, growing organisms, 98% of them beneficial to plants. You can't see these microorganisms (over a thousand species of algae, bacteria, viruses, protozoa, fungi and mites), but you can check for life in your soil by just counting earthworms. Ideally, you should find at least five in every cubic foot!

In attempting to build good soil in our gardens, we need to think like Mother Nature. "In a natural environment there is no waste," wrote Malcolm Beck in his charming book of essays, *Lessons in Nature*. "One form of life dies and decays so that another form can be born and grow. The circle continues in perfect harmony, as long as Nature is allowed to control the process." This chapter is about recreating healthy layers of earth, just as nature replenishes the forest floor.

SOIL DEPTH

The topsoil is very shallow in many areas of the state. Because plants growing in shallow soil require more water and nutrients than those grown in deep soil, Texas homeowners often must import new topsoil before even beginning to garden. In some areas, it's necessary to build raised beds to grow vegetables and/or ornamental plants such as roses. For new planting beds, I always recommend a blended soil mix that contains lots of organic matter.

Whenever you need large quantities of soil mix, ask a trusted local nursery owner to recommend a reliable source. How you apply the new topsoil is also important. Break up the surface of the existing soil and till or fork-in some of the new soil. Then apply the remainder of the new soil mix. This step is especially critical in areas where the existing soil is compacted by construction or clayey by nature. Otherwise, the plants will remain shallow-rooted or, worse yet, will expire as quickly as a house-plant in a pot without a drainage hole. Plant roots have difficulty penetrating abrupt changes in soil texture.

Raised beds allow gardeners to control the soil medium

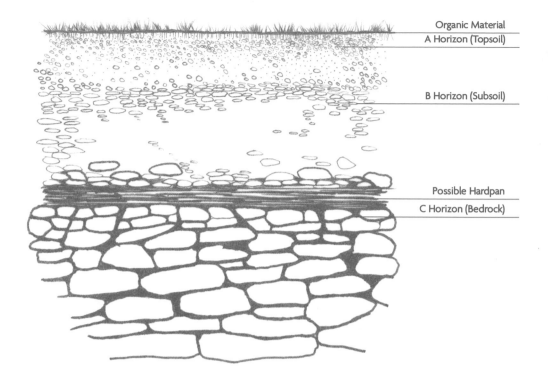

Organic Material
A Horizon (Topsoil)

B Horizon (Subsoil)

Possible Hardpan
C Horizon (Bedrock)

SOIL TEXTURE

Rock weathers into soil in the form of clay (with particles so fine they can only be seen with an electron microscope), silt (intermediate-size particles) and sand (coarse particles). The ideal soil is a soft, crumbly mixture of about 40% sand, 40% silt, 10% clay and 10% organic matter. Soil that's too sandy doesn't retain water; soil that contains too much clay won't drain properly. Squeeze a handful of damp soil. If it will hold together, but not clump into a tight ball, you probably have pretty good soil texture. You can get a better handle on the texture of your soil by performing a couple of easy tests.

Surprisingly, the addition of composted organic matter and/or soil inoculants (naturally occurring, beneficial soil organisms) is the remedy for soils that are too porous *and* for those that are too heavy. Clay soils also benefit from the addition of crushed granite or sharp builder's sand to improve drainage. Enlivening existing soil is a labor of love. The project consists of loosening it to improve aeration and amending it with compost to improve structure and fertility.

The "Mason jar" test for soil texture:

To determine the proportions of sand, silt, clay and organic matter in your soil, take random samples from the areas where you're going to plant and make a representative composite sample. Put a cup of dry, pulverized soil, four cups of water and a teaspoon of liquid Ivory detergent in a large jar with a lid. Shake vigorously. The sand will settle to the bottom in about a minute. Mark its level with a crayon. The silt will settle out in about two hours. Mark its level. The clay particles will need a couple of days to settle. The organic matter will rise to the top. Once the water is clear, compare your sample to the ideal proportions listed in the preceding paragraph.

The "coffee can" test for drainage:

Cut both ends from a one-pound coffee can and force the can into your garden soil to a depth of four inches. (If that's impossible, you *know* you have a problem!) Fill the rest of the can with water and let it drain through. Then fill it again and measure how long it takes the water level to drop an inch. If it drops immediately, the soil is too sandy and porous; if it takes more than four hours, the soil is too clayey and your plants are likely to drown from lack of oxygen.

SOIL CHEMISTRY: THE PH FACTOR

The pH scale is used to measure soil acidity. The numbers of the scale run from zero (the most acid) to 14 (the most alkaline). The neutral point is 7. Most plants thrive in a slightly acidic environment (6 to 7); some plants such as azaleas absolutely require acidic soil. Acid soils occur mainly in East Texas, where damp conditions and thousands of years of decaying leaves and pine needles reduced the pH. If the soil is too acid (below 4), it can be neutralized with agricultural limestone or wood ashes. Don't ever use your wood ashes in alkaline soil.

Alkaline soil, which is common in dry climate regions (i.e., most of Texas), is far more difficult to correct than acidic soil. The biggest problem with alkaline soil is that it makes iron, phosphorus, zinc, manganese, copper and several other important nutrients unavailable to your plants, even when these minerals are present in the soil. There are products available that help neutralize the soil temporarily, such as sulfur and gypsum. Finely ground sulfur, used at the recommended rate, may lower the pH by one point. Gypsum is mainly used for its soluble calcium, which helps leach sodium out of the soil, so it should not be applied without a soil test and expert advice.

Sphagnum peat moss also helps acidify alkaline soil, but it is too expensive to employ throughout the garden. I've incorporated peat moss into planting holes around acid-loving plants in Dallas, but having watched clients struggle to grow azaleas in Austin's limestone soil, I'm inclined to confine acid-dependent plants to the eastern region of Texas where the soils naturally accommodate them. By the way, peat moss must be moistened or it will stay dry in the ground forever. If you're going to use it to acidify, make a slurry of peat moss and water in a wheelbarrow before incorporating the product into the soil.

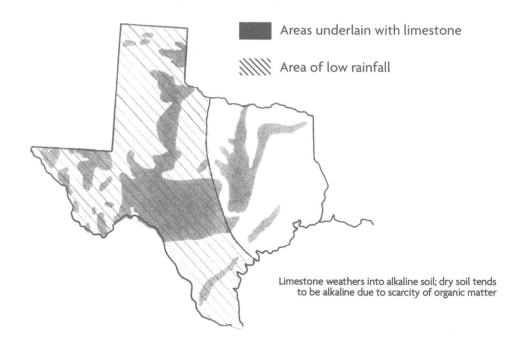

Areas underlain with limestone

Area of low rainfall

Limestone weathers into alkaline soil; dry soil tends to be alkaline due to scarcity of organic matter

Gardeners in the western three quarters of the state, everywhere but East Texas, routinely struggle not only to lower the pH of their soil, but also to compensate for the lack of available iron, which is essential to the production of chlorophyll. The telltale symptom of iron starvation is yellowed leaves with dark green veins, so even without the benefit of a soil test, many experienced Texas gardeners add chelated iron every growing season. Again, this is a temporary "fix." Where I live, the water is also very alkaline, so it is a losing battle. The only real solutions to gardening with an extremely high pH are 1) planting the species that prefer, or at least tolerate, alkaline soil, 2) adding humus and 3) making sure the soil is well-drained.

SOIL FERTILITY

In addition to sunlight, air and water, plants need nutrients to flourish. Nitrogen (N), phosphorus (P) and potassium (K) are essential to plant growth. These three macronutrients are always listed on fertilizer labels in order N-P-K. Plants also use magnesium (Mg), calcium (Ca) and sulfur (S) in relatively large quantities. These are known as "secondary nutrients." Small amounts of iron (Fe), zinc (Zn), molybdenum (Mo), manganese (Mn), boron (B), copper (Cu), cobalt (Co), chloride (Cl) and nickel (Ni) are also needed for plant growth. These elements are called "micronutrients." There are other trace elements that have been identified as beneficial, but are not yet classified as essential.

Fertilizer is erroneously called "plant food." When we fertilize, we are simply adding one or more elements. For an element to be useful, first it must be dissolved, and then absorbed into plant cells by way of complex chemical reactions. Conversion from a raw element into an available nutrient occurs in symbiosis with microorganisms, hence the importance of humus. Temperature, the availability of water and oxygen, and the relative alkalinity or acidity of the soil also influence the chemical processes that allow plants to make food from nutrients.

Basic soil tests analyze the three primary nutrients: nitrogen (N), phosphorus (P) and potassium (K). More sophisticated tests will measure organic matter, secondary nutrients and micronutrients. Other tests are available to measure acidity and/or determine if there are toxic substances (soluble salts, etc.) in your soil. Inexpensive color chart kits available at local garden centers allow you to measure the presence of the most basic nutrients and test for acidity/alkalinity levels with some degree of accuracy, but professional soil testing is the best way to determine your soil's chemical composition. There are several qualified labs in the state listed at the end of this chapter.

Once you've gotten the soil tested, add only the elements you need (preferably in an organic form) to correct deficiencies. The addition of fertilizer will help plants exist in nutrient-deficient soil, but the best long-term strategy is to build up the natural health of the soil. You may discover that all you need is a liberal dose of compost!

Moneysaving Tip: Determine what your soil needs before investing in fertilizers or additives.

What *is* Compost?

The word "compost" is both a verb and a noun. To compost (v.) is to expose organic material to microorganisms and other creatures, bacteria, time, heat and moisture to accelerate natural decomposition and sanitize the raw materials. Compost (n.) is used to describe any organic material (cottonseed meal, blood meal, aged manure, garden debris, etc.) that has been composted. When the mixture breaks down, it forms humus. Although organic matter represents only a small percentage of the overall composition of the soil, the addition of compost will increase the depth and improve the texture of your topsoil. Compost can be used both as a soil amendment/fertilizer and as a mulch/ topdressing. Only "finished" compost is suitable for use as a soil amendment, but partially decomposed materials can be used for mulching.

Compost improves the chemical, physical, and biological characteristics of soils. This miracle material also helps regulate moisture retention and soil temperature. It is typically not characterized as a fertilizer. However, composted organic material feeds the soil by providing a reservoir for nutrients as well as food for the many beneficial organisms that help decompose dead organic matter. These organisms, in turn, make nutrients available to plants and provide aeration.

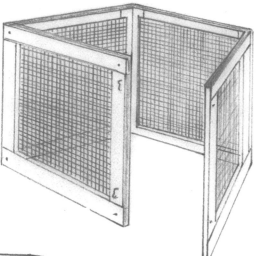

Compost Bin (Slow, but inexpensive)

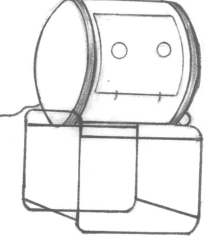

Tumbler (Faster, but more expensive)

HOW TO MAKE COMPOST

Libraries and bookstores are replete with books that tell you how to make your own rich compost. Cities are putting out free pamphlets on the subject and setting up demonstration sites. Basically, it's a simple matter of layering brown (shredded leaves) and green (grass clippings) in a well-ventilated bin. Compost bins can be purchased at garden centers or made with lumber, pallets, concrete blocks, wire fencing, or other materials. Bins help retain moisture and heat, deter pests, and keep your yard tidy. Special worm composting bins can be used to compost food scraps and paper, even in an apartment.

The layers should be kept about as moist as a damp sponge and stirred about once a month. You can toss coffee grounds, tea bags, nutshells, raw vegetable scraps, fruit peelings and other non-fatty kitchen wastes into the mix. Many gardeners also add some garden soil and manure to speed decomposition. It's not rocket science.

Composting goes faster when you break everything into small pieces. Try chopping the food scraps and mowing the leaves before adding them to the pile. If you have an existing pile that's not breaking down, sift the materials through a 3/8-inch mesh screen. Shred the materials that you cannot sift through the screen or start a second pile. A pile that is composting properly will get up to 160°F. Temperatures this high will kill weed seeds and pathogens that cause disease, but will allow the beneficial organisms to remain. If you're unsure, use a special compost thermometer to monitor the temperature of your pile.

Provided that the materials stay moist, the mixture should compost within a year without producing an odor or spreading diseases or attracting pests. There are different opinions about what should be composted. Most people avoid meat and dairy products, which can cause odors and attract rodents, and pet droppings, which they fear may harbor diseases. Others don't compost weeds with seeds or any diseased or insect-infested plants. All agree that it's best to avoid treated wood or other materials that may contain preservatives or other toxins. Temperature and moisture seem to be key to avoiding problems.

A bad odor indicates that your compost has too much "fresh" material or is too wet. If your pile is dry, turn it and add water until the whole pile is evenly moist. If it's too damp, turn the pile and add dry leaves. If your pile is attracting ants, flies or roaches, make sure you bury any food materials under a layer of leaves. Any other insects in your pile are probably harmless composters. Should problems persist, bury the compost and start another pile.

Perfect compost looks like rich, friable soil. You'll know when it's ready to use because it will smell pleasantly earthy. One of the funniest stories I've ever heard was told by an extension agent who got a call from an irate gardener saying, "I followed your directions for making compost, and all I got was dirt!"

WHY BOTHER?

First, home composting is good for the environment. Yes, it involves some work, but your little compost bin will hold kitchen scraps, leaf clippings and other yard wastes that otherwise might end up in landfills where it will generate methane gas. Yard debris makes up at least 15% of all municipal solid waste generated in Texas! Second, it's good for your garden. The finished product will be available as backfill each time you want to tuck a new plant into the landscape. You may be able to generate enough to top-dress your lawn every spring, saving the cost of packaged fertilizer.

Moneysaving Tip: Composting saves gardeners and taxpayers big bucks.

If you're beginning a new garden or renovating an established landscape, you'll need to spend the first season working lots of organic material into the soil, especially in areas where you'll be putting nonnative trees, shrubs, lawn grass, flowers and vegetables. Since you won't have the compost to meet your garden's needs, there are numerous private companies and city waste management departments set up to convert yard trimmings into compost and mulch, successfully diverting tons and tons of yard trimmings from landfills each year.

THE STATE OF COMPOSTING IN TEXAS

There are far too many composting companies to list in this book. I did, however, talk to several of the most respected in the state. I was amazed to find out what kinds of waste products are candidates for recycling. This is not the compost your granddad made! Some Texas entrepreneurs are converting reject vegetables from local farmers or horse manure from riding stables into "black gold." Others have used zoo manures, out-of-date beer or the refuse of businesses that must dispose of massive quantities of wood pallets.

Some compost-making companies and municipal composting departments accept, for a fee, tree trimmings and grass clippings from landscape companies. (For the landscape company, the cost of selling to a composter is about half the cost of taking the material to a landfill, which is actually a plus for taxpayers, as well.) The composters first separate and pulverize the waste materials, and then they heat them to 160° to produce high-nutrient organic matter.

What I also learned from my research is that there are no industry-wide quality standards in place, so it's important for homeowners to question suppliers about their methods and finished products before ordering compost. Composting companies are regulated as to any pollution they might create, but no Texas agency is currently regulating the industry's products.

Raw manure tops the list of products that I *never* use in the garden. (Uncomposted manure is easy to recognize; it has a strong, distinctive odor of ammonia.) A few years ago I ordered a load of compost from a supposedly reputable dealer. I wasn't home when it was delivered. The maintenance person who worked it into my planting beds noted that it smelled bad. Within a week, my plants looked burned, and I had an astounding crop of weeds that took months to eradicate. I learned the hard way not to buy compost over the phone. I go look at it, smell it and feel its texture!

Moneysaving Tip: Be wary about the source of any bulk compost, mulch or soil mix; good gardens have been ruined by products filled with weed seeds.

HOW TO USE COMPOST

When planting a new lawn, I till a one-inch layer of compost into the top six inches of soil. Before establishing a planting bed, I mix a three-inch layer of compost into the top 12 inches of soil. To maintain an established lawn, I recommend an annual application of a half-inch layer of finished compost, which only needs to be watered well. (I maintain planting beds with mulch, but I'll get to that subject in a minute.)

Working the soil on a bare lot in a new subdivision or in a vegetable garden that sits empty over the winter is relatively easy. Here, you can use a mechanical tiller to loosen the soil to a depth of 12 to 18 inches and then fork in the composted organic matter. Never cultivate wet soil — you'll eliminate the air spaces and compact it even more. Work from one end of a bed to the other so that you won't step on the soil you've just loosened. Expect your tilling to bring weed seeds to the surface where they germinate with great abandon. Be vigilant about weeding. Fortunately, it's relatively easy to pull weeds out of loose, fluffy soil.

Adding compost to enrich the soil in an established bed takes time and patience. In this case, you'll need to work carefully around the roots, cultivating the compost into the soil between the plants, by hand if necessary. In spots where you're adding new plants beneath existing shrubs and trees, excavate as large an area as possible and fill with a mix of your garden soil and a rich compost.

Mulch, Mulch, Mulch

There's so much to recommend mulch. It ultimately contributes valuable nutrients, but initially it serves to inhibit nutrient-robbing weeds, insulate the soil from sun and wind, retain moisture and prevent erosion. Mulching is the simplest, most obvious way to conserve plant life, labor and money. What is amazing is that when I began gardening 45 years ago, nobody told me about the benefits of mulching. Now I know that it's the most effective way to keep a well-established garden healthy.

On a forest floor, dead twigs and leaves form a natural mulch each winter. This mulch continually enriches the soil as it decomposes and enables the soil to feed the plants. To mimic Mother Nature's methods, I routinely cover my planting beds with a two-inch layer of organic mulch twice each year — in late fall to protect plant roots from winter cold and in late spring to preserve soil moisture during periods of heat and drought. There is one caveat. As mulch breaks down, it uses nitrogen, so most gardeners add a slow-release nitrogen fertilizer such as blood meal or composted manure (for good measure) beneath the mulch. This is a step nature doesn't need because an undisturbed forest floor has had thousands of years to create humus between the bedrock base and the leaf-litter mulch on top.

By gently forking the older mulches into the soil before adding new mulch year after year, I've reclaimed some pretty poor patches of earth. (Okay, I'll be honest. I *hire* someone to man the spading fork and shovel. My old back can't take the strain, and my sweet husband has never been fond of a garden tool.) It has been my experience that plants tend to grow at a reasonable rate with this regimen. In the long run, plants are hardier and more pest-resistant if they are not fed excessively or encouraged to put on great spurts of growth. I continue to monitor the pH and fertility, however, and add nutrients as needed to maintain a balanced soil.

WHAT'S THE DIFFERENCE BETWEEN COMPOST AND MULCH?

While compost is completely decomposed organic matter, which is mixed into the soil or can be used to top-dress a lawn, mulch is any material that's used to blanket a bare soil surface. The mulches I prefer are partially composted shredded hardwood or pine bark. I've also used cypress mulch, which is especially good for slopes because it is very fibrous and holds together. Pine needles, if you have access to them, are good for mulching acid-loving plants. Mulches often contain partially decomposed leaves and grass clippings, as well. There are such non-organic mulches as shredded tires and pea gravel available, but I only use mulches made from organic matter because they will slowly turn into compost as the ingredients break down.

Earthworms are a gardener's best friends

There are some commonly used organic materials that are poor choices for mulch. I won't use bark mulch that has not undergone a partial composting process. Not only does a raw wood look unnatural in a refined garden, but also it depletes the soil of nitrogen as it decomposes. Composted manure, peat moss and sawdust are too fine in texture to be used as mulch. Raw grass clippings compact to form a pancake layer that inhibits water penetration. Straw is sometimes recommended, but it may contain weed seeds, and cottonseed hulls tend to blow away.

"Store-bought" mulches are pretty pricey. A two-cubic-foot bag of mulch can cost as much as $5.00. Assuming you apply a two-inch layer, one bag will cover only 12 square feet. So, it makes sense to recycle your yard debris even if you don't have a compost bin. You can shred all your twigs and leaves, layering them with grass clippings and pile them up in an unobtrusive spot in the garden. Don't put weeds or the autumn remains of your flower garden into the pile because it may not become sufficiently hot to kill weed seeds and/or plant diseases. Turn the pile periodically and let the lawn debris decompose for several months before "harvesting" it for mulch. Don't worry, however, if your yard waste is only partially decomposed when you use it as mulch. If it smells OK and has a loose texture, it will continue decomposing and disappear down into the soil with a few months. Because many cities now recycle yard wastes on a large scale, it may be more convenient for you to send off what you can't use and buy it back after it has been properly treated.

Moneysaving Tip: If you use bagged compost or mulches, stock up whenever you see the products marked-down.

HOW TO USE MULCH

A two to three-inch layer of mulch is sufficient for any planting bed. Heavy mulch inhibits gas exchanges and prevents rainwater from penetrating the soil. Be aware that mulch may attract snails and rodents, so keep it an inch or two away from the plant's trunks and low branches. The benefits from mulching your garden far outweigh any problems you may encounter. You can create a self-mulching lawn by waiting to mow until your grass is three to four inches high. A mulching lawn mower is ideal for the job. Mow only the top one-third of the grass, and don't rake up the clippings, which will slip between the blades of grass and slowly decompose to feed your soil.

Fertilizers

Fertilizers, both synthesized and organic varieties, are labeled according to their content of nitrogen (N), phosphorus (P) and potassium (K). For example, a 10-10-10 contains 10% of each; the other 70% is filler. As a landscape architecture student in the 1970s, I was taught that plants couldn't tell the difference between organic and synthesized nutrients. So why are so many people switching to organic fertilizers these days? Let me explain.

Most synthetic fertilizers are designed to be rapidly absorbed into the roots of the plant, and many of these fast-acting products contain more nitrogen than the plants can actually use. What's not absorbed is flushed out by rain and wasted. Moreover, chemical fertilizers do nothing good for microorganisms and earthworms.

Ammonium sulfate (21-0-0), which is a commonly used lawn and garden fertilizer, has actually been used for the purpose of killing earthworms on golf courses.

The earthworm, which Malcolm Beck calls "nature's plow, chemist, cultivator, maker, and distributor of plant food," enriches and aerates the soil. Its tunnels allow water and oxygen to penetrate deeply into the soil, promoting the growth of helpful microorganisms and, in turn, healthy plants. Mr. Beck notes that organic fertilizers are released gradually into the soil, where the plants can extract them as needed. Composted manures, bone meal, blood meal, alfalfa meal, cottonseed meal, kelp meal, fish meal, etc., which are derived from by-products of once-living organisms, and rock powders (lava sand, greensand and colloidal phosphate) are all classified as organic. In addition to these products, a number of organic gardeners apply biostimulants, which are formulated to invigorate microbial activity in the soil.

Organic fertilizers are more expensive than the synthetic products, and they are generally lower in nutrients per pound, so they must be applied more liberally to be effective. What has discouraged a lot of gardeners from "going organic" has not been so much the cost factor as the fact that shoveling a truckload of composted manure is a lot harder work than broadcasting granulated fertilizer. Happily, there are now numerous organic fertilizers in easy-to-apply liquid and granular forms.

Howard Garrett's *Texas Organic Gardening* book provides an excellent list of the various organic fertilizers on the market. It also has a helpful rate-of-application chart. Use your soil test and your own good common sense, however, to determine which products your plants really need. Going into a garden store to buy "plant food" is not unlike going into a health food store to buy vitamins. The array is overwhelming, and if you ingested one of everything, it would probably kill you.

Moneysaving Tip: Determine what your soil actually needs before investing in fertilizers. Test a small amount in your garden before ordering large quantities of any product.

A Cold Frame allows gardeners to start seeds in an ideal soil mix, as well as getting a head start on the season

REDUCING THE NEED FOR FERTILIZERS

There are basically two ways to reduce your need for fertilizer. First, build healthy soil. Have you ever noticed that nobody ever fertilizes a forest? The fallen leaves provide the mulch, and microorganisms that live in the next layer of woodland soil turn that mulch into compost (humus), continually renewing the soil. We do the same when we recycle nature's waste materials into nutritious composts and mulches.

The second strategy is to "go native." A plant growing in soil that's natural to its needs does not require much supplementary enrichment. The shrubs and wildflowers of the Hill Country, for example, evolved in shallow, alkaline soil and perform best in those conditions. As one company that's in the organic fertilizer business says, "Don't ask a plant to do something it's not genetically designed to do."

At the end of this chapter, you'll find Texas companies that produce bagged compost and mulches, fertilizers and soil additives. Many of the products are available at regional garden centers and home improvement stores. I've used a variety of these products in my garden and my clients' gardens. I cannot attest to the effectiveness of any of them for your particular garden situation, but I can heartily recommend compost for every Texas garden.

Resources for Soil Building:

Soil Testing

A&L Plains Agricultural Laboratories
P.O. Box 1590
Lubbock, Texas 77408
806.763.4278
www.al-labs-plains.com

Founded in 1971 to serve the agricultural industry, this lab is part of a national company that does comprehensive analysis of soils, plants, water, feed and fertilizers. The services are available to homeowners, as well, and its catalog is online. The company maintains an established set of procedures for checking the accuracy and precision of all tests and for maintenance of all instruments.

Extension Soil Testing Lab
Texas A&M University, Dept. of Soil and Crop Sciences
College Station, Texas 77843
979.845.4816
http://soiltesting.tamu.edu

Ten years ago, you had to go to your county extension agent for a form and soil bag, but the computer age has changed all that. The costs haven't changed! Basic tests still range from $10 to $30, depending upon the level of testing you want. The website explains the procedure for collecting the sample. You can print out a Submittal Form and place the soil in a sealed plastic bag or pint-size plastic container. They'll even accept Visa and MasterCard.

Texas Plant and Soil Lab, Inc.
5115 West Monte Cristo Road
Edinburg, Texas 78541
956.383.0739
www.tpsl.biz

If you don't think that gardening has become chic, consider the fact that this Texas soil-testing lab was featured in *Town & Country* magazine! The company began serving citrus farmers in the Valley in 1938. It is now operated by Esper K. Chandler, an agronomist and soil scientist. The lab uses a natural extraction testing method that employs carbon dioxide to determine actual nutrient uptake availability. In addition to data on nutrients, the Standard Comprehensive Topsoil Analysis provides (for $30) information on pH, soil texture, humus content, thorough salt evaluation and other factors that allow "the most accurate soil fertilizer interpretations and recommendations possible." The method works equally well for acid or alkaline soil. "We mimic the plant's natural method of extracting nutrients from the soil," says Mr. Chandler. The company also offers a basic lawn and garden test ($15). It provides analysis of fertilizers, composts, plants and irrigation water at various prices. Write, call or visit the website for information on sample collection. Use Ziploc sandwich bags and send a complete history. "We offer sustainable educational information with our analytical services — we do not sell or endorse products."

Texas Manufacturers of Soil Amendments and Fertilizers

Back to Nature, Inc.
P.O. Box 190
Slaton, Texas 79364
888.282.2000
www.backtonaturecompost.com

This is one of several companies on the High Plains turning feedlot wastes and cotton gin "trash" into treasure. The company's cotton burr composts are rich in carbon and protein. They also contain significant amounts of plant macro- and micronutrients. The composted cattle and chicken manures and special blends for flowerbeds, rose gardens and general landscape use provide food sources for beneficial soil organisms.

Desert Peat Humate
P.O. Box 635
Alpine, Texas 79831
432.837.2393
www.desertpeat.com

Desert Peat™ is a naturally occurring organic humus soil conditioner that is especially valuable for use in arid and semi-arid areas of the state. High in primary nutrients and micronutrients, it helps retain soil moisture and lowers the alkalinity level of the soil.

Garden-Ville
7561 East Evans Road
San Antonio, Texas 78266
210.651.6115
www.garden-ville.com

Garden-Ville was a pioneer in the field of organic gardening. The company, which was begun by Malcolm Beck, continues under new ownership to make excellent bagged soil and soil amendments and a remarkable array of organic supplies. The approach here begins with good soil. Two San Antonio locations and three in the Austin area offer everything for the garden except plants — composts, mulches, soil blends, specialized soil amendments, fertilizers, insecticides and herbicides. Garden-Ville's products are also sold in garden centers throughout the state, and packaged products can be ordered through the company's online store. You can find a jar of mycorrizal fungi or a pecan mulch that discourages cats from planting beds. This "store" has educational components, as well. There are online classes offered, and you can order any or all of Beck's books and sign up for an e-mail newsletter.

Lady Bug Natural Brand
8648 Old Bee Caves Road
Austin, Texas 78735
512.288.9740
www.ladybugbrand.com

John Dromgoole can lay claim to the longest running radio garden show that promotes natural gardening methods, and it's an unpaid job! When he talks dirt, people hang on to his every word. On Saturday and Sunday mornings after the show on Austin's KLBJ, his customers at The Natural Gardener wait in line to talk to him. His website features essays on garden care, and, of course, mentions his Lady Bug Brand natural gardening products. He has carefully formulated them all — fertilizers, soils and soil amendments — for the organic-minded grower. They are bagged from the bulk supply at The Natural Gardener. "We are continuing to build a line of specialized quality bulk products for a variety of situations," he says. "Have clay soil? Revitalizer Compost is for you. No soil? Build raised beds with our Hill Country Soil or Rose Magic. Trees stressed? Mulch with our Sylvan Formula that is modeled after the forest floor." He emphasizes that an organic lawn care program works with nature, not against it, giving plants just what they need to be green and healthy. Click "Where to Find Us" and enter your zip code to find the nearest retailer who carries Lady Bug products.

Maestro-Gro, Inc.
P.O. Box 869
Hamilton, Texas 76531
254.784.0396 or 888.378.4976
www.maestro-gro.com

Maestro-Gro is a family-operated fertilizer and plant food manufacturer. Founded in 1987, when Gary DeMasters (the Maestro) formulated the original product line, the company's wares have always been 100 percent organic or natural. His son Brian runs the business now. "We use only the finest ingredients and best natural practices to offer safe, non-toxic alternatives," he says. Maestro-Gro makes fertilizers, specialized plant foods, soil amendments, insecticides, microbials and non-selective herbicides. In 2008 the company bought Rabbit Hill Farm, which had developed a popular soil amendment from rabbit manure and worm castings. The products can be purchased online or through retail distributors.

Medina Agricultural Products
P.O. Box 309
Hondo, Texas 78861
830.426.3011
www.medinaag.com

Medina started in 1962 when a local farmer, Arthur Franke, met James Martin, who had spent several decades developing a catalyst for growing huge quantities of microorganisms to stimulate worn-out soil. As Stuart Franke, company president and son of the firm's first farmer/backer, explains, "The idea is to duplicate the way the earth developed the soil. However, for farmers to be willing to use a product, we had to be able to show practical, profitable results." The company has grown slowly, but steadily, as more and more people have become loyal to the label and enthusiastic about organic growing. The product line has expanded beyond the original Medina® Soil Activator ("yogurt for the soil") to include Medina® Plus, which is fortified with micronutrients and growth hormones, Hasta Gro® (a liquid fertilizer available in formulations for lawns or gardens) and HuMate Liquid Humus, which is described as "concentrated compost in a bottle." The products can now be purchased online.

Nature Life, Inc.
P.O. Box 207
Ropesville, Texas 79358
800.839.3781 or 806.562.3781
www.naturelifeinc.com

Composted cotton burrs from West Texas are the raw materials for this organic soil conditioner. It's higher in nitrogen, phosphorus and potash than manure. Available in bag or bulk, Nature Life is guaranteed to be free of weed seeds, defoliant chemicals and disease organisms. The company's products are sold through retail nurseries and landscape contractors. Royce Acuff says, "We have been active in agriculture for nearly 50 years; consequently, the care and use of our land is of primary importance to our business." He notes that with proper use this product will give the gardener a rich, mellow soil. "Call if you can't find the product in your hometown."

Nature's Guide
2317 Cullen Street
Fort Worth, Texas 76107
800.299.1881
www.natures-guide.com

Nature's Guide is the product label of Harvest Supply Company in Fort Worth. More than 95 percent of the products are Texas-made, and all are environmentally

(LISTING CONTINUED ON THE NEXT PAGE)

(CONTINUED)

friendly. In addition to everything from dry and liquid fertilizers, soil amendments to weed and disease controls, the Nature's Guide name is on sprayers, herbal soaps and even healthy snacks. Time-lapse photography over a 20-day period on the website shows the difference between cuttings grown in plain water and in Nature's Guide Root Stimulator. I'm impressed.

Rohde's GreenSense
1651 Wall Street
Garland, Texas 75041
972.864.1934
www.greensense.net; online catalog through Amazon.com

Greg Rohde's Nursery and Nature Store was one of the first in the Dallas area to carry only organic fertilizers and employ pest control using beneficial insects, microorganisms and bacteria products. His knowledge in the use of organic gardening techniques has grown from more than 35 years of practical experience in the landscape maintenance business. The Garland store offers all of the GreenSense products his company developed and now formulates, and they are available from a few other high-quality garden centers in Texas, as well. "GreenSense organic gardening products are blended to enrich your soil, protect your plants from insects and help you create a beautiful, healthy landscape without the use of chemicals or pesticides," says Greg. You can buy the products online only at Amazon.com. It takes six mouse clicks to get to the right place: Home & Garden; Patio, Lawn & Garden; Plants & Planting; Soils, Fertilizer & Mulches; Brand; GreenSense. I actually found and ordered the product I wanted, *Lawn & Garden Microbial Treatment* (item #36 of 44), which Greg had discussed in his informative July 2008 newsletter. You'll find newsletters dating back to 1997 at greensense.net.

Soil Mender Products
7355 FM 928
Tulia, Texas 79088
800.441.2498
www.soilmender.com

Greg Birkenfeld and his two brothers are farmers. They got into what has become a very substantial enterprise through their desire to improve the land they owned. "Our goal," says Greg, "is to form a relationship with our customers and offer them a consistent, high-quality line of soil-conditioning products." Soil Mender Products manufactures four soil amendment lines: Back to Earth, Soil Mender, Hu-Max and Yum Yum Mix, each unique in its own way. Altogether there are 50 different products, as well as custom mixes and blends for bags or bulk available from these energetic people. Their facility encompasses over 200 acres producing aerobic, windrow composts. "Our composting, bagging, and packaging equipment are of the highest standard in the industry. We strive to meet as many people's needs as possible. We're learning and growing alongside you." The products are available at retail nurseries throughout the state.

Vital Earth/Carl Pool
PO Box 1148
Gladewater, Texas 75647
800.245.7645 or 903.845.2163
www.vitalearth.com

In 1992, Vital Earth Resources Inc. acquired the well-known Texas fertilizer manufacturer, Carl Pool Products, which celebrated its 60th anniversary in 2005. Among other things, Carl Pool has been a leader in the water-soluble fertilizer field. Its Earth-Safe Organic products include diatomaceous earth, rock phosphate, bone meal, fish meal, bat guano, seaweed extract and much more. The products contain no excess salt or other impurities, and the water-soluble fertilizers are adaptable to drip or foliar applications. Vital Earth Resources was founded in 1983 by Buck Hammer and Eric Eweson, inventor of the Eweson In-Vessel Composting System. Vital Earth bagged products are all-natural. They include Premium Potting Soil, rose and azalea mixes and numerous compost and top-dressing mixes.

6
The Planting Plan

The Planting Plan

Assess What You Have

Trees, shrubs and ground covers are the landscape's green foundation. Texas gardeners prefer a primarily evergreen landscape, and the good reason is that our widely used lawn grasses turn brown in the winter and most of our native trees shed their leaves for a few months. We rarely have a cover of snow to soften the landscape, so without greenery our gardens look bleak. But because winter will reveal your garden's weaknesses, it is the *best* time for evaluating what you have and creating a new Planting Plan.

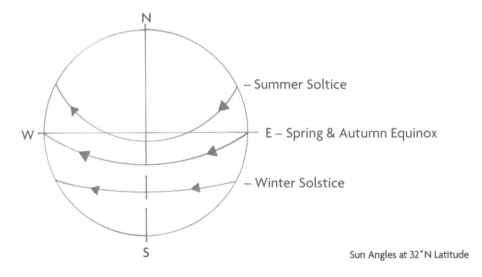

Sun Angles at 32°N Latitude

If you've bought a building site or recently acquired a home with an existing landscape, take a year to become acquainted with the property before making any big decisions. Walk around each day; observe the patterns of sunlight at different times of the year. After every rain, watch for standing water or rapid runoff. Take photographs of different areas of the landscape in each season. Keep a notebook for recording information about the plants you have. If you've bought in an older neighborhood, chances are that the soil is depleted and the plants are overgrown. In many cases, the landscape is replete with invasive species and filled with plants that have been pruned into little misshapen balls and boxes over the years.

Start jotting down ideas for plants to add. Cut out pictures from magazines. Window-shop at area garden centers. If you find a plant you simply can't live without or a friend gives you an unidentified plant from his or her garden, store it somewhere until you can determine where it would best serve your garden plan. Consider starting your own "nursery" in a garden utility area somewhere out of sight.

If your home is a newly developed suburban area, it's safe to assume that the land was formerly a farm or ranch. The builder may have planted some shrubs and grass, but that doesn't mean what has been planted needs to remain or that any care was taken with soil preparation. There may be construction debris that was simply covered over. The existing topsoil was probably depleted and made worse with compaction by the construction crews. If the house was built on an urban infill lot, there may be residues from previous industrial uses. (Go back to Chapter Five for information on improving your soil.)

If you are new to the state or even to your region, you will have a lot of catching up to do. You may or may not know your planting zone, and even if you do, it could get you into trouble. If you've moved to Dallas/ Fort Worth from Detroit, for example, Zone 8 might sound like the tropics compared to the winter temperatures you experienced in Zone 5. If you've moved to Abilene from Atlanta (both in Zone 7), you could be tempted to think that the climate will be similar. You would be wrong in both instances. The USDA Hardiness Zone Map, which only addresses average winter temperature, doesn't begin to tell you everything you need to know about Texas weather!

Perhaps you have lived in the same house for twenty years and have become tired of all the work and expense associated with keeping an older landscape attractive. In the last few years, people have begun critically rethinking their landscapes. The most important new trend in gardening is the idea of "naturescaping," which is primarily about returning to the species that evolved within the region. When our properties are covered with nonnative lawn grasses and our planting beds filled with an array of imported ornamentals, we've not only created more work for ourselves, but we've also made our yards uninhabitable to birds, butterflies and other attractive wildlife.

Moneysaving Tip: Take it slowly and choose your plants carefully. Trees, shrubs and ground covers are major investments.

By the time you are ready to start purchasing new plants for your landscape, you will have made a design plan and considered the climate of your region and the specifics of your site. You will have analyzed and improved your soil. Now, the process involves finding the right plants for the right places.

CONSIDER GOING NATIVE

Thousands of gardeners are now participating in the Texas Wildscapes program, which encourages homeowners to make their properties more attractive to birds, butterflies and other wildlife. They begin by replacing undesirable trees and shrubs with a few native species that produce seeds, nuts and berries as food for wildlife, adding native trees to serve as nesting sites and providing water in the form of shallow ponds or birdbaths. Then they discover the beauty of native plants!

Numerous books and magazine articles have dispelled any lingering notions that using native plants means sacrificing "beauty." Colorful new varieties of such drought-tolerant perennials as salvias, lantanas and verbenas are the darlings of the gardening world these days. Once these plants are established, they require less water than their nonnative counterparts. Natives rarely need fertilizer or pest controls because they have an affinity for the local soils, coping mechanisms to deal with climate extremes and natural resistance to insects and disease. However, simply calling a plant a "native" is to omit a key question: Native to where?

We must begin by understanding the incredible diversity of our state's climate zones and soil types. See *The Texas Garden Resource Book* for detailed information about each of the state's 12 regions. Each has its own unique sets of relationships between different kinds of plants and between plants and animals. Every native plant evolved to fit a narrow range of site-specific variables, which include climate, availability of water, soil chemistry and soil composition.

A fern that grows in the Big Thicket would be a poor choice for a garden in Big Spring! Many of the native shrubs and herbaceous perennials found in East Texas evolved in the shade of large trees; few would survive in an open, sunny location. Our challenge is to match the plant with its normal niche. Not only are plants more likely to thrive where they evolved, but also they appear to "belong." The ancient Greeks had a name for it, *genius loci*, sense of place.

The Lady Bird Johnson Wildflower Center has done more to encourage the propagation and use of "wild" plants in planned landscapes than any other organization in the country. When Mrs. Johnson spoke of living in a place "as the Lord made it," she backed up her conviction with tools that make the idea possible and practical. The Wildflower Center has developed plant lists suitable for every region of the state. I would not recommend that anyone plant a garden anywhere in Texas without obtaining a basic plant list from the organization. (See page 52 for information on navigating its website.)

While Mrs. Johnson is still associated in the public consciousness with "beautification," she was eager to emphasize that her commitment to native wildflowers (and trees, shrubs and grasses) was much more than pure aesthetics. As she expressed it, "I think of beautification as making the world more beautiful within the context of what will grow. Native plants are our best hope for ensuring continued habitation of this country, and of the planet."

Unfortunately, Texas native plants have been more difficult to obtain (and often more expensive) than imported species. The horticulturists who began promoting Texas natives thirty years ago were real pioneers. A sort of "catch-22" existed at the time — the average gardener knew little about our wild plants, and the wholesale growers avoided investing time in plants for which there was little demand. The few tiny nurseries that were growing natives had very limited supplies. Design professionals were sold on the ecological value of natives, but most were unwilling to specify plants that were difficult to find or were too small for landscape use. (Homeowners are not amused when their landscape contractor arrives with a ten-inch-tall "shade tree.") Until recently, the propagation of native plants was a lonely and unprofitable venture.

New awareness about the advantages of "going native" has turned the growing of Texas plants into a booming business. Several large-scale wholesale nurseries are growing ornamental trees such as Texas mountain laurel, Texas redbud, Mexican buckeye and desert willow as good alternatives for small gardens. Neighborhood garden centers are making room for native shrubs alongside the popular Indian hawthorns (native to China), Japanese yews and Chinese hollies. And, at long last, homeowners are truly embracing native plants.

BEWARE OF INVASIVE SPECIES

Two places I visited recently have convinced me that nurseries should stop selling and homeowners should stop buying plants that are listed as invasive. (For a complete list, go to www.texasinvasives.org.) Both of my excursions involved train rides. The Texas State Railroad runs 25 miles between Rusk and Palestine where I expected to enjoy the fragrance of pine trees and to see lush understory native to the Piney Woods. In many places I spotted rampant bamboo and a host of other species that had to have escaped from gardens. Obviously these plants had choked out dogwoods, plums, hawthorns and farkleberries that should have been blooming there. A few weeks later I rode the little train in San Antonio's Brackenridge Park with my five-year-old granddaughter, chugging through a half-mile of what the engineer's canned speech called "woods." Much to my horror, it was composed almost entirely of Japanese ligustrum! Where were the retama, huisache and Texas mountain laurels that belong there? My granddaughter asked why I was so upset about woods that just looked shady and green to her...

The sad truth is that more than 80 nonnative plant species are wreaking havoc on Texas's croplands, woodlands and waterways. Landscape professionals are only now discovering that many commonly used trees and shrubs are invading Texas preserves and forests. Plants, like animals, colonize rapidly in areas where they have no natural predators. When land is uncovered to bare soil by road construction, overgrazing, poor farming practices or haphazard home and industrial development, people have given carte blanche to uninvited plants. The very agricultural industry that has been the foundation of our state's economy has been the land source most negatively impacted by invasive species. Millions of dollars have been lost in diminished yields, and many more spent trying to deal with unwanted weeds and brush. But the same is now true for our natural forested areas, as well as natural waterways in the state.

"Invasive plants are those that have a tendency to spread and invade both healthy and unhealthy landscapes, ultimately causing some kind of negative impact," explains Dr. Barron S. Rector, who serves as a Range Scientist for the Texas AgriLife Extension Service in the Department of Ecosystems Science & Management at Texas A&M University. "Invasive plants are often best defined as 'plants that do not stay where they are planted." Invasive plants occur all over the state of Texas and today are recognized as a serious environmental threat." He points out that invasive plants are successful "because the biological or ecological factors and mechanisms that kept these plants under control in their native land are not present here (disease, insects, biological predators, exact nutrient requirements and soils, prevailing weather conditions, etc.)."

Many invasive plant species have been inadvertently introduced to wildscapes by gardeners. We've paid a higher price than we realized for the plants our grandparents eagerly bought from nurserymen in the 19th and 20th centuries. Today gardeners are being asked to avoid planting such shrubs as Chinese pistache, ligustrum, photinia, pyracantha, vitex and berrying varieties of nandina, which are easily carried by wind and birds into woodlands and riverbottoms. Also, such spreading plants as English ivy, elephant ears, holly fern, vinca and wisteria, which are not generally transported long distances, are to be avoided if your property adjoins parks or waterways.

It is not just introduced species that can cause a change in nature's balance; even a Texas native plant can become invasive when circumstances change. With native grasses declining from overgrazing and efforts to control naturally occurring wildfires in the late 1800s, populations of our native cedars (*Juniperus ashei*), which had formerly been sparsely dotted throughout Central Texas grasslands, began exploding. Other native species such as mesquite, huisache and prickly pear often contribute to the economic decline of a farm or ranch. These plants have spread out of their normal ranges because of poor human management decisions, lack of natural fire and continued disturbance.

"Humans seldom knew the biology of an introduced plant or speculated on where a plant might be in the next 30 years," says Dr. Rector. "Plants from foreign countries are often planted without humans having knowledge of what the plant might do in the future. Who would have guessed that Macartney rose from Japan, introduced in the 1850s as the 'living fence,' would now be a major invasive plant of pastures in the eastern half of Texas? Or that King Ranch bluestem, a noted grass useful in the recovery and protection of played-out farmland, would be the number one weed on roadsides in central Texas today? It must be remembered that bad decisions made today can create the natural resource problems of tomorrow." The 21st century has ushered in a new sense of urgency about how we should manage the land, and responsible gardeners will respond by planting species that "belong" here.

HOW TO READ PLANT LABELS

While some plants are too successful in Texas, other plants common in Oregon, Michigan or Florida may have little chance for success here. Most gardeners are familiar with USDA (United States Department of Agriculture) Hardiness Zones. But what many may not know is that plant hardiness, as defined by the USDA, refers only to the plant's ability to withstand cold. When you see a plant labeled for Zone 8, all you have learned is that the plant can be expected to withstand temperatures down to 10 degrees. The plant should certainly survive the winter in the warmer Zone 9 (where average minimum temperatures range from 20 to 30 degrees), but it is a poor candidate for Zone 7 (where the range is from 0 to 10 degrees). As you begin selecting the plants for your landscape, you'll need to be aware of your

Summer Heat AHS Zones

ZONE 7	60 to 90*
ZONE 8	90 to 120
ZONE 9	120 to 150
ZONE 10	150 to 180
ZONE 11	180 to 210
ZONE 12	More than 210

* Number of days per year above 86°

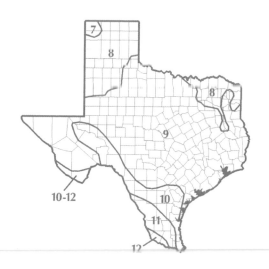

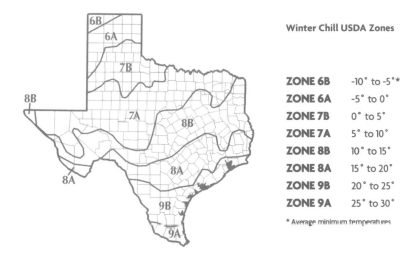

Winter Chill USDA Zones

ZONE 6B	-10° to -5°*
ZONE 6A	-5° to 0°
ZONE 7B	0° to 5°
ZONE 7A	5° to 10°
ZONE 8B	10° to 15°
ZONE 8A	15° to 20°
ZONE 9B	20° to 25°
ZONE 9A	25° to 30°

* Average minimum temperatures

USDA Zone, but it's important here to caution novice Texas gardeners that minimum winter temperatures are the least of your problems! 'Hardy' is a very misleading word.

Camellias are labeled for Zone 7; Wichita Falls is in Zone 7. So why are these plants not among the best choices for a garden there? When you read more about camellias, you'll discover that camellias do best in moist, acid soil. Oops! They prefer sites that are not excessively hot. Oh my! They are susceptible to tea scale, thrips and botrytis. Oh no! Camellias are gorgeous, but are they really worth acidifying soil, adding iron, watering every day in summer, and battling a host of insect and disease problems? For sensible gardeners west of Fort Worth, the answer will be, "No way."

I'll cite the low-growing junipers as another example. These plants make dandy ground covers in some regions of the state. They are drought-tolerant and they're "hardy" in Zones 2-6, meaning that they'll withstand the worst winter Texas can offer. This is a plant that requires fast drainage, however. In moist soil and conditions of high humidity, the roots rot and spider mites devour the sap. In either case, the needles will quickly resemble little pieces of brown wire. For gardeners in Southeast Texas or along the Gulf Coast, junipers are simply not a good option.

Such plants as tulips and apple trees provide other good examples of plants poorly suited to most areas of Texas because they *require* exposure to a certain number of hours of winter chill to flower. Yes, there are a few apple varieties that will set fruit in Texas. Yes, one can refrigerate tulip bulbs. However, many of the plants that are beloved in northern climes simply do not like our hot-as-Hades summers or our winters, which tend to alternate between unseasonably warm and frigid.

Many growers are including Heat Zone information along with the USDA hardiness zone ratings on their plant labels and in their catalogs. In 1997, the American Horticultural Society produced a Heat Zone Map that complements the USDA Zone Map and is based on the number of days over 85 degrees. This information is very helpful to gardeners. For example, I live in USDA Zone 8. The USDA map might make me think I could grow lilacs and rhododendrons. Wrong! The Heat Zone in the Austin area is 9, and that's way too many hot days for such plants. While the two Zone Maps are imperfect (neither take into account rare temperature extremes or factor in humidity), these maps do help gardeners select plants most likely to thrive in their particular areas.

Moneysaving Tip: Carefully read plant labels to determine sun requirements, ultimate height and width of the plant, and zone information.

In creating a plant list for your garden, there's not only the climate of your region to consider, but also the several different microclimates around your home. Obviously, the north side of the house will be cooler and shadier than the sun-drenched south side. However, because the summer sun actually sets in the northwest, a portion of the north side of your house may get a blast of late afternoon sun. And, unless shaded by tree canopy, a fence or a tall building next door, a planting bed on the east side will get full Texas sun until at least 1 p.m. Therefore, a plant such as oakleaf hydrangea, which is labeled for "partial shade," may not be a good candidate for an open, east-facing location.

On the other hand, the east side of your house may provide the perfect environment for shrub roses and crepe myrtles. Because these plants are susceptible to powdery mildew, they perform best in spots where there is morning sun to evaporate any dew that might collect on the foliage at night. Whole books have been written about the cultural requirements of plants suitable for Texas gardens. I've only space here to remind people who are new to gardening or new to Texas that you must do

your homework to determine a plant's suitability for your particular garden. Zone Maps are only the starting point.

Before you choose the exact species that will go in a specific place, you should be aware that certain varieties are more resistant to pests and disease than others. Unfortunately, some of the state's most beloved plants (azaleas, dogwoods and roses) are the very ones most often brought into the Master Gardener's clinics with problems! Most plants you'll see featured in popular lifestyle magazines are not adapted to the western half of Texas at all.

Think of the Garden as a Work of Art

As you begin to choose new plants, consider the colors and textures of the trees, shrubs and ground covers in your existing landscape. Beyond basic greenery, these plant materials should be woven together to create a rich tapestry. Repetition is used to unify a garden, but variety is truly its spice.

A landscape composed entirely of medium-textured plants, for example, can be greatly enlivened by interspersing such finely textured plants as yaupon or mesquite and a few plants with leaves as bold as those of magnolias or loquats. Texture can even be used to fool the eye. If you are attempting to make an area of your garden look larger than it is, you can employ an old Japanese trick. Planting coarsely-textured shrubs in the foreground, medium textures in the middle and fine-textured plantings at the rear of the garden will increase the perception of depth.

To create more interest in the planting scheme, look for variety in the shades of green. You can use variegated plants to create subtle color harmonies. Use bronze, yellow or red-leafed plants as warm accents. Such silvery plants as artemisia and Texas sage not only serve as strong elements of contrast, but also they tend to add a cooling element. The purple leaves of 'Forest Pansy' redbuds and Chinese fringe flowers punctuate the garden. Also remember that sheen often attracts the eye as much as color, so the introduction of such plants as hollies may be in order. There are even a few plants that produce splashes of fall color in Texas, such as Mexican bush sage (Salvia leucantha) and Goldenrod (Solidago spp). For winter interest, consider shrubs and trees with attractive bark, sculptural forms and/or berries.

In landscape design, you are painting a picture in three dimensions. Consider the shape of each plant at maturity, as well as its ultimate size. As I've continuously told my clients, you'll rarely have to prune if you choose plants that fit the spots for which they are intended. Never plant tall shrubs or trees under eaves or power lines, and make sure that broadly branched plants are spaced at proper distances from one another.

Eventually the plants will grow together, and the shrub mass will shade out most weeds. Your ultimate goal should be to let the plants do the garden work. Create a tree canopy if there is none. Group shade-loving shrubs and ground covers beneath the trees and encourage a community of self-sustaining plants. And, if you let the autumn leaves lie where they drop in your planting beds, you'll need little fertilizer and minimal water. Mother Nature has been gardening this way for years!

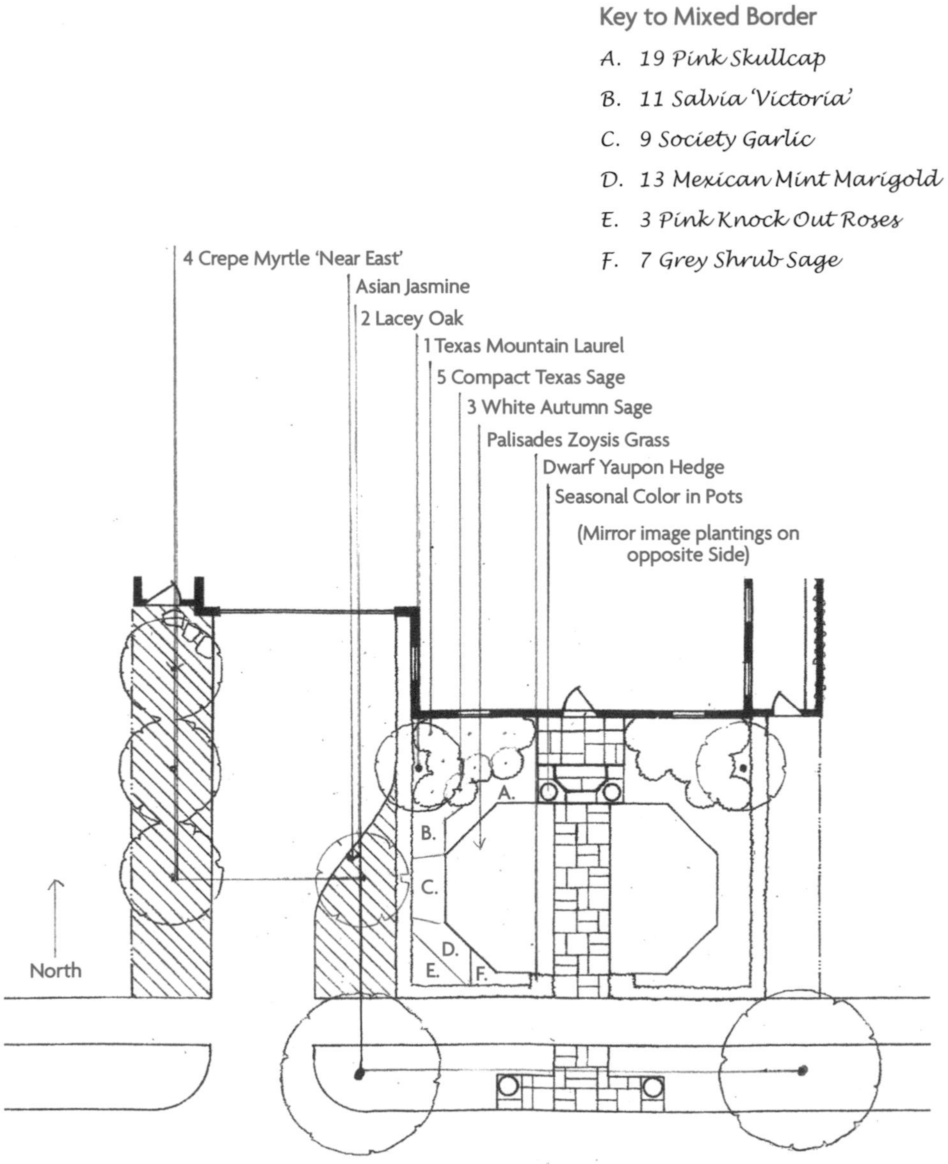

Key to Mixed Border

A. *19 Pink Skullcap*

B. *11 Salvia 'Victoria'*

C. *9 Society Garlic*

D. *13 Mexican Mint Marigold*

E. *3 Pink Knock Out Roses*

F. *7 Grey Shrub Sage*

4 Crepe Myrtle 'Near East'

Asian Jasmine

2 Lacey Oak

1 Texas Mountain Laurel

5 Compact Texas Sage

3 White Autumn Sage

Palisades Zoysis Grass

Dwarf Yaupon Hedge

Seasonal Color in Pots

(Mirror image plantings on opposite Side)

North

Planting Plan for Formal Front Garden – Texas Hill Country

CHOOSING NEW TREES

Your first priority should be your existing trees. If the property has large trees, count yourself blessed and make sure they are healthy. When I bought a home in Austin in the early '80s, I called an arborist to evaluate the 27 trees on my quarter-acre lot. Much to my surprise, he found encircling roots that were threatening to choke out a large sycamore that we desperately needed to provide afternoon shade. He also found symptoms of iron deficiency in several trees and recommended thinning out a few of the smaller live oaks to allow the rest of the grove to grow more fully. It was money well spent!

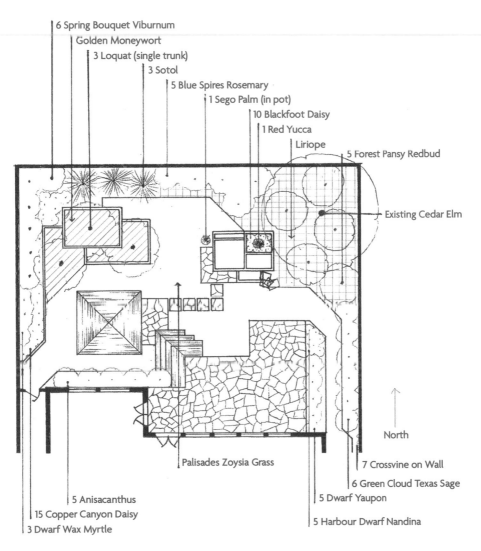

6 Spring Bouquet Viburnum
Golden Moneywort
3 Loquat (single trunk)
3 Sotol
5 Blue Spires Rosemary
1 Sego Palm (in pot)
10 Blackfoot Daisy
1 Red Yucca
Liriope
5 Forest Pansy Redbud

Existing Cedar Elm

North

Palisades Zoysia Grass

7 Crossvine on Wall
6 Green Cloud Texas Sage
5 Dwarf Yaupon
5 Harbour Dwarf Nandina

5 Anisacanthus
15 Copper Canyon Daisy
3 Dwarf Wax Myrtle

Planting Plan for Naturalistic Rear Garden – Texas Hill Country

Making the decision to remove a tree is always difficult. Even when you know that a tree is ugly or diseased, it's tempting to wait for an act of God. But if it has brittle branches that may fall onto your roof, encroaching roots that make your walkways hazardous or messy fruits that make outdoor living area unlivable, you might as well admit the truth and remove the tree. Replace it with a new tree (preferably native to Texas) that will provide shade and sustenance for the future.

Well-placed trees can reduce the cost of heating in winter and provide cooling benefits in summer. You'll want deciduous shade trees on the south and west sides of the house to mitigate summer sun. You may need large evergreen trees or shrubs on the north side to serve as a windbreak in winter. Well-placed trees can reduce the cost of air conditioning by up to 50% and lower temperatures by as much as nine degrees. A single large tree releases about 13 pounds of oxygen and removes 26 pounds of carbon dioxide each year. It can mask noise levels with the soothing sound of rustling leaves. Every young $100 tree you plant can be expected to mature into a plant with an appraised value of between $1,000 and $10,000.

Moneysaving Tip: Shade trees significantly appreciate the value of your property.

Before buying a tree, however, consider its ultimate size and mature form in relation to the size of your house and garden. Does it need lots of open space? How quickly will it grow? Is the wood strong enough to withstand wind? (The fastest growing trees usually produce weak wood.) Will its roots allow other plants to grow beneath its canopy? Be especially careful about the trees you plant within 20 feet of a power line — they should never exceed 20 feet in height at maturity.

Many of our most dependable ornamental trees are simply too big for today's urban lots. Small trees such as crepe myrtles and yaupons will be better choices than oaks or pecans, which need ample growing room. The trees you select to surround your patios or line your walks and driveway should be especially attractive and tidy. What is the tree's branching pattern? Will its form, bark or berries be interesting in winter? Does it flower? Will it drop large seeds or fruit on people, pavement and cars?

Let me tell you about a deodar cedar purchased about 50 years ago by a young couple who thought it would be nice to have a "living Christmas tree." Assured by a store clerk that it would never grow taller than 12 feet, they planted the tree in their small front lawn, unaware that its normal mature height is 40-60 feet, with a 20-foot spread. They still live in the house, but the tree's sweeping branches have taken over the entire front yard. It has shaded out all the other plants, and it poses a threat to power lines and passing cars. The owners have had the tree topped three times (it's hideously ugly), but the price for removing it is beyond their retirement income.

The moral to the story is that trees are too crucial to the landscape to plant indiscriminately. Don't be tempted to haphazardly plant a "gift" tree or order some fast-growing, weak-wooded species out of the newspaper's Sunday supplement. Your trees will probably outlive you. Seek advice from the Wildflower Center, your extension agent or a trusted nurseryman on the best species for your area. (Use that living Christmas tree as a container plant or donate it to a park department.)

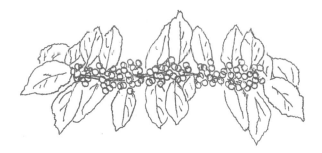

SELECTING THE SHRUBBERY

The garden's shrubbery should be your next priority. Start by reconsidering the "foundation plantings." Like most homes built in the '50s, the house I bought in Austin had a row of Burford hollies lined up like soldiers across the front. The planting scheme was boring, and the heavy shrubbery made the low ranch-style structure look squat. Left alone, these plants would have covered the windows, but some previous homeowner has pruned them into tight little balls in a vain attempt to keep them under control. I dispensed with all of them, and the pair of arborvitaes at the corners of the house, too!

Perhaps some of your foundation plants can be salvaged by renewal pruning. (See page 191 for ideas and instructions.) Remove those that aren't worth saving and plant some colorful annuals until you've had time to make a new plan. Garden centers now offer a plethora of dwarf shrubs that will not obscure your windows or overgrow the beds. Consider redrawing the line of the planting beds to make them deeper or more interesting in shape. In addition to shrubbery, consider richly-textured ground covers and small trees to set off the lines of the house. Start anew and let the plants retain their soft, natural forms as they mature.

Evergreen shrubs provide the garden's year around good looks. Such plants as hollies, Texas sage (a.k.a cenizo), yews and other evergreens appropriate for your region should represent the majority of your selections for privacy screens, accent plants and foundation plantings. However, flowering deciduous shrubs such as roses, spiraea, hydrangeas and flowering quince (a.k.a. japonica) contribute much-needed seasonal color. I prefer to plant deciduous shrubs against a backdrop of evergreens so that conspicuous holes do not appear in the winter landscape. Because many of the wonderful old deciduous shrubs tend to become "leggy," I either tuck ground covers at their base or choose the new, more compact varieties of barberry, mock orange, pomegranate and a host of other colorful shrubs.

Be sure to select flowering shrubbery that will complement the color of your house. If a client has an orange-tone brick house, I would never plant anything with bright pink blooms anywhere on the property. Likewise, pink brick and bright red flowers do not usually combine happily. I've often suggested painting a brick house some shade of white, gray or taupe simply because the client's colorful landscape plantings would play best against a neutral background.

Avoid "one of everything." Too much variety results in a fidgety-looking landscape. A garden should be like a symphony with recurring themes. Pick a few of your favorite plants, and mass shrubs of the same variety in groups of three, five or seven for maximum impact. Always buy an uneven number of the same species unless you are using a matching pair to flank a formal entryway or mark a gate to some other part of the landscape. (Don't ask me why planting in uneven numbers is more visually pleasing, just trust me on this one. It works!)

WHAT ABOUT GROUND COVERS?

Don't overlook ground covers as a means of creating interesting patterns and textures in the landscape. Large swaths of vinca or liriope can serve as evergreen transition areas between lawn and planting beds, keeping the garden lively through the winter. Asian jasmine is often employed as a lawn substitute in areas too difficult to mow or under a grove of trees where mowing would damage the roots. Ground-hugging ajuga or dwarf mondo is ideal for areas too shady for grass. Perennial ground covers such as mountain pea, lamium, violets and ferns may serve to tie together the many colors, forms and textures of a mixed shrub border. They act as living mulch, suppressing the weeds, conserving the soil moisture and shading the roots of valuable trees and shrubs.

ADD SPLASHES OF SEASONAL COLOR

Fashion can be as heartless to flowers as to hemlines. Annuals fell out of favor after World War II, when homeowners became more interested in perfect lawns than in flower gardens. Now rediscovered by the gardening press, annuals are all the rage. What's interesting is that many of today's trendy annuals were mainstays in early 20th-century gardens. "Out" are the hybridized orange marigolds and purple petunias of the '70s. "In" are such mellow old favorites as cosmos, cleome and sweet peas. Even biennials such as foxgloves and hollyhocks are back in demand as gardeners restore old homesteads or create "period" gardens. And, families are once again passing down seeds like heirlooms from generation to generation.

The hundreds of new and old varieties touted by garden writers and resurrected by specialty growers are rapidly becoming available at local garden centers as a new generation of gardeners looks for plants that provide a long season of bloom. Annuals have lots of landscape uses beyond the most obvious. They are wonderful, of course, in containers and hanging baskets. They also make excellent "fillers" in new planting beds and at the base of mature shrubs, where they add a touch of color in midsummer when few plants are at their peak.

Annual vines are also back in vogue. I remember my mother planting morning glories to clamber up strings in front of west-facing windows. Now gardeners seeking quick sunscreens can find a wide range of flowering vines, including hyacinth bean, black-eyed Susan vine, passion vine, mandevilla, and tender jasmines to perfume the summer garden.

According to the Professional Plant Growers Association, the most popular annuals remain the tried-and-true impatiens, geraniums, petunias, begonias, pansies, lobelia, marigolds and sweet alyssum. In Texas the list would also have to include such heat-tolerant standards as zinnias, periwinkles and verbena. Texas gardeners are also buying great quantities of bedding plants to color the winter landscape — flowering kale, pansies, calendulas, Iceland poppies and snapdragons.

When designing with annuals, plan your color scheme carefully. Just because impatiens come in 20 colors does not mean you should plant one of every color. Pick a harmonizing scheme of no more than five colors that coordinate with your home's exterior and interior, and repeat that scheme throughout the landscape. To achieve the most impact for your money, avoid "mixed" flats. Plant large drifts of a single color of each species you choose. For example, a flat of lemon-yellow French marigolds, a flat of deep purple salvia and a half-flat each of white vinca and coral geraniums could be combined to make a whale of a show along an entrance walk.

To brighten shady areas or play against a dark wall or hedge, let the light colors predominate. To play against a white house or fence, go for maximum impact, but remember to separate and soften bright red and gold with cool blue hues and splashes of gray foliage. Consider unusual color combinations such as lime green with a deep burgundy or a bright salmon with pale blue. Any color scheme is enhanced by the liberal addition of white, which can be used to tie the garden together and can be seen at night.

The best thing about annuals is that they can be grown easily and inexpensively from seed. Beginner's mistakes include failing to thin the plants, planting tall varieties in front of the shorter ones, and sowing every tint in the botanist's palette. The second best thing about annuals is that next year you can make a fresh start! And, if you haven't the time or patience to plant from seed, your local garden center will have flats and flats of newly available annuals. Only the most indifferent gardener could resist their appeal.

START A WILDFLOWER MEADOW

Lady Bird Johnson's book, *Wildflowers Across America*, coauthored by distinguished horticulturist Carlton B. Lees, includes many photographs of Texas wildflowers. Mrs. Johnson wrote, "Often I am asked what my favorite wildflowers are. Since there are nearly five thousand species in Texas, that is a hard question to answer. Bluebonnets would certainly be on the list, although I am a little frustrated when people know only about bluebonnets and nothing at all about the vast panoply of others." She made a convincing argument that these lovely little plants should be used not only for roadsides and parks, but also to make our home gardens bloom and grow.

As our water resources dwindle, fields of wildflowers are returning to favor as substitutes for lawn grasses. In medieval times before there were mechanical mowers, scythed meadows were used for recreation and known as "flowery medes." For our less romantic era, turf grass is admittedly more practical. It's hard to play touch football when you're knee-deep in bluebonnets. But how much grass do we really need? Certainly the parking medians and other sunny, seldom-used corners of our lawns are good candidates for conversion to flowery medes.

There are obstacles to overcome when you attempt to get a wildflower meadow established. Mrs. Johnson described wildflowers as "capricious." Certainly they have defied artists' ambitions to "paint with wildflowers." The most notable attempt took place about 25 years ago when a well-known Dallas painter thought of creating colorful abstract designs adjoining the runways at DFW Airport. The patterns of color worked reasonably well the first year, and then the plants reseeded themselves into a cheerful hodgepodge. John Thomas at Wildseed says people often call him wanting to replicate the Texas flag in wildflowers. Good luck. Why do you think we call them "wild" flowers?

Choosing wildflowers native to your region of Texas will increase your odds for success in establishing a wildflower meadow. Many of the readily available, prepackaged "wildflower mixes" contain a high percentage of commonly cultivated annuals that create a burst of color the first year, but do not reseed the second year. Some may even contain potentially invasive nonnative species that may create an ecological imbalance with other plants in the same habitat. Buy only from reputable regional seed producers, and don't expect to scatter the seed and let nature take its course.

You'll want to select a well-drained sunny site and clear it of nonnative grasses and weeds before attempting to simulate a meadow or prairie. It takes time and patience. The Lady Bird Johnson Wildflower Center suggests only shallow tilling (no more than a inch deep) and then employing soil solarization with clear plastic for several months or using two applications of a non-residual, post-emergent herbicide to remove existing vegetation. Water the site for a week or two to promote germination of weed seeds and let the weeds grow for a couple of weeks before applying the herbicide. Repeat the process once more before planting. The organization also recommends combining wildflowers with native grasses such as buffalo grass, little bluestem or sideoats grama to more closely simulate natural prairie conditions.

The primary mistakes people make are planting and mowing at the wrong times. Follow the seed producers' instructions for planting times and techniques. Many of the perennial species will not even bloom until the second year. For the annuals to return in subsequent years, you'll need to delay mowing until after the flowers have set seeds. While the plants are drying out after the blooming period, the foliage may look ragged for a few weeks. Therefore, if you're growing wildflowers in a small, highly visible area such as a median between the street and a sidewalk, you may want to simply cut them down and replant seeds each year.

It is fair to say that the Texas Department of Transportation has been the state's most energetic gardener. It distributes more than 60,000 pounds of wildflower seeds annually to more than 800,000 acres of highway right-of-way. With so much property to maintain, the Department has gained a wealth of experience in wildflower management. By trial and error over a sixty-year period, it has perfected mowing techniques that keep the native grasses healthy and the wildflowers blooming year after year. (These include less frequent mowing and leaving the native grasses taller to discourage invasive non-natives.) In the process, the Department gained national recognition as a leader in highway beautification.

April is the prime time for enjoying wildflowers in bloom along Texas roadsides. There are several widely publicized Trails and Festivals during the month, but if you want to strike out on your own, you can call Texas Tourism's Wildflower Hotline (800.452.9292) or log onto www.dot.state.tx.us and select Travel. Take a field guide such as Geyata Ajilvsgi's *Wildflowers of Texas*, and don't forget your camera!

You'll find a list of reputable Texas wildflower seed producers at the end of this chapter.

Ten Tips for Success with Wildflowers

1. Choose mixes or plants native to your region. Calculate the number of square feet you wish to cover and follow the recommended seeding rates. Wildflowers grow best in the company of wild grasses, but only those that do not form dense, spreading mats such as annual ryes or fescues.
2. Select the site carefully; it should be well-drained and should receive eight hours of sunlight each day.
3. Remove lawn grasses or weeds before planting. Use herbicide or soil solarization under clear plastic.
4. Because wildflower seed is very fine, mix it with masonry sand at a ratio of four parts carrier to one part seed.
5. Sow seed in fall (September through December), except in the Panhandle, where early spring planting is recommended.
6. Sow very shallowly and rake to barely cover the seed. Press the seed into the soil by walking or using a roller over the newly planted area. Water it in.
7. Keep the soil moist during the period when the plants are becoming established, but don't soak it. Gradually reduce the water after the seedlings reach two inches in height.
8. Avoid commercial fertilizers, pesticides or herbicides on or near wildflowers.
9. For wildflowers to return year after year, they must be allowed to dry out and set seed. Mow or cut them down in fall after seeds ripen (seedpods or seed heads turn brown and dry), or leave stalks standing to provide fall and winter food for birds. In either case, the annuals will reseed themselves. If some of the wildflowers begin to reseed too freely, remove the aggressors' seedpods, and thin unwanted seedlings.
10. If you're growing wildflowers in highly visible areas, such as streetscapes, it's best to simply cut them down when they turn brown and replant seeds each year.

Shopping for Plants

The first moneysaving tip in this chapter (Take it slowly) should be reiterated here. Read plant labels. Look at everything that's available in your area. Shop around. Ask to speak to a person in charge. It shouldn't take you too long to figure out where the plants are of the highest quality and the personnel most knowledgeable. Your garden deserves only the best!

Moneysaving Tip: Buy your plants from trained nursery personnel.

You'll find that the trees and shrubs offered in garden centers come in three different forms: bare root (which must be planted while dormant); balled-and-burlapped; and container-grown plants. I've had equal success with plants sold in all three forms. B&B stock is field-grown, dug during the cool months and normally planted soon thereafter. The advantage to container-grown material is that it can be planted at any time. A container-grown plant is generally more expensive, however, and if the plant has been in the container too long, it may be root-bound. Be suspicious of plants that have been drastically marked down.

Look for supple branches and plump buds that would indicate a young, vigorous tree or shrub. Plants should show evidence of recent increase in size. Don't be afraid to pull a plant out into the aisle to inspect it. If a container-grown tree has a stake in it, ask the salesperson to untie it. If the tree bends, the trunk is too weak. Look for healthy leaves and a full branching pattern. A gnarled, misshapen tree that nobody else wants might work as a picturesque focal point, but generally you will want a plant with a consistent shape and evenly spaced branches.

Moneysaving Tip: "Bargain plants" are rarely a bargain.

Poor root development and unbalanced or dried-out roots are the most difficult defects to detect when you walk through a nursery, yet the roots are key to the plant's survival. Reject plants that have roots growing out of the container or roots that encircle the trunk. Don't be afraid to ask the salesperson to remove a shrub or tree from its container so that you can inspect for encircling roots. (Once you get the plant home, if you find that it has tightly wound roots, take a spray nozzle, wash the roots and spread them out by hand. Otherwise, they'll continue to grow in circles and the plant will never develop properly.)

Moneysaving Tip: Learn how to select a healthy plant.

When you're planting a new landscape or doing major renovation, you may be able to get a "volume discount" from your local garden center. It never hurts to ask. Do what the professionals do: Mail or fax a plant list to several suppliers to check on availability and prices.

Moneysaving Tip: Shop around. If you're thinking big, ask for a price break.

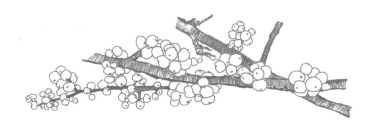

Protecting Your Investment

The major cause of plant loss is improper planting. Remove tags, wires and everything else that is not biodegradable. Cut the string from around burlap. Remove the top six-inches of the fabric after the plant is in the hole. If it becomes obvious that the balled and burlapped plant has been grown in heavy clay soil, remove the burlap completely and wash away some of the original soil with a spray nozzle as you're backfilling the hole. I've been called to clients' homes to inspect a dead tree as long as two years after it was planted. After digging it up, we discovered that the roots were still growing in the shape of the container or that the burlap was intact, with no roots penetrating the surrounding soil.

Avoid planting too deep. There's an old maxim, "Never plant a $50 tree in a $5 hole." The concept is correct, but it doesn't tell you enough. Carefully measure the depth and width of the soil in the container. The ideal planting hole will be exactly the same depth as the depth of the root ball, and at least twice its width. The depth of the hole is critical because the plant will die from lack of oxygen if it is planted too deeply. (I take a yardstick and measure the root ball before any digging begins.) The width is important because all of the feeding roots are in the top six inches. They'll want plenty of room to spread quickly.

Planting Detail

If the plant is not native to your region, mix existing garden soil with composted organic matter (half and half). Native plants will not need the compost. Fill in around the sides of the plant, gently tamping the back-fill and moistening the soil as you go. Water thoroughly. If the soil settles, add more back-fill around the edges. Do not pile soil on top of the root ball. Apply a two-inch layer of mulch over the top, but don't place mulch up against the trunk of the plant. Be sure that the dark ring or stain (usually found just above the root ball) remains above the finished ground surface. Never use fertilizer on a newly planted tree or shrub because it may burn the roots.

Moneysaving Tip: Learn proper planting techniques.

Stake young trees if they're in a location that is subject to high wind or if the root ball is small in proportion to the height and branching pattern. Three evenly placed stakes work best. Use a soft strapping material or guy wires covered with a piece of rubber hose to avoid damaging the trunk. Remove the stakes after the first year. Keep the soil moist, but not waterlogged. Build a low mound around the outer rim of the root ball to act as a water-retaining basin. Be sure to remove the ring of soil before spring rains begin.

Keep a watchful eye for pests, disease and dieback. Reduction in new shoots and a scarcity of new leaves are reliable clues that the tree or shrub needs attention. Be sure to replenish the mulch around the trees and shrubs in late spring and late autumn to cut down on climatic stress. If a tree is planted in a lawn area, maintain a ring of mulch around its base to prevent damage by a lawn mower or string weeder.

Moneysaving Tip: Keep your garden healthy by employing proper maintenance techniques.

P.S. Don't put this book on a shelf without reading the last chapter!

Online Resources for Wildflower Seeds in Texas

Browning Seed, Inc.
3101 South I-27
Plainview, Texas 79077
800.243.5271 or 806.293.5271
www.browning seed.com

This company carries all kinds of native grasses of the High Plains, and it offers a good variety of wildflower seeds, including plains coreopsis, gray-headed prairie coneflower, house mint, moss verbena, native sunflower, and ox-eye daisy. There are also several clovers suitable for the region.

Native American Seed
3791 North U.S. Highway 377
Junction, Texas 76849
325.446.3600 or 800.728.4043
www.seedsource.com

This business is a real labor of love that kindles enthusiasm and appreciation for Texas wildflowers and grasses. Talking with owners Jan and Bill Neiman about native wildflowers and grasses makes us want to join in the harvest! Perhaps a better idea is to go online and spend some time with the catalog. It's a visual treat, and it contains the most specific information you'll find anywhere on individual wild-flowers and native lawn grasses for various regions of Texas, hand-collected seeds of 55 species of rare wild plants, live roots, special mixes to attract birds and butter-flies. There are informational articles, suggested books and gift items, as well. According to Jan, "We have been in the plant business since 1975 and started to specialize in hard-to-find native seeds in 1985. What makes us different from many other wildflower seed companies is our commitment to offering only those plants that are native to our bioregion." Bill adds, "You won't find African daisies, blue-bonnets that have been grown in China, or even California poppies in any of our mixes. Not because we don't think they're pretty, but because we understand that every ecosystem is a delicate web of relationships that have evolved over centuries. And humans, with all their power of creativity and imagination, must respect the wisdom of those centuries before entering into the processes of nature as active participants."

Turner Seed Company
211 CR 151
Breckenridge, Texas 76424
254.559.2065 or 800.722.8616

Turner Seed Company is a grower and conditioner of native and improved grasses, legumes, wildlife, field and wildflower seeds. It offers a fall and spring mix each year, plus a special Xeriscape mix. The online catalog is very complete. Family owned and operated, this company was started in 1961 by Bob Turner whose dozer business specialized in applying conservation practices to the land. He and his wife retired recently but still live next door and help out if needed. Their son, Darcy, graduated from Texas A&M with a Bachelor of Science degree in agronomy in 1978, and has been actively expanding the business in wildlife and wildflower areas for the past 20 years. Their daughter, Julie Turner Vick, who graduated in 1985 from Tarleton State University, runs the office located 3 miles south of Breckenridge off Highway 183.

Wildseed Farms
425 Wildflower Hills
Fredericksburg, Texas 78624
830.990.8080 or 800.848.0078
www.wildseedfarms.com

[txt] Wildseed Farms is one of the world's largest growers of wildflowers! John Thomas began his company in 1983 when he was hired by the Houston Park Department to seed lawn grasses and discovered that there were no large-scale wildflower seed producers in the entire country. A farmer first, he now grows single-species wildflowers in rows, like crops, on several thousand acres. Small and large quantities are available, and there are over 70 species from which to choose. Wildseed's catalogs (both printed and online) are beautiful and informative. In addition to single species, the company offers two good mixes, a butterfly/hummingbird blend and a Texas/Oklahoma mix that may be especially appealing to urban dwellers with little space to plant. (The store is located on Highway 290, seven miles east of Fredericksburg.)

7

A Gardener's Garden

A Gardener's Garden

Those of us who pore over magazines and books looking for ways to make our gardens special are forever on the lookout for unusual plant varieties and new ideas in design. Perhaps you've become passionate about antique roses or want rare varieties of daylilies in your perennial border, or maybe you want to introduce gorgeous edible plants into your landscape. When you are ready to transform a basic landscape into a sophisticated garden, this chapter is for you!

In the previous chapter, I discussed trees, evergreen shrubs and ground covers as the "bones" of your basic landscape — these provide the foliage textures and shades of green. Annuals are used on most properties to add quick, disposable color. In envisioning a "real" garden, however, flowers that return year after year come to mind. Flower color is relatively short-lived and seasonal in any garden, but because color *is* the most memorable element, I encourage my clients to first choose an overall color scheme and stick with it.

I have never hesitated to remove or transplant existing shrubs that exhibit color clashes. One of my clients in Seattle bought a home that had one of every imaginable color of azaleas. It looked like a bubble gum machine. We removed all the reds and oranges and grouped the remaining pink and purple varieties by hue, using white varieties as "separators." To add color through the seasons, we augmented the garden with deciduous flowering shrubs, perennials and grasses to introduce other shades of pink, yellow, blue and white. The result was pretty stunning, if I do say so myself. With literally thousands of varieties from which to choose, creating a beautiful garden in the Pacific Northwest is actually made more difficult by an over-abundance of options. Our choices in Texas are fewer, but even here, careful editing is essential to good garden design.

English Gardening, Texas Style

Perennial gardening has become an art form. Texas gardeners are well-advised to study the pictures in English gardening books and then to studiously ignore the text! Few of the perennials that grace England's gardens would survive the first season in our hot clime. Happily, Texas nurseries are making available a wide array of our very own native perennials, and never has it been more possible to create a lavish mixed border. In addition to the tried-and-true daisies, daylilies, iris, phlox and chrysanthemums our grandmothers grew (exotics all), now we can pick from over thirty species of native salvias, as well as penstemons, prairie verbena, betony and winecups.

PERENNIALS

The most sought-after characteristics in the perennial border today are fragrance, soft color and resistance to pests and drought. A garden of perennials, bulbs and flowering shrubs is most appealing when its colors are carefully orchestrated. It's hard to go wrong with the color schemes Gertrude Jekyll designed over a hundred years ago. The English cottage gardens in which she painted yearlong successions of living pictures have inspired and delighted several generations of gardeners. Her secret was in the way she set off the vivid colors with soft drifts of white and gray and green.

The other factor that makes English gardens so visually enchanting is that the beds are deep and layered. Plants are arranged in graduated heights, from tiny border plants and ground covers at the front to tall plants at the rear. Often the perennials are mixed with old roses, forsythia, spiraea and other deciduous shrubs and played against a wall or a richly textured screen of evergreens.

A perennial garden requires faithful care and some advanced gardening skills. The word "perennial" is not a synonym for "permanent." Different perennials have different needs: some require staking, and most need to be deadheaded during the blooming season, cut back in July to rebloom in the fall, cut down after the first freeze, mulched in spring and fall, and periodically divided. Few perennials have the sustained bloom period of annuals, so Texas gardeners who want a big summer show may still want to tuck in some annuals, especially at the front of the bed.

BULBS

From the first cheerful daffodils to the later spring iris and into the summer with daylilies, glads and dahlias and completing with fall-blooming lycoris, bulbs lend elegance to the flower garden. They combine beautifully with ferns, perennials and flowering shrubs. Bulbs have an important role to play in the perennial border. For the sake of simplicity, I'm calling a "bulb" any plant that stores its life-cycle underground. Actually, the group includes corms (gladiolus), rhizomes (agapanthus, cannas and most iris), tubers (begonia, anemone and caladiums), tuberous roots (daylilies and dahlias), and true bulbs (allium, amaryllis, crinum, hyacinths, daffodils, tulips, etc.).

Bulbs are most effective en masse and more natural-looking when planted in soft, flowing drifts. It's tempting to order one of every variety. To make a big impact, however, buy at least two dozen bulbs of the same variety. Plant "minor" bulbs in groups of 50 or more, lest they be lost in the landscape. Like all the garden's permanent plantings, bulbs should be orchestrated by color. Consult a bloom-sequence chart to prolong the joy and ensure pleasing color combinations of the varieties that bloom at the same time.

Since spring-blooming bulbs begin showing color while the weather is still cool and rainy, I like to plant them where I can enjoy the display from a kitchen window or outside my living room. However, the best site for bulbs is where *they* will be happiest. Success begins with quality bulbs. All are easy to grow, but most prefer sun and well-drained soil. If your drainage is slow, plant bulbs over a sand or grit base.

One difficulty with using bulbs in the perennial garden is that the bulb's foliage shouldn't be cut down until it has begun to turn brown (the bulb rejuvenates itself by drawing down nutrients from the leaves). Therefore, to hide the bulbs' foliage as it withers and dries, I usually interplant spring-flowering bulbs with deciduous ferns or set them among a drift of later-blooming perennials.

Few garden centers carry a wide variety of bulbous plants. The daylily and iris selections seem especially *vin ordinaire* when compared to the array of varieties available from specialty nurseries. The American Hemerocallis Society (AHS) has registered more than 20,000 named varieties of daylilies bred by amateur and professional growers. Moreover, it promotes display gardens throughout the country, where daylilies are grown with companion perennials. Daylilies are no longer the orange and yellow varieties I remember from my childhood. As Mabel Matthews, a large-scale Texas hybridizer, told us, "As the quality of daylilies has improved in form, substance and color variation, there is a noticeable trend toward wider segments, more corduroy texture, extremely ruffled segments, many with extremely heavy gold edges and gold picotee edges as much as ¼-inch wide. Deep wide eyes and halos enhance the beauty of these cultivars. Colors range from almost snow-white to a deep black red."

Likewise, hundreds of new iris hybrids are developed each year from the 300+ species that grow throughout the world. By acquiring several varieties, you can extend the blooming season well into summer. Both iris and daylilies rank among the toughest, most trouble-free plants. Just give them enough sunlight, moderate water and decent soil, and soon you'll be sharing divisions with your friends.

ROSES AND OTHER FLOWERING SHRUBS

Roses are without doubt the most popular shrubs in America. But until the mid-1980s, the roses available to Texas gardeners ranked among the most difficult plants to grow. I've never included hybrid roses in my designs for Texas landscapes unless the owner specifically asked for them. Few of my clients have time for the expert pruning, the regular feeding and the spraying for black spot, powdery mildew and a variety of insects that most hybrid varieties require. Rose bushes cannot be termed the world's most attractive landscape shrubs, but who can resist their fragrance and blossoms?

The roses I appreciate most in Texas were found growing around abandoned homesteads, in old cemeteries and along fencerows. Any plant that can tolerate zero care and our seasonal temperature fluctuations is my kind of plant. Fortunately for Texans, a fellow named Mike Shoup saw the beauty in these neglected plants and started collecting cuttings to begin the Antique Rose Emporium less than 25 years ago. His roses are now worth their weight in gold.

There's renewed interest in the older, hardier varieties of roses throughout North America. Old roses are wonderful as shrubs in a mixed border. They flourish with sensible pruning and very little "doctoring." The downside to many of the old roses is that they bloom for only a brief period and produce less showy flowers than hybrids. The new Earth Kind roses and Knock-out roses, which bloom continuously from spring through fall, are offering Texans even more good choices. These plants "play well with others" in perennial gardens, and they produce longer periods of bloom and more wonderful fragrances than the hybrid tea roses ever did.

Because properly pruned hybrid teas look ratty several months of the year and because they prefer a bed all to themselves, I'll pick an out-of-the-way spot for a rose garden if my client wishes to grow roses for cutting. This will also allow the owner to plant varieties that may not complement the overall color scheme of the landscape. Of course, we'll choose only the most disease- and pest-resistant varieties on the market and find a location in the landscape that will provide full sun and good air circulation to lessen the possibility of fungal diseases. We'll water with a drip irrigation system and instruct the gardener to prune off infected parts and attempt to keep these hybrids happy with good soil and a clean growing environment.

Moneysaving Tip: If you're investing some of your money in roses, invest some of your time in education.

Rose societies offer classes and demonstrations on the care and feeding of roses. Different categories of roses have different pruning requirements. Because all roses bloom on new growth, you'll want to master pruning techniques that promote strong plant development. The severe pruning practices your grandmother may have taught you have fallen out of favor. Even experienced rosarians say they never stop learning about roses and seeking better ways to grow this very special plant.

There are many other deciduous shrubs that work well with perennials and grasses in a mixed border or lend a splash of color in front of an evergreen screen. These once-popular plants are often overlooked in today's gardens. For example, red-leaf Japanese barberry is a tough-as-nails adapted plant that graces the garden with its contrasting foliage. Japanese snowball and various hydrangea, spiraea and weigela cultivars thrive in partial shade and contribute an old-fashioned charm with their blossoms. Sun-loving shrubs such as altheas, small crepe myrtles, forsythia, flowering quince, butterfly bush and pomegranate also color the garden. There are a number of flowering native shrubs making their way into the nursery trade, including gray-leaf wooly butterfly bush, flame acanthus, American beautyberry and, of course, lantana.

ORNAMENTAL GRASSES

Ornamental grasses have been the darlings of the gardening press for about the last 20 years. Their spiky leaves and plume-like flowers make a lovely addition to a mixed border. The category includes true grasses, sedges, reeds, and some members of the lily family, including yucca, mondo grass (*Ophiopogon*) and the ever-popular monkey grass (*Liriope*). Most ornamental grasses are tough and drought-resistant, and therein lies the bad news for Texas gardeners. When I hear the word "grass," I immediately worry about introducing potentially invasive plants.

Consider two very tenacious grasses that evolved elsewhere: bamboo and Johnson grass. Tall running bamboos, which were widely planted in the 1950s, have been known to send shoots under a house foundation and come up on the other side! Johnson grass, which was introduced to Texas for cattle feed, now grows wild in every urban alley and vacant lot. When its seeds blow into your garden, you've got a serious problem.

Many of our native Texas grasses are making appearances in the best gardens. With its feathery pink plumes in fall, gulf muhly (*Muhlenbergia capillaris*), has become a popular alternative to fountain grass (*Pennisetum setacceum*), which is native to Asia and Africa and has proven to be very invasive. Mexican feathergrass (*Nassella tenuissima*), with its soft, low-growing habit, is a natural for slopes, but it does tend to reseed. The young tufts are easy to pull up, so I'm willing to tolerate its wanton ways. Bear grass (*Nolina spp.*) makes a handsome specimen plant in dry gardens. Inland sea oats (*Chasmanthium latifolium*) is beautiful in partial shade. However, it tends to reseed, so it should be planted in carefully restricted areas in the moist regions where it is native. Where it is not native, such as the Hill County, it can grow in big drifts in complete shade and remain nonaggressive. For expanses of native countryside or arid, sunny suburban areas with alkaline soil, blue grama (*Bouteloua gracilis*) can be seeded as an attractive ground cover.

There is a reason why I am careful to add the botanical name of the grasses I've used in Texas gardens. It's very important to know what you are buying before you take home some cute little four-inch pot of grass — it may turn into a monster. I've used clumping bamboos in clients' gardens because the texture adds a graceful touch in a water garden or an Oriental landscape, but I would never advise planting a running bamboo in any landscape. Even the most rampant of ornamental grasses *can* be utilized as accent plants in containers; just don't allow them to go to seed. Know what you are getting and use caution in their application.

Actually, it's never wise to buy any plant without knowing its characteristics and cultural requirements. You'd be well-advised to take a horticultural reference book with you when visiting a nursery that specializes in rare plants. I know from experience that a dear little vine can grow up to consume an arbor, and that an innocuous-looking perennial can overrun everything in its path. As one of my friends puts it, "Don't go home with strangers!" It's very easy to fall in love with every new perennial variety that comes on the market and such a temptation to buy one of every rare bulb you encounter. I'll repeat, a good garden requires careful editing. Plant collecting is only a virtue if your garden is established and you're willing to remove an existing plant to replace it with something extra special.

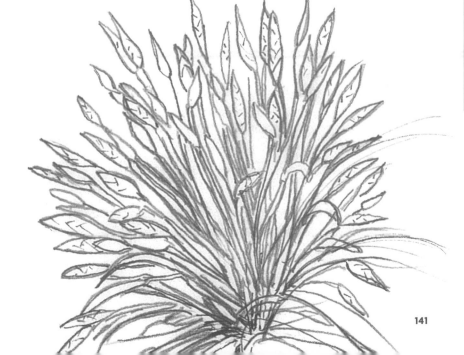

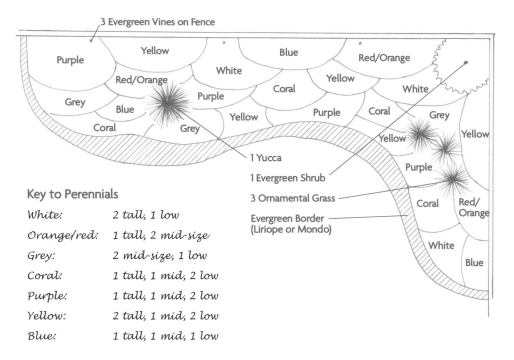

3 Evergreen Vines on Fence

Key to Perennials

White:	*2 tall, 1 low*
Orange/red:	*1 tall, 2 mid-size*
Grey:	*2 mid-size, 1 low*
Coral:	*1 tall, 1 mid, 2 low*
Purple:	*1 tall, 1 mid, 2 low*
Yellow:	*2 tall, 1 mid, 2 low*
Blue:	*1 tall, 1 mid, 1 low*

1 Yucca
1 Evergreen Shrub
3 Ornamental Grass
Evergreen Border
(Liriope or Mondo)

Notes: Select plants suitable for your region of Texas!

Use steel edging on both sides of the evergreen border to maintain a "ribbon" effect.

Substitute deep and light pink blooms for orange/red and coral if you prefer pink color scheme.

HOW TO DESIGN A MIXED BORDER

The biggest pitfall to avoid is concentrating all your efforts on a single season of the year. One of the best aspects of gardening in Texas is our long growing season, and with such a wealth of perennials, bulbs, shrubs and grasses from which to choose, we can extend the border's color throughout most of the year.

I keep a notebook that lists all the flowering plants that thrive in Texas. I've organized the book with columns for height, color and season of bloom and sun/shade requirements. Being a "lazy gardener," I put a big star by the varieties that require the least water, fertilizer and general TLC. Then, when I need a 24-inch-tall, pale pink, summer-blooming sun-lover, I have a ready resource book that offers me several choices that fit the bill.

I plan the planting bed on ¼" grid paper, drawing in big overlapping oval shapes. Based on the normal width of the plant, I assign the proper number of squares per plant, which allows me to estimate the number of plants I will need. I never plant fewer than five of a variety, usually nine or eleven. I lay out the bed on the ground with stakes and string to make a one-foot grid. This makes it simple to translate the plan-on-paper to the actual garden plot. (I always make a few eye-pleasing changes as I do the planting, but at least I've got the right number of plants to fill the bed.)

I'm especially fond of flower gardens that offer a wide variety of textures and a carefully chosen range of colors, so the garden of a dahlia collector or a chrysanthemum fancier is seldom appealing to me. But gardens are made to please the gardener, and if you want to "specialize" in a particular plant, it's still possible to create an attractive display using the same design principles and arranging the plants by color and height.

The possibilities for beautiful combinations are unlimited. For example, one of my plans for a sunny spot might include purple coneflowers, white obedient plant, tall yellow yarrow, majestic blue sage and Louisiana iris at the rear. Large drifts of shasta daisies, yellow daylilies, purple salvia, artemisia, Mexican feathergrass and burgundy chrysanthemums could fill the middle ground. For the front, I might choose miniature white roses, pink skullcap and daffodils for spring, with dwarf coreopsis to replace the daffodils and continue the splash of yellow until the first frost. I might edge this bed with an undulating ribbon of mondo grass for an evergreen border. I almost always include chrysanthemums in a perennial garden, not only because I enjoy the late fall show, but also because chrysanthemums serve as a moisture meter! When chrysanthemums begin to wilt, you know it's time to water. They bounce back quickly.

Perennials are normally sold in four-inch pots or one-gallon cans. If you are planting in the fall, purchase one-gallon plants so that the root systems are sufficiently developed to get the plant through the winter. When planting, inspect the root ball for matted or encircling roots. If you find a problem, you can cut half way up the root ball and gently spread the roots. Plant in a hole up to twice the size of the diameter of the root ball. Amend the garden soil if it is low in organic matter, and backfill the planting hole with good soil. Water thoroughly. After the first freeze, cut perennials to the ground and mulch over the roots for winter protection.

Once the plants are established, you'll need to start dividing to keep the more vigorous growers from taking over and to rejuvenate the plants. Most perennials produce inferior blooms when crowded. As you become an experienced perennial gardener, you'll get to know the individual needs of each species. In general, you'll divide spring and summer bloomers in late fall, and fall bloomers in spring.

Be willing to correct your mistakes. No matter how much planning has gone into a perennial garden, there are always a few surprises. One drift of plants grows taller than the species behind it or the color combination isn't just right. Perennials are easily moved, and that's part of the fun. Don't get discouraged if it takes three or four years to get everything the way you want it.

The Edible Landscape

I'm embarrassed to admit that, at a ripe old age, I'm planting my first real vegetable garden in the spring of 2009. I did it for the same reason that gardeners all over the country plant "Victory Gardens." Being able to go outside and pick your own organically grown vegetables makes sense from the standpoints of both the economy and a desire for fresher, safer food. Even the White House has a vegetable garden this year! So, in a raised bed in the courtyard garden I fenced last year to deter deer, I'm growing tomatoes, eggplant, sugar snap peas, lettuce, carrots and whatever else strikes my fancy.

A front-page story in the *Austin American-Statesman* in February of this year reported, "Natural Gardener owner John Dromgoole says his vegetable plant and seed sales have gone up 300 to 500 percent in the past year... Dromgoole attributes at least part of the interest to modern techniques that emphasize intensive gardening in small raised beds. A technique called Square Foot Gardening, created by national gardening guru and author Mel Bartholomew, is one of the raised-bed methods that new gardeners are finding appealing. They are virtually weed-free and low maintenance. You can even build these beds on an apartment patio."

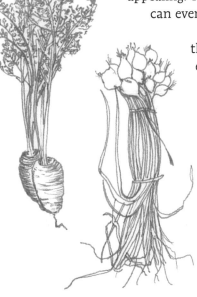

I've always believed in a landscape that both pleases the eye and teases the palate! There's nothing inherently homely about food plants. Fig trees are no less attractive than yaupons, and grapevines are as good for covering an arbor as wisteria. I've used parsley as a lacy border, strawberries as ground cover and purple basil as a colorful filler in perennial beds. Attractive edibles not only make a landscape more interesting, but also make better use of limited garden space.

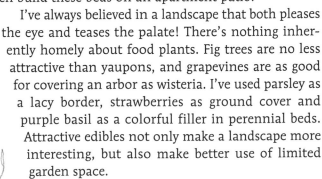

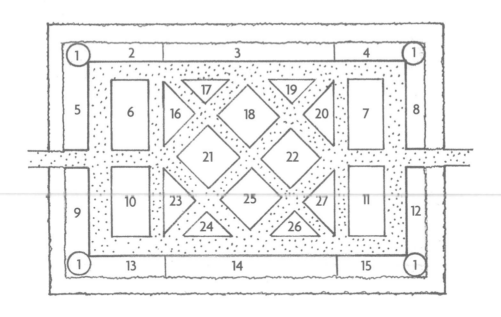

Key to Herb Garden

1. bay (in pots)
2. Silver Bush Germander
3. Tuscan Blue Rosemary
4. Roses 'Carefree Beauty'
5. Mexican Mint Marigold
6. Golden Sage
7. Provence Lavender
8. Curry
9. Lemon Verbena
10. Sweet Basil
11. Israeli Sage
12. Florence Fennel
13. Italian Flat Leaf Parsley
14. Purple Basil

15. Garlic Chives & Onion Chives
16. Curly Parsley
17. Caraway Thyme
18. Lemon Grass
19. Golden Variegated Thyme
20. Marjoram
21. Purple Coneflower
22. Monarda
23. French Tarragon
24. Silver Variegated Thyme
25. Calendula
26. Lemon Thyme
27. Italian Oregano

HERB GARDEN

HERBS

Throughout the millennia, mankind depended upon herbs for food, dyes, cleaning products, cosmetics and medicine. Many of the earliest writings, on clay tablets and papyrus, were herbals that described useful plants — where they could be found and how they could be preserved. No home garden was without its herbs. Then, in the early twentieth century, commercial products replaced traditional herbal remedies, and herb gardens almost disappeared from the landscape.

When I set up housekeeping in the early '60s, the only culinary herbs I knew were those available on grocery shelves, dried and bottled. In the last few years there has been an explosion of interest in fresh herbs that add exquisite flavors without salt or fat. The first plants I put out each spring are my basils, and the last thing I do before the first freeze is to salvage the last of the basil, making pesto and freezing it in ice trays to use over the winter. Mint and oregano are the other two flavors I could not live without. Other, more serious cooks grow a far wider range of herbs than I, but it's easy to incorporate at least a dozen different herbs into a landscape even without an organized herb garden. Herbs are also wildly popular in products for personal health and beauty. And, there's new enthusiasm for these ancient, beneficial plants as decorative elements and for freshening the air.

Traditionally, herbs were arranged in formal gardens. Most herbal books offer photographs and drawings of historical patterns — knots, stars, circles, cartwheels, diamonds, squares-within-a-square. Today, enthusiasts are recreating Chinese medicinal gardens and "literary gardens," based on herbs mentioned in the Bible or the works of Shakespeare. A well-designed herb garden can easily become the focal point of your landscape.

Their soft colors, interesting textures and wonderful fragrances are enough to recommend herbs in any garden. They are among the easiest plants to grow, so they're rewarding for a beginner. Herbs are highly decorative in perennial borders, and because they require little space, they're ideal in containers on small terraces and on sunny windowsills in urban apartments. Moreover, deer tend to avoid herbs, so gardeners in suburban areas plagued by these ravenous creatures often use evergreen herbs such as trailing rosemary, lavender, creeping germander and oregano as border plants in the landscape.

FRUITS, VEGGIES AND NUTS

Texas is one of the best places on earth to cultivate a kitchen garden because there are edible plants for every season. It must be noted that the only native plants of Texas available in supermarkets to feed the human population are pecans and prickly pear pads in the form of nopalitos. All other edible plants are introduced species.

Apple, apricot, cherry, fig, pear, peach, persimmon and plum trees make lovely ornamental trees for small gardens in Texas. Pecan and walnut trees can provide a canopy for larger landscapes. If your space is limited or you have a bare wall to cover, dwarf fruit trees can be grown in pots or espaliered. Pomegranates and blueberries make attractive shrubs. Of course, not every fruit- and nut-producing plant is right for every region in the state. The apple trees that grow well in the cooler winter climes of West Texas give way to citrus trees in the Rio Grande Valley.

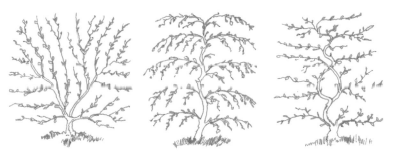

Espalier Patterns for Fruit Trees

Because most vegetables are annuals, they can be grown anywhere in the state. Your local county extension agent is your ultimate source of information on the best varieties to thrive where you live. Veggies are easiest to tend in a conventional "patch" with raised rectangular beds, but if you don't have time or space to spare, they can be sown successfully amidst an ornamental landscape. Historically, farmer's wives mixed flowers in with their vegetables, so urban gardeners are simply reversing the trend when they tuck lettuce or okra into the flowerbed and run cucumbers or beans up a trellis.

Moneysaving Tip: Buy only the best varieties for your region.

Having easy access to these wholesome plants in your garden allows you to harvest at the exact moment of ripeness. The produce is fresh, and the price is right. If your space is limited, it may make sense to concentrate your efforts on herbs and vegetables such as arugula and exotic peppers that are expensive in supermarkets and to leave the watermelons and corn for farmers to grow. Most beginning gardeners make the mistake of thinking too big, anyway. One little plant can produce an appalling number of cherry tomatoes or summer squash!

Good soil is key to successful food crops. (Refer back to Chapter Five.) You'll need to add liberal amounts of organic compounds, which in turn will encourage worms and microorganisms to flourish in a symbiotic relationship with plants, adding their own body secretions to the soil. Without microorganisms, air, water and nutrients become less available, and plants become more susceptible to disease and insects.

Remember, too, that you're making a commitment to managing without chemical pesticides. With the advent of new technologies, gardeners have more control over disease, pests, even the weather. Organic farmers' secrets include choosing disease- resistant varieties, using crop rotation and companion planting. In winter, they'll employ cover crops, which they dig back in to enrich the soil. Expecting some insect damage, growers compensate with a few extra plants.

I am always tickled when I see gardeners grabbing up tomato starts at the garden centers on the first warm day in March. Sure as the world, their plants will be zapped by one last hard freeze. You can get a head start on the season, however, by getting your vegetable starts a couple of weeks before your local extension agent says it's time to set them out. Move them into larger pots and give the roots a stimulus with a dose of organic houseplant fertilizer. Place the pots in a sunny spot outdoors and move them in at night. Meanwhile, you can be increasing the soil temperature in your planting areas by covering the soil with a layer of clear plastic, which also inhibits weeds. Fall and winter vegetable gardening presents different challenges and rewards. Experiment for the fun of it! And, wish me luck with my first "real" veggie patch!

Container Gardening

Plants in handsome containers add significantly to the graciousness of any outdoor space. A single, elegant container plant can be used to serve as a focal point in the landscape. Paired, potted plants lend warmth to entrances and frame gateways. While distinctive specimen plants (such as a tree rose, a handsome cactus, an azalea or gardenia in full flower) can stand alone, I generally like plants displayed in groups, with a variety of textures and leaf shapes, especially when played against a bare wall, descending a staircase or surrounding a seating area.

Throughout the growing season my entrance courtyard and rear patio are brimming with blooming tropical plants and seasonal annuals. I also enjoy growing vines on pyramidal wire trellises in pots. One good decorator trick I've learned is to mass potted plants on both sides of a glass door or low window wall, doubling the impact inside and out.

Mixed plantings in a single container are very popular again. All the home magazines are featuring "how-to" articles on window boxes, Victorian-style hanging baskets and urns overflowing with multicolored flowers. I like something tall and possibly spiky in the center of a mixed container and trailing plants around the edges. I fill the remaining space with medium-sized plants chosen for color harmony. (Think: thriller, filler and spiller.)

If you are reusing an old pot, clean out the inside with a half-cup of bleach to a quart of water. Test to make sure it doesn't damage the container. Always use fresh potting soil when planting or repotting. I prefer to begin with new bags of soil each spring. To save on soil cost and facilitate good drainage, I fill the bottom half of large containers with Styrofoam packing peanuts and add a layer of filter fabric before filling the pot with soil. Several layers of coffee filters are good for covering drainage holes of pots you plan to completely fill with soil.

Containerized plants of any kind require more attention than plants in the ground. Most of the houseplants you buy are grown in a potting soil, which contains no actual garden soil, but rather a blend of composted bark, sphagnum peat moss, vermiculite and other ingredients blended to provide good drainage, aeration and moisture retention. Because plants quickly deplete the nutrients in the potting soil, they need regular doses of fertilizer and periodic repotting. If the roots become too large for the pot size, the plant can't store enough water to sustain itself. Always repot your plants into a good packaged soil mix rather than common garden soil, which will be too heavy for container plants and may contain weeds or pathogens.

In hot weather, container plants on your patio or porch may need daily watering. The upside to gardening in containers is that not a precious drop of water is wasted to surrounding soil. By adding biologically harmless polymers to the soil, you can further reduce the water needs of containerized plants up to 75 percent. There are kits available at home improvement stores and garden centers for watering container plants from outdoor spigots. They come with timers, and I'm told they are easy to install. This past year I put all of my pots on a drip system that operates off the automatic sprinkler controller. Now I would be free to take a summer vacation if I didn't have a book to write!

HOUSEPLANTS

In winter, I turn my full attention to indoor gardening. My husband has always grumbled when asked to haul in all the tropical plants that decorate the outdoor living areas throughout the growing season, but we are both pleased with the effect when our sunny breakfast room is filled with blooming hibiscus and bougainvillea on cold days. Especially in winter, a home is incomplete without houseplants to brighten bare walls, spill from bookshelves and flower on tabletops.

The design ideas you use for the placement container plants on a deck or patio apply equally well to houseplants. Big tropical plants are very useful for camou-

flaging architectural flaws. I've used plants to fill one end of a long narrow room, to divide space in an overly large room and always to soften the corners. I use fluffy ferns to fill the empty fireplace in summer (rotating them weekly between the garden and the house). In choosing houseplants, it's important to consider the scale of both the room and the plants. Too many small plants can make a room look "fussy." On the other hand, huge plants or plants with large leaves may look menacing in a small space.

I first learned the visual impact of indoor plants many years ago when friends bought a house with a huge formal living room. Like most young couples, they couldn't afford much in the way of furnishings, so they invested in several large ficus trees. The "garden room" effect was so pleasing that they never did buy all the fine furniture they had originally envisioned.

Tropical plants are literally lifesavers for people who spend long hours confined indoors. Houseplants not only provide vital oxygen, but also raise a room's humidity level, which is a gift to anyone who suffers with dry skin. Used in large numbers, houseplants have even been shown to cleanse the air of noxious household chemicals.

A two-year study by NASA and the Associated Landscape Contractors of America proved that 'Janet Craig,' 'Warneckii' and marginata dracaenas, peace lily, English ivy, mother-in-law's tongue, green spider plant, golden pothos and bamboo palm are among the best plants for removing concentrations of chemicals from the air. The researchers estimated that fifteen to twenty potted plants of these species can purify the interior of a typical 1,800-square-foot house. The other good news is that these common plants are easy to grow and among the most attractive for interior plantscaping.

It's important to know that most of the tropicals available in the United States are grown outdoors (in Texas' Rio Grande Valley or in California, Florida or Hawaii). Specialty shops and better garden centers know to acclimatize tropical plants for several weeks before offering them to the public. By gradually reducing light and moisture levels and withholding fertilizer, they prepare the plant for the drier conditions and lower light levels of a home environment. It's worth asking a nursery manager how the plants you buy have been grown and acclimatized.

Moneysaving Tip: Inspect houseplants carefully before making your purchase.

Avoid buying plants that have brown edges on the leaves, which may indicate sunscald or excessive fertilizer. Pale or yellow leaves may be a sign of improper watering. Sparse or leggy plants may have been subjected to abnormally forced growth. Roots that grow above the soil surface or out the drainage hole are a sure sign of a plant that has become root-bound. Inspect for insects on the undersides of leaves and at the junctions between the stem and the leaves. A "bargain" plant is certainly no bargain if it expires within a week or introduces an insect infestation to your existing plants.

It's probably a good idea to place a new plant in quarantine in any case. To reduce the shock of moving it into a dry environment, mist the foliage every day with tepid water. It's also good practice to flood new plants with water to flush out salts that may have accumulated from heavy fertilizing by the grower. Run a slow stream of water through the soil for a full five minutes and let the plant drain thoroughly. (A bathtub or shower works well for this task.) Periodically, I run water through all of my house plants to prevent the buildup of salts.

It's normal for a few older leaves at the bottom to die as the plant adjusts to new conditions. Instead of pinching off yellowed leaves, allow them to drop naturally; nature has a mechanism for sealing the wound. If the plant loses a lot of leaves, you're probably watering too much or have placed the plant where it isn't getting enough light. If it dies within the first month in spite of your TLC, take it back and ask for a replacement.

Most garden centers have huge houseplant departments these days, and tropical plants have become almost ridiculously inexpensive. The ferns and potted palms favored in Victorian times are popular once again, but your options only begin there. With worldwide transportation improved, exotic species from tropical regions all over the world are now available to the discriminating shopper. Never has there been such a vast array of colorful blossoms and fanciful forms from which to choose.

Online Resources for Serious Gardeners in Texas

We've found some sources that even avid gardeners may not know. These are growers who really know and love gardening, and whose wares are available all over the state through websites and printed catalogs. You'll enjoy meeting these people as well as exploring their nurseries and private display gardens, so by all means go visit them if you are in their area. (Many of these gardens are located at private residences, so please call ahead to arrange a convenient time to visit.) We expected to find more resources than were available ten years ago because of the Internet, but we've discovered that shipping costs have made many growers unable to sustain a mail-order business. One orchid grower told us that her clients were unwilling to pay a $28 shipping charge for a $25 plant, and rightly so!

Bulbs and plants such as daylilies, roses and fruit trees that can be shipped bare-root are about the only plants now available. Yucca Do is an exception, and its fabulous Internet catalog lists plants that fit under almost every category in this chapter.

Bulbs and Other Perennials

Argyle Acres Iris Gardens
910 Pioneer Circle East
Argyle, Texas 76226
940.464.3680 or 866.320.4747
www.argyleacres.com

Joe and Donna Spears offer a wide variety of historic and modern iris. The website features photos of numerous varieties, and you'll be tempted to order vast quantities of at least a dozen varieties! Call for a descriptive catalog. The Speares ship all over the country; orders are accepted until the end of July each year. (Gift certificates are always available.) Visitors are invited to their display garden during most days of April during the blooming season.

Hillcrest Iris and Daylily Gardens
3365 Northaven Road
Dallas, Texas 75229
214.352.2191
www.hillcrestiris.com

Hooker and Bonnie Nichols began work on their AHS Display garden almost 20 years ago, and it's one of the loveliest in the state. They grow thousands of daylilies and iris in traditional raised beds, accented with pots of annuals. Hooker is the hybridizer in the family, and his daylily collection consists of about 1,000 varieties. The iris collection focuses on bearded, with 2,000+ varieties, and also includes 30-40 spuria and 300 Louisiana iris varieties. The website provides ordering information and will list times for Open Garden in Mesquite, where the Nicholses grow this vast array of colorful plants.

Hurst Park Daylily Garden
405 Crosstimber Drive
Hurst, Texas 76053
817.268-5189

This AHS display garden specializes in daylilies and carries thousands, hybridized from the latest cultivars throughout the United States. Some iris and other perennials are also available. As Mabel Matthews tells us, "Growing and hybridizing daylilies has been a pleasure of mine for over 45 years." Mrs. Matthews carries over 700 named cultivars and approximately 10,000 seedlings from which the most distinctive ones (about 10) are selected to introduce into the National AHS. "I like to have customers take time to sit and discuss their problems and my planting and growing procedures. We ship between March and May and then again in October," she says.

The Lily Farm
7725 Highway 7 West
Center, Texas 75935
936.598.7556
www.lilyfarm.com

Jack Carpenter is well-respected in the world of daylilies, and his beautiful website will show you why! "I am a hybridizer of top-notch hybrid daylilies. It is obvious that we would not be using shadehouses if there were not some good reasons for doing so. Many people who grow lilies live in areas that have conditions more similar to those created by shadehouses. In fact, in our area, shadehouses cannot even approach creating the milder temperatures in air and soil that are found naturally occurring in much of the Northern, Great Lakes, and coastal areas of the U.S. Our 30 percent shadecloth may give us a 95- 97-degree temperature instead of the 100 degrees outside." You can order by mail during March and April and September and October. Lilies may be purchased from the field during the two- to three-week Open House that runs from the last week of May through the middle of June. This farm is located 19 miles northeast of Nacogdoches. There's a sign on the highway during that time.

Payne's In The Grass Daylily Farm
14103 Melanie Lane
Pearland, Texas 77581
281.485.3821
www.paynesinthegrassdaylilyfarm.com

As Paula and Leon Payne explain, "Our business evolved from our love of daylilies, and we take special interest in hybridizing. We offer many of the latest cultivars and our own introductions as well as those for the beginning collector or casual gardener. We grow over 800 different registered cultivars, and we plant approximately 5,000 seedlings each year. We also grow many different perennials. It is a lot of work, but there is something special about going out early in the morning and seeing a daylily bloom its maiden bloom. It has turned into a labor of love, but worth the rewards." Leon has also become interested in bamboo, and they now grow about a dozen different species of large clumping bamboo. They sell bamboo in the garden, but don't ship it. At least once a year during the daylily blooming season, the Paynes hold an "Open Garden" where the public is welcomed. Send an e-mail (payne@hal-pc.org) for a price list.

Plantastik Nursery
713 Spring Street
Granbury, Texas 76043
817.736.0833
www.plantastikdaylilies.com

Plantastik Daylilies, a division of Tana Tomlinson's nursery in Granbury, carries approximately 400 registered cultivars of *Hemerocallis* for sale, as well as seedlings produced in her hybridizing programs with partner Gail Rasberry in Arkansas. Plantastik Nursery, where plants may be purchased on-site, specializes in Texas hardy perennials. Some of her best perennials, such as columbines, cannas, coneflowers, cardinal flowers, salvias and a particularly pretty penstemon, are also available through the online catalog. The website provides a link for questions regarding plant availability, pricing, shipping charges, etc.

Shimek's Gardens
3122 County Road 237
Alvin, Texas 77511-8690
281.331.4395
www.hal-pc.org/~neshimek

Shimek Gardens was a 2008 AHS National Convention Tour Garden and boasts 800 named daylilies plus thousands of seedlings. You'll also find hundreds of other plants, including roses, hibiscus, jatropha, bauhinia, ginger and plumeria. Harvey and Nell Shimek are serious collectors! Quotes Nell, "When one of our many visitors commented that we couldn't possibly want for another daylily, I just laughed and replied that my want-list of daylilies was probably longer than his!" You can buy overstock from October through February. Garden advice is freely offered, and visitors are welcome. Don't miss the Open Garden Days; this is a spectacular display garden. Dates and directions are on the website.

Southern Bulb Company
P.O. Box 350
Golden, Texas 75444
903.768.2530
www.southernbulbs.com

Chris Wiesinger, now 27, started the Southern Bulb Company in 2004 with the aim of reintroducing flowers long out of fashion, committing himself exclusively to those that had survived hot weather and droughts for decades. The company is based on a business plan he devised as a senior in TAMU's horticulture program. After graduation he began combing old towns for abandoned buildings and houses and "other places where people couldn't afford to plant new things." His catalog includes such heirloom bulbs as crinum lilies, rain lilies, spider lilies (*Hymenocallis*), Byzantine gladiolus, oxblood lilies, hardy amaryllis and several varieties of narcissus. There is even a tulip that will naturalize in Texas! His efforts have made him a popular lecturer around the South and earned him a place on the *House & Garden* list of most important American tastemakers.

Spring Creek Daylily Garden
25150 Gosling
Spring, Texas 77389
281.351.8827

Mary & Eddie Gage's half-acre of daylilies includes some 1,500 varieties. Of course, not all are in the free descriptive catalog, but once a year they eliminate some and add others. With four registered varieties of their own, they are continuing to hybridize, and they enjoy sharing both their wares and their storehouse of knowledge with other "plant people." There is no website, but you can call for a catalog or e-mail (mary@springcreeklily.com).

Wild Prairie Farm
4361 Ridgedale Avenue
Odessa, Texas 79762
432.230.9776
www.wildprairie.com

Wild Prairie Farm is exclusively about reblooming iris. What this means is that these beauties will bloom several times during a growing season, depending on your zone and garden care. "These iris require a bit more moisture and very regular fertilizing since they are actively growing and blooming throughout the year," says Reneé Shearer. "Irises prefer to be left alone most of the time, so when I don't have my hands in the soil, I have it in clay." You'll find her pottery in the online catalog as well.

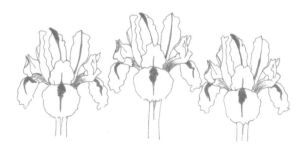

Roses

The Antique Rose Emporium
9300 Lueckemeyer Rd.
Brenham, TX 77833
800.441.0002 or 979.836.9051 (customer service)
www.antiqueroseemporium.com

The Antique Rose Emporium is one of our "Texas Treasures" and a visit is always a delight, but the website is beautiful, informative and close-by! As Mike Shoup explains," We offer old garden roses that are especially versatile for landscape use. Old roses are noteworthy not only because of their survival, but because they retain the characteristics of fragrance, disease resistance and diversity of form. You plant them with perennials and companion plants, not in perfect rows so you can spray all the time." Order directly from the website or request a catalog. The website also has the addresses of both the Independence and San Antonio retail stores/display gardens.

Chamblee's Rose Nursery
10926 Highway 69 North
Tyler, Texas 75706
800.256.7673
www.chambleeroses.com

As Mark Chamblee told us, "We ship 300 varieties of miniature roses and old garden roses nationwide." As owner of the largest retail rose nursery in East Texas, his family-owned company has been in business since 1953. Chamblee knows roses! The online catalog offers own-root garden roses, as well as David Austin, Dr. Griffith Buck and Earth Kind roses.

Rare and Endangered Plants

Yucca Do Nursery, Inc.
P.O .Box 1039
Giddings, Texas 78942
979.542.8811
www.yuccado.com

This very special nursery's specialty is drought- and heat- tolerant plants and trees. It received the American Horticultural Society's 1996 Commercial Award, "given to a firm/company whose high standards have made significant contributions to gardening. The award recognizes outstanding work in collecting seed of rare and endangered plants of Mexico and Texas and reintroducing them into cultivation." The plants available from Yucca Do are not easily categorized. There are bulbs, tropical and hardy perennials, grasses, cacti, succulents, palms, cycads and ornamental trees and shrubs among the more than 300 plants these people grow.

Nursery manager Wade Roitsch sent shock waves through the world of plant collectors a couple of years ago when he announced that the company would no longer produce a printed catalog, but the online version is superb! There are scads of sculptural agaves, rare buddlejas, the most beautiful canna I've ever seen and more species of rain lilies than I knew existed. You'll spend several hours perusing this site. You'll want to become a collector!

Edibles

Bob Wells Nursery
17160 County Road 4100
Lindale, Texas 75771
903.882.3550
www.bobwellsnursery.com

Bob Wells' website is unbelievably comprehensive. This fourth-generation nursery has always specialized in fruit and nut trees and berry bushes, but its selection surprised even me! Would you believe eight types of berries, with several varieties of most? The list even includes the only raspberry that will produce crops in West, Central and North Texas. Exploring the site further, I found asparagus and rhubarb. But what I really didn't know is that this is a source for some of the heirloom shrubs I had mentioned in the text earlier in the chapter — altheas, forsythia, flowering quince, weigela and Japanese snowball.

Dixondale Farms
2007 Highway 83
Carrizo Springs, Texas 78834
877.367.1015
www.dixondalefarms.com

This fourth-generation, family-owned business is the largest and oldest producer of onion plants in the country. According to Bruce Frasier, "If you haven't planted your onion transplants by the end of January, it is probably too late for this year. But if you're planning for next year, our little onion factory in South Texas has the freshest starter plants and best advice."

Teas Herbs & Orchids, Inc.
32930 Decker Prairie Road
Magnolia, Texas 77355
281.356.2336
www.teasherbsandorchids.net

Teas is a lovely specialty nursery that carries a wide variety of herbs, vegetables, perennials and orchids. The plant material is unusual, and customers can often choose from a crop instead of a few flats. Janis Teas is willing to ship her wares in small pots to customers throughout the state. As far as we know, she is the only source of mail-order herbs in Texas at this time. You can join her mailing list online and call for availability and shipping information for any type of plant she offers.

Willhite Seed Company
911 Sparks
Poolville, Texas 76487
817.599.8656 or 800.828.184
www.willhiteseed.com

In the business for over 80 years, Willhite Seed Company provides quality garden seeds for everything from asparagus to zucchini. There are herbs and flowers in there as well. The company offers many standard and open-pollinated vegetable varieties as well as hybrid varieties and All America selections. All of the varieties are described in the catalog (most with color pictures). Parker County is noted for its watermelons, and T.A. Willhite got his start selling watermelon seeds, so you'll find plenty of listings for melons. "Our goal is the same as it has always been... to continue to provide the highest quality seed to our customers," says office manager Carole Clark, who has almost 25 years of experience and personally tries many of the new varieties in her home.

Womack Nursery Co.
2551 Hwy 6
DeLeon, Texas 76444
254.893.6497
www.womacknursery.com

Since 1937 Womack's has been a respected name in the Texas nursery business. There's no online catalog here because the family is too busy growing and shipping thousands and thousands of grapevines, berry plants and fruit and nut trees to customers across the country. You'll find several varieties of peach, pear, plum, apricot, nectarine, persimmon and fig trees, plus various berries available. They also grow pecan and some shade trees. This is a great source for top-quality tree-pruning tools and everything you need for budding and grafting. Call for a catalog or send an e-mail (pecan@womacknursery.com) Shipping season for the bare-root plants is from mid-December to mid-March.

8
Finishing Touches

Finishing Touches

Please Be Seated

Just thinking about garden furniture revives happy memories. As a child in the 1940s and '50s, I spent lazy afternoons watching the world go by from my grandmother's porch swing. I often think about the hammock where I loved to curl up and read. I remember reclining in a sling-back canvas chair as my father pointed out the constellations on starry summer nights. I have faded photographs of family picnics and children's tea parties held around a big tile-topped table.

People are rediscovering such simple pleasures in the twenty-first century. But today's furniture is not your grandmother's furniture. It's far better! Visit any outdoor furniture store today, and you'll see dining tables and chairs in a splendid array of new finishes and colorful materials. There will be sofas and occasional tables, teacarts and etageres, bar stools and bright market umbrellas — all reflecting fresh flair and elegance. Some of the pieces look like they belong indoors, and several outdoor furniture dealers have told us that people are buying good-looking patio furniture for indoor family rooms because it is so durable.

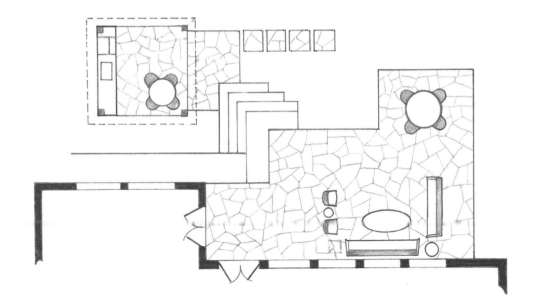

DESIGNING A "COMFORT ZONE"

Over the years, I've learned the hard way some facts about buying outdoor furniture. If you get it right the first time, maybe you (unlike me) will only need to make this investment once. Before you buy anything, think about how you want to use your porch, terrace or deck. Perhaps you need lots of seating or a big dining area for entertaining, or maybe you simply want a private place for quiet relaxation. Measure your space and draw it on ¼-inch grid paper. Then visit furniture stores and get measurements of standard tables, sofas, chairs, etc. You can use construction paper to cut out little rectangles, squares and circles at ¼-inch scale to represent the furnishings you want.

Arrange the pieces and move them around on the grid paper to see what furniture will best fit the space and meet your needs. In addition to the space required for a seating arrangement, allow ample room for walking around and through the outdoor sitting room. If you're designing an outdoor dining room, you'll need a minimum of eight by eight feet for a four-foot round table and chairs. You may want a barbecue grill and perhaps a service bar nearby, and you'll want to allow a minimum of four feet as a transition area between the cooking and eating areas. You may discover that a rectangular table would work better than a round one. If all this seems too complicated, outdoor furniture stores often have professional designers to help you. Outdoor rooms require the same kind of spatial planning as interior rooms.

FINDING THE RIGHT FURNITURE

Once you've determined your requirements in terms of type, size and quantity, you'll need to select the furniture you buy based on the look you want, the environment it will occupy (covered porches are more benevolent to furniture than open spaces), and your commitment to maintaining outdoor furniture. Your first priority should be comfort. Designers are responding to new consumer demands by studying human proportions and seeking the best fit for the widest possible range of human body types. While a garden bench does not need to be the ultimate in comfort, the chairs you use for dining and lounging should be as carefully selected as any that go into your home.

The choices in materials are wide, and manufacturers are emphasizing durability. Romantic Victorian styles are in vogue again, but now the pieces are fabricated of cast aluminum or all-weather vinyl wicker rather than traditional wrought iron or real wicker. Contemporary designers are drawing on stylistic trends from art deco to post-modern and using stainless steel and cast aluminum to produce sleek new furnishings. You'll still find the classical designs. There are many faithful reproductions of English-style wooden garden benches and comfortable new versions of the Adirondack chair. To complement the country lifestyle, Texas craftsmen are creating new versions of the old picnic tables, porch swings and gliders I remember from childhood.

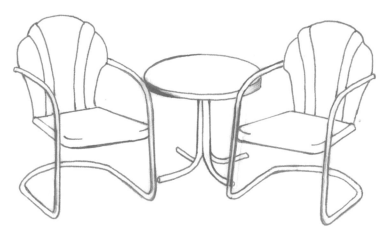

CHOOSING FRAME AND FABRICS

Wood is timeless and traditional. It grays as it weathers, so if you want to preserve the rich color and smooth finish, you will need to oil it regularly. If your furniture will be exposed to the elements, do not buy wood that has been sealed with a varnish or paint. Wood needs to breathe. An oil-based stain will protect the wood and allow it to expand and contract with changes in the weather. Wood furniture should be joined with brass, stainless steel or galvanized fasteners.

Wood remains popular because it doesn't feel hot in the summer or cold in the winter. Many of the exotic hardwood species once used for garden furniture come from ecologically sensitive areas of the world, so manufacturers are increasingly fabricating their wares from domestic woods which, if properly selected and well-maintained, should hold up almost as well as tropical species. Responsible companies that use woods such as teak certify that their material has been harvested from sustainable-source plantations. Responsible — should consumers demand it.

Antique wrought iron pieces lend a certain charm to your garden, but they rust and will need to be sandblasted and repainted every few years. If you buy new wrought iron furniture, use it on covered patios and porches. New powder-coated cast aluminum furniture is not as heavy as wrought iron, but it's rustproof, can be used in open areas and is available in myriad finishes and styles. Designs in other noncorrosive metals such as steel, tubular aluminum and welded wire-mesh are also manufactured with baked-on finishes to provide a far longer life span than simple paint.

Stone and concrete furniture, the most durable of choices, have a tendency to collect water and are very uncomfortable for seating, but these, too, have their place in the garden; stone is a beautiful material for table tops. And, furnishings made of high-tech plastics and resins treated with ultraviolet inhibitors have become viable alternatives. New vinyl wickers, if they are made in America and if they are properly treated to resist sun damage, are said to hold up well, but I'm of the opinion that they are a better choice for covered patios and porches than for the great outdoors. (I recently disposed of a five-year-old set of vinyl wicker that cracked and unraveled in the sun.) Molded-resin furniture and pieces made of PVC-type tubing are light-weight and easy to clean, but they are not good choices where they will be subject to high winds.

Take a look at the frame colors available in cast aluminum! White, green and dark earth tones remain favorites, but today's site furnishings also come in wild and wonderful hues. In the right setting, red or bright blue chairs can make a memorable statement. Cushions lend both pattern and color to seating areas, and here we are talking about a *lot* of choices. (If the furnishings will be visible from indoors, be sure the colors complement your interior design as well as the exterior setting.) All the national and regional manufacturers offer catalogs or brochures, and many are willing to customize orders to accommodate your special requests.

New furniture often comes with cushions made of Sunbrella® all-weather fabric. The solution-dyed acrylic fabric won't fade or deteriorate if left outside year-round. (Threads holding the cushion together may disintegrate before the fabric does.) If your old garden furniture needs new cushions, you can buy inexpensive seasonal cushions and replace them every couple of years, or you can invest in durable cushions, which can take the sun and rain.

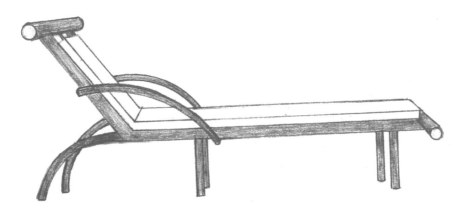

With garden furniture in general, there are two ways to go. You can buy cheap, planning to discard the furniture when it falls apart. Or you can go for quality. It's hard to argue with the logic of stackable welded wire chairs that cost $5.95. (I've seen them at all the hardware stores, even the drugstore chains.) They're "knock-offs" of great-looking Italian chairs that sell for about $100 apiece. Sure, if you leave them outdoors, the welds break and the paint peels, but at that price, who can complain? They are handy to pull out when you're entertaining large crowds. For the furnishings you are going to see every day and plan to use year in and year out, buy the highest quality furniture you can afford.

Moneysaving Tip: Shop around. Look for bargains online and compare prices. You may pay less online for the product itself, but you may pay dearly for shipping. Be sure items are in stock when you order, and ask if you can cancel at no charge if the order doesn't arrive by a guaranteed date.

Many of the retail Garden Furnishings sources we've listed in the twelve regional chapters of *The Texas Garden Resource Book* mark down their products in late summer or early fall. It's hard to justify spending money on something you aren't going to use for several months, but you can save up to 50% just because a store needs to make room for other merchandise. Sometimes the sales begin as early as September, and this is usually about the time of year when we Texans venture back outdoors! During the season, check out discount merchandisers such as Home Depot and Lowe's. If you've shopped around and know what to look for in quality, you may unearth some real bargains.

Moneysaving Tip: Buy off-season.

Pat and I were surprised to discover that there are very few retail stores devoted solely to outdoor furnishings in the smaller towns of Texas. It became apparent that people may have to travel quite a distance to find high-quality garden furniture. At the end of this chapter, we are listing some manufacturers that ship their products. Often the retail stores in the major market area of your region will offer catalogs and shipping or delivery services to outlying areas.

PROTECTING YOUR INVESTMENT

You'll want to follow the care instructions that come with any outdoor furniture you buy. Most manufacturers recommend regular cleaning for the frames of metal and plastic furniture. If you don't have instructions to the contrary, it's generally safe to hose off dust and dirt. If the piece needs more thorough cleaning, wash it with mild soap, rinse well and dry it with a soft towel. Do not use abrasive materials or strong detergents on metal or plastic furniture. Some people use auto polish to brighten metal surfaces that have become dulled over time, but I'd suggest testing a small unobtrusive area. Waxes are not recommended for textured frame finishes.

Wood furniture can be cleaned with water and a soft brush, but never use any type of soap on wood. It is best to allow wood to dry in direct sunlight. I disagree with manufacturers' instructions that recommend sealing wood; you are setting yourself up for removing all the old sealer, and continually resealing it. I repeat, *wood needs to breathe*. I prefer to let wood weather naturally. It can be lightly sanded if the grain becomes rough and kept nice with an oil made for outdoor wood finishing.

Marble, granite and tile tabletops have become popular. For basic cleaning, hose or dust off the dirt. For thorough cleaning, use a neutral pH cleaner such as Simple Green®. Never allow spills such as wine, soda or coffee to stand on the surface of tile or stone for extended periods of time. If the finish becomes dull due to a collection of autumn leaves, hard water or air pollution, clean with a non-abrasive pad or sponge and apply a coat of polish, such as Goddard's Granite and Marble Polish. Clean woven wicker with your vacuum cleaner's soft bristle attachment, and use a damp sponge to wipe away heavier soil.

The fabrics and fibers used for cushions today are very durable. For basic cleaning, hose off the dirt and dust; for a more thorough cleaning, spray a mild soap and water solution on the fabric and lightly scrub with a soft bristle brush. Rinse and stand the cushions on edge to allow them to dry inside and out. Umbrella fabrics can be cleaned the same way. The umbrella should be closed when not in use and stored indoors during the winter. Although some manufacturers recommend it, I don't like using vinyl furniture covers during the winter because we have so few harsh days in Texas and often it's warm enough to enjoy the outdoors for a few hours on a winter day. Who wants to pull off covers to enjoy a little sun in February? So, ladies and gentlemen, please be seated.

The Artful Garden

Exteriors are as thoughtfully accessorized as home interiors these days. Envision a rear garden or entry court as an outdoor room. A large piece of sculpture might be used as its focal point, just as a fireplace compels attention in the living room. A water feature could be used as the center point of a courtyard or to draw the eye out into a corner of the landscape. A handsome tile mural could fulfill the same purpose as a landscape painting hanging in the dining room. A series of billowy hanging baskets hung between porch columns or handsome urns holding topiary trees might "finish" the outdoor space in the same way that lamps and objects of art complete a guestroom.

SCULPTURE AND DECORATIVE OBJECTS

To make a strong impact, garden accessories generally must be more massive than interior furnishings. It's important to understand that exterior spaces are larger in scale than interiors. Even if an enclosed courtyard is the same size as an adjacent living room, the sky makes an outdoor space seem larger. A small piece of art can easily become lost.

Also keep in mind the viewpoint from which a piece of garden art will be seen. Consider not only its size, but also its shape. Remember that works of garden art don't exist in isolation, but rather they compete with other elements in the landscape and with one another.

I've giggled over front yards packed with concrete gnomes and whirligigs, but if these pieces bring pleasure to the owners, well, who am I to judge? I have a friend (a fellow landscape architect) who owns a flock of plastic flamingos purchased when Woolworth's went out of business.

About two hundred birds alight in his front yard for party occasions. They are a hoot! However, I generally suggest restraint and caution clients against cluttering the landscape with too many decorative objects in view from one spot.

Moneysaving Tip: One nice piece of garden art may be all you need in the way of ornamentation.

The placement of garden art is an art in itself. It affords the collector an opportunity to be creative with the artist. The idea is to make the piece appear effortless and permanent. It should be used to delight rather than confront the viewer. Remember, too, that garden art will be seen in varying light conditions and changing seasons. Try the piece in several spots within the garden. Dare to be experimental.

Garden art is often used to create balance within the garden, although the balance may be asymmetrical. For example, a large contemporary sculpture might be placed at the edge of a wooded area or on a rise within the lawn as a counterweight to the house and its more intensively landscaped environment. Formal gardens, on the other hand, call for symmetrical or rational placement of sculptural elements. A classical piece might be used as a central feature in the garden or placed in a niche at the end of a walkway. A pair of antique urns could set off a doorway or flank the head of a staircase.

If you're considering commissioning a piece of art for your garden, you might want to contact the art department of a local college. A well-made sculpture will last a lifetime, so it's a great investment. It's no coincidence that stone and bronze have been the preferred materials of sculptors through the ages. Today, artists are also making wonderful works of garden art from aluminum, resins and concrete. Unfortunately, security is a factor in the placement of art in the landscape. If its weight is not sufficient to deter a would-be thief, consider bolting, welding or mortaring the piece onto a base. A base may also serve to raise the piece, making it more "important" in the landscape. Of course, you must also secure the piece if it might fall over and hurt someone.

Moneysaving Tip: Look for craftsmanship and durability in outdoor accessories; avoid metals that rust and materials that deteriorate.

Garden art doesn't have to be expensive to be wonderful. An inset of hand-painted tile, grouping of stone plaques or a big clock might brighten a bare wall. Whimsical pieces, like an amusing garden sign or a stone bunny peering out of a planting bed, add elements of surprise. A birdhouse or a wind chime can be used to attract the eye upward into a beautiful tree, while a sundial or birdbath could be used to focus attention on the center of a formal garden. I love to explore garden emporiums, art galleries and antiques shops when I travel, and I always visit the gift shops when I go to botanical gardens. Often they will carry the work of local artisans who make birdhouses, banners, wind chimes, topiary and fountains that might add just the right touch to a corner of my garden.

Living Sculpture

Some plants are just meant to grab your attention! Bonsai (the ultimate in restraint) and topiaries (on the opposite end of the scale) are hot gardening items these days. And, cacti and succulents can turn an ordinary clay pot into a piece of sculpture. I've lumped all of these kinds of plants together as "living sculpture," and found a few good sources to share at the end of this chapter. Several nurseries in Texas specialize in the ancient art of bonsai, but none of them ship plants, as far as I know. There is one good Internet source for bonsai tools and equipment.

GREAT POTS

A few strategically placed pots might be used as sculptural elements in the garden. I've used pots to separate a seating area from the dining area or to divide an overly large planting area. In working out an arrangement of plants in pots, remember that the plants will show to best advantage if they are placed against a wall. When the grouping is placed against foliage, the pots will predominate. Bigger is better when it comes to garden containers. Small pots require more frequent watering, and too many can make a garden look cluttered.

The pots you select should blend well with the style of your garden. You'll find handsome ceramic pots in every imaginable shape and size, plus a wide array of wood, stone, concrete and glazed containers available throughout the state. There are also great-looking lightweight plastic, fiberglass and metal containers that can be easily moved and will hold soil moisture better than ceramic pots. Lightweight pots are especially good for balconies, decks and steps where you'll want to keep weight to a minimum. Old-fashioned unglazed ceramic pots will never go out of style, but they do require more water, so I prefer to use them out in the landscape where they can be watered with the sprinkler system.

Be sure that any clay container in which you plant directly and use year-round is high-fired. Thin-walled glazed ceramic pots and low-fired pots from Mexico are subject to cracking with winter freezes, so I use them as cover for plain black plastic pots. This works well for quick and easy seasonal color changes, and it allows me to store my decorative clay containers in the garage over the winter.

Moneysaving Tip: If you cannot afford "important" garden art, try a handsome topiary in a great container or a group of containers holding sculptural plants to function as works of art.

Water Features

Water is the elemental source of life and beauty. Quiet or dancing, no other substance adds as much pleasure to a garden. The very words we use to describe its sights and sounds — bubbling, gurgling, rushing, trickling, shooting and spilling — suggest water's magical ability to play on our emotions. Flowing lazily along a natural stream, water is relaxing; tumbling down rocks, it has the power to excite. Be it fountain, fishpond, reflecting pool, bog or stream, a water feature seems to cool the hottest summer day. Whatever shape the water takes, gardening possibilities in and around the pool include a range of delicate and colorful plants that would be out of place in a dry landscape — luscious ferns, bog plants and water lilies. The Wildflower Center (www.wildflower.org) has a list of Texas Native Pond Plants.

A recirculating fountain can serve as kinetic sculpture, with water tumbling down a rock waterfall, bubbling up from a pool like an underground spring or pouring out of a piece of classical statuary. A delicate wall fountain, a ceramic bowl filled with water lilies or a Japanese lantern beside a little pond could be used to establish the motif of a small garden. A water feature may serve utilitarian purposes, as well. Splashing water can be used to neutralize traffic noise. A naturally occurring depression, which is usually a liability in the landscape, can be widened into a charming little bog garden. A rock-lined streambed that channels water away from the house may suggest a pleasing creek, even when dry. Swimming pools and spas can be designed to appear as natural ponds or formal fountains, thus serving decorative as well as practical functions.

The latest thing in water features is the disappearing fountain, in which the water flows up through and then over a glazed ceramic pot or drilled stone onto a pebble surface and "disappears" into the ground. Beneath the pebbles is a heavy-duty plastic grate over a hidden reservoir large enough to hold a pump and sufficient water to keep the fountain flowing. The system has become popular because it requires less maintenance and is safer than an open pond for someone with small children. Such fountains are also easy to install and relatively inexpensive, which may mean that they may soon become "ordinary," but I've seen them used very effectively.

Fishponds, which were much in vogue early in this century, fell out of favor in the '50s, primarily for maintenance reasons. They're popular once again, partly because improved materials have made them less expensive to build and easier to maintain. Traditional geometric garden pools are usually constructed of reinforced concrete and capped with brick or cut stone. Often they will incorporate a fountain. Naturalistic free-form ponds can be made with inexpensive PVC pond liners or pre-formed fiberglass. These new fish-safe liners will last for decades. Designed correctly, the pond should sustain itself: the plants will keep the water clean, and the fish will eat the mosquitoes.

To get maximum emotional effect, a water feature should be placed where it will reflect sky, trees and flowers. Add colorful koi and special-effects lighting, and you have a real treasure. Let your imagination run free. You may even want a bridge to cross or an island to conquer. Now, a few words of caution! Do not dam or alter a natural stream that runs through your property without a permit; observe carefully how nature builds her waterways (natural-looking streams and ponds are difficult to achieve); and remember that children can drown in a few inches of water. Check regulations in your municipality before beginning construction, and secure your pool or pond as soon as it is begun.

FIRE

For the enjoyment of a backyard fire, as well as the functionality of providing outdoor heating to extend the season, nothing is more satisfying than an outdoor fireplace. Just as you would create a seating area around your family room fireplace, an outdoor fire suggests camaraderie on a covered or open patio on a chilly evening. Full-size fireplaces are expensive to build, but fire pits and chimineas are inexpensive alternatives.

Chimineas originated in Mexico as ovens for baking bread, but today they are mainly used for making outdoor fires and rarely for cooking. Because the Mexican chimineas caught on, small portable fire pits have also become popular sources of outdoor heating. Within the past few years, several of my clients have asked for permanent fire pits to be built into their outdoor entertaining areas. Fire pits and chimineas add to the ambience of a patio in ways that electric patio heaters (popular choices in the 1980s and '90s) never did.

Online Resources for Garden Furnishings in Texas

Furniture and Accessories

In the listings that follow, you'll discover interesting online resources for all kinds of outdoor spaces, from rustic country porches to sophisticated city landscapes. Also look within your own area under Garden Furnishings; some of the companies listed will ship their wares. As you travel, keep in mind sources outside your region. Shopping for unusual garden furniture and art is an especially worthy pursuit when it is too hot to work in the garden!

Accents of Salado
3366 FM 2484
Salado, Texas 76571
877.947.5938
www.accentsofsalado.com

"The beauty of things imperfect, fresh and simple" is the tag line on this company's website. It specializes in Mediterranean-style accessories, and if you click on Old World Tuscan Gardens, you'll discover all kinds of containers and planters, window baskets, plant stands and candle sconces. There are pictures of gardens that will make you drool! Other "pages" of the online catalog offer gorgeous dinnerware and accessories for elegant outdoor entertaining.

Adkins Architectural Antiques & Treasures
3515 Fannin Street
Houston, Texas 77004
713.522.6547 or 800.522.6547
www.adkinsantiques.com

Adkins Architectural Antiques & Treasures has been chosen as one of the top architectural salvage dealers in the country by *This Old House* magazine. Its eclectic mix of architectural salvage and period design elements for the home and garden has been wildly popular for almost 30 years. Adkins Architectural Antiques maintains an extensive selection of garden décor, including street lighting in 40 different styles, garden gates, patio furniture, urns, benches and fountains. Call the store to order the treasures you find online.

AntlerWorx, Inc.
1909 East U.S. Hwy 80
White Oak, Texas 75693
903.746.2395 or 866.902.9679
www.antlerworx.com

"We build quality antler furniture out of the finest naturally shed antlers available. Each work of art is its own distinction, since no two antlers are alike," said Shaun Baker, who assured us that his one-of-a-kind table bases and the log furniture he carries are suitable for outdoor use on covered patios and porches. The company also offers replicas of vintage lanterns and advertising signs.

Christopher Smith Galleries
578 Wood Duck Lane
Caldwell, Texas 77836
979.567.9620
www.smithbronze.com
Hours: By appointment

Sculptor Christopher Smith has received national acclaim for his work in bronze for more than a decade. His elegant fountains and wildlife sculptures (all cast in the Old World lost wax method) are sold in exclusive limited editions to collectors throughout the country. As a place to live and work, this Montana-raised artist and his wife chose the Central Texas countryside for its inspirational diversity of wildlife.

Cunningham Living
18700 Carrot Street
Spring, Texas 77379
800.833.5998
www.cunninghamliving.com

The three-year-old online catalog of Cunningham Gas encompasses so much more than the gas grills, lights and logs and the kitchen equipment the company has been selling for 50 years. Cunningham Living offers practical and decorative items for outdoor living from an entire ready-built kitchen to old-fashioned wall-hung bottle openers. (Remember them?) There are bars, attractive gas fire pits, barbeque grills, unobtrusive wall-mounted electric heaters, outdoor ice chests, handsome patio torches, etc. The newest feature of the website is a link to "Kitchen-ator," which allows customers to design their own outdoor kitchens.

El Dorado Trading Post
13710 RR 12
Wimberley, Texas 78676
512.393.9353
www.willowfurniture.net

People who couldn't afford any other type of furniture used willow, and it was traditionally crafted by people who traveled about the country. When they came to areas where willow grew in abundance, they made chairs and tables to sell to local residents. Today the furniture is romantic, and while it is not made for cushy comfort, it looks charming in a garden setting and makes a pleasant place to perch awhile. This company's source of furniture is willow grown and harvested from the banks of creeks, lakes and swamps of East Texas. (Also natural to this area are alligators, snakes, mosquitoes and wasps!) Willow is classified as a weed in Texas and can be freely harvested if a person doesn't mind broiling sun and unfriendly creatures. It's all lovingly handmade. See the website for photographs and ordering information.

The Garden Gate
5122 Morningside Drive
Houston, Texas 77005
713.528.2654
www.gardengateco.com

Fine English reproduction limestone castings of pedestals, statuary and fountains and English lead garden ornaments, urns and handmade, galvanized ironwork. These are a few of our favorite things, and whatever you fancy on her website, owner Donna Lokey will be happy to ship to you. She carries English reproduction sundials, birdbaths, plaques, pedestals, pools, finials, balls, plinths, columns and obelisks, plus planters, fountains and tables from Provence. You'll also find an ever-changing inventory of garden antiques.

Jackson's Home and Garden
6950 Lemmon Avenue
Dallas, Texas 75209
214.350.9200
www.thepatiostoreandmore.com

For many years Jackson's has carried the largest selection of containers in the Southwest. Its wholesale division supplies many of the garden centers in the state. So, it is wonderful for people in other parts of the state to have this company's wares available at the click of a mouse! In addition to a wonderful array of pottery, you'll find great-looking garden decor (statuary, fountains, furniture and more), plus a very complete Grill Store online.

Lars Stanley — Architects & Artisans
1901 E.M. Franklin Avenue
Austin, Texas 78723
512.445.0444
www.larsstanley.com

Mr. Stanley's firm designs and fabricates custom garden elements, which are handcrafted from forged steel, copper, brass and other metals. His work includes elegant entry gates, gazebos, lighting, furniture and sculpture. It has been featured in leading magazines, and each piece is unique. Staff architects help homeowners and designers elaborate their own ideas into well-detailed reality.

Lone Star Forge
6691 Hawkeye Road
Krum, Texas 76249
940.482.6982
www.lonestarforge.com

The artist/owner Paul Matthaus got his initial training when he lived with a master blacksmith in Germany from ages fifteen to eighteen. He came to America when he was 31, and moved to Texas in 1977. Paul is an artist who pays loving attention to the details. His artworks and tables shown on the website can be

(LISTING CONTINUED ON THE NEXT PAGE)

(CONTINUED)

customized to the buyer's specifications or new works commissioned. He and his wife, Becky, make an effective team with whom you feel comfortable doing business.

Mind Over Metal
4050 North Hwy 183
Liberty Hill, Texas 78642
800.320.1076
www.mindovermetal.com

As Richard Schultz told us, "Mind Over Metal has been in business since 1976, making heirloom-quality metal furnishings and architectural appointments. The pieces are produced by a small, tight-knit group of Texas artisans who pride themselves on dedication to their craft and attention to detail." They've produced handsome chairs, rockers and tables, plus garden gates, fountains, figurative and abstract sculpture, gazebo spires, railings and trellises. They work in bronze, copper, wrought iron and stainless steel, and they supply fossilized limestone tops for tables. Call Richard for an appointment if you are interested in the work. They can custom-make almost anything to meet your special needs. The website shows a multitude of creative items and 12 different metal finishes. The Squash Blossom fountain and the intricate railings for stairways and balconies especially impressed us.

Music of the Spheres
4909B East Cesar Chavez
Austin, Texas 78702
888.324.4637 or 512 385 0340
www.musicofspheres.com

In business since 1989, Music of the Spheres®, Inc. has become one of the country's leading manufacturers of tuned wind chimes. In fact, its slogan is "the Stradivarius of windchimes®." Designed by the late Larry Roark, who held a degree in music theory from the University of North Texas, the chimes are tuned to standard orchestral pitch and come in seven voices/sizes ranging from soprano to basso profundo. They also come in a variety of musical scales. You can actually listen to the choices on-line and choose the one most pleasing to you! Once you have settled on your favorite musical scale, you can start collecting all the voices so that you can create an ensemble in your own garden. Created from tempered aluminum alloy, the matte black electrostatic powder-coat finish protects the tubes from environmental issues like salt air and even acid rain. Activity level is controlled by the detachable "wind catcher" and by sliding the clapper up the central cord to turn off the music. The company also designs one-of-a-kind acoustic sculptures.

Statement Furniture, Inc.
1131 Slocum Street
Dallas, Texas 75207
214.760.2450
www.statementfurniture.com

Christopher Wynn began making furniture in 1995. Now he and his wife Adrianne are shipping his beautiful work all over the country. You can commission unusual outdoor dining tables, coffee tables, console tables and much more. The tops are made of exotic marble, onyx, granite and limestone, and the bases may be wrought iron, stainless steel or bronze castings. Whether your look is Old World or contemporary; this custom-factory will help you with the design. Visit the website to see his work and call for photographs of work similar to what you are visualizing. They will send stone samples and help you in every way to achieve a "statement" piece.

Texas Backroads Furniture
7006 Clear Valley Drive
San Antonio, Texas 78242
210.670.0891
www.texas-backroads.com

"We offer a wide range of custom, rustic/ Western-style furniture built from reclaimed woods, from chairs and garden benches to tables of all sizes and styles," says Bill Groppel. "Photos on the website are just examples of our custom work and illustrate the types of furniture and accessories that we can construct. We have been building custom furniture from old barn wood and other reclaimed woods since 1996. The lumber comes from a variety of sources, some with quite an interesting story. From antique, longleaf yellow pine found on the old firing range at Fort Sam Houston in San Antonio to cypress from the banks of the Cypress Creek in Comfort, each piece is virtually one of a kind. Our Alamo Adirondack Chair is similar in design to the original Adirondack chair, but not quite. Actually, it is a whole lot more comfortable, with a Texas flair."

Texas Hill Country Furniture
19280 Hwy. 281 South
Lipan, Texas 76462
254.646.3376
www.txhcountry.com

Larry Dennis constructs gliders, rockers, swings and barstools out of native cedar, oak, mesquite and pecan. While not all of his attractive, rustic furniture is recommended for use out in the garden, most of it is perfect for country porches and covered patios. His signature piece is a beautiful wooden rocking chair with a five-point star meticulously carved into the headrest. Much of his work is custom. You may find a piece you like on the website, and he will make it in unfinished cedar for garden applications, if that is where you want to use it. His wife Sherry does all of the design work for their retail store, which is between Mineral Wells and Stephenville.

Tradiciones
6990 Gateway East
El Paso, Texas 79915
866.373.9292
www.southwesternfurniturerustic.com

(LISTING CONTINUED ON THE NEXT PAGE)

CH 8

(CONTINUED)

"We began manufacturing 35 years ago with the notion of spreading traditional southwestern furniture and unique Mexican decor across the nation," says Jesus Reza. While most of the company's furniture is for interior use, the wrought iron chairs, benches, barstools and tables are unusual in design and very suitable for covered patios and porches. The company also offers gorgeous wool Zapotec rugs. "Our years of experience and attention to detail should be reassuring when you order from Tradiciones. All of our Southwestern furniture can be modified to your dimensional needs, and/or finish and design."

Living Sculpture

Dallas Bonsai Garden
4460 West Walnut Street, Suite 218
Garland, Texas 75042
800.982.1223 or 972.487.0130
www.dallasbonsai.com

Dallas Bonsai Garden promises you the most complete line of Japanese bonsai supplies on the planet. Included in the online catalog is everything from aluminum wire to Zeolite soil additive. "Each year we travel to the Orient to purchase directly from the very best manufacturers of supplies in Japan and to China for figurines and pots. We have been in business since 1965, and offer you the widest selection at the very best prices because you are basically buying direct from the manufacturer, with us as their warehouse. We offer potting soils, decorative sands, a large selection of books in English, instructional videos, and seeds from Japan."

River Oaks Plant House
3401 Westheimer
Houston, Texas 77027
713.622.5350

As one of the leading topiary makers in the nation, River Oaks Plant House revived the ancient art of shaping plants into decorative sculptures. Says owner Daniel Saparzadeh, "Our firm is the largest manufacturer of topiaries in the world." Its artists have handcrafted a menagerie of deer, birds, elephants and many more animals, as well as other whimsical custom designs. To ensure quality control, each topiary is locally made in the company's studio greenhouse. The galvanized metal frames are designed, welded together and stuffed with sphagnum moss while being wrapped with monofilament, which brings out the detail. The frames are guaranteed to maintain their shape for at least 10 years under normal conditions. A sprinkler system, usually for larger pieces, is an optional feature and can be installed prior to filling the frame. The final step in creating a topiary is planting either fig ivy or Asian jasmine in the moss. The pieces are shipped to customers throughout the state. According to Architectural Digest, "River Oaks Plants represents the state of the art in topiary design." The company does not have a website, but you can call to request a free catalog.

Water Garden Supplies

Aqua-Tec Aquatic Farms
5916 Johnson County Road 402
Grandview, Texas 76050
817.996.1741
www.aqua-tec.net

"We are water garden specialists at Aqua-Tec," owner Wiley Horton told us. A certified Texas-grown aquatic plant source, Aqua-Tec offers not only a large collection of lilies and bog plants, but also carries ponds, fish, supplies, equipment and books. The company offers direct shipping for pond supplies, fish and plants, plus custom aquatic- plant growing for residential and commercial settings. You can call regarding availability of plants at any given time.

Dickson Brothers, Inc.
204 North Galloway
Mesquite, Texas 75149
972.288.7537
www.dicksonbrothers.com

As they proudly proclaim at Dickson Brothers, "For 35 years, we have been your water gardening headquarters!" This company's 20,000-square-foot showroom and ½-acre outdoor site sells absolutely everything you need to build and enhance your water garden. There are underwater lighting systems, floating fountains, self-contained fountains, decorative bridges and every imaginable product for maintaining a water garden. The company does not ship fish. Plants are available, but only in quantity, so if you need only a water lily or two, you should find a local source. There is a lot offered on the company's new website, and products are shipped by UPS or common carrier.

Garden Accents, Inc.
14907 Treichel Road
Tomball, Texas 77375
800. 256.0393 or 281.351.4804
www.gardenaccentsinc.com

Bob Folger creates a beautiful rock waterfall, then makes a mold of it and casts the piece in concrete. He also collects all sorts of concrete fountains and ornaments from his travels. "We are the largest manufacturer of realistic concrete waterfalls. We also manufacture fountains and fiberglass ponds of various shapes and sizes. We have statuary and benches, landscape boulders and panels, filters and pumps, anything you would need to create the perfect paradise in your yard." Call or e-mail to order anything you see on the website.

Water Garden Gems, Inc.
3136 Bolton Road
Marion, Texas 78124
210.659.5841
www.watergardengems.com
Hours: Mon–Sat 9–5 (Nov-March), Mon–Sat 9–6 (April–Oct), Sun & holidays 11–4

Founded in 1990 by Burt Nichols, Water Garden Gems is now the largest full-service water garden center in Texas and surrounding states. It offers a complete range of water gardening supplies — plants, pumps, filters, pond liners, fountains, books, water quality products, fish (koi and goldfish), fish food, statuary, stepping stones, lighting (pond and outdoor), consultation and design. The online catalog is very thorough, and any product they carry can be shipped to customers (at the right time, if it is a plant or a fish), but the owners are emphatic that this is not some Internet business that knows little about water gardens. The retail store is on 3.3 acres with 10 fully landscaped ponds, a 3,000-square-foot indoor koi facility, and hundreds of water plants, including 80 water lily varieties and 60 bog plants. It has a large selection of fine statuary, filtration and pond supplies. When you need help, you can call them for guidance.

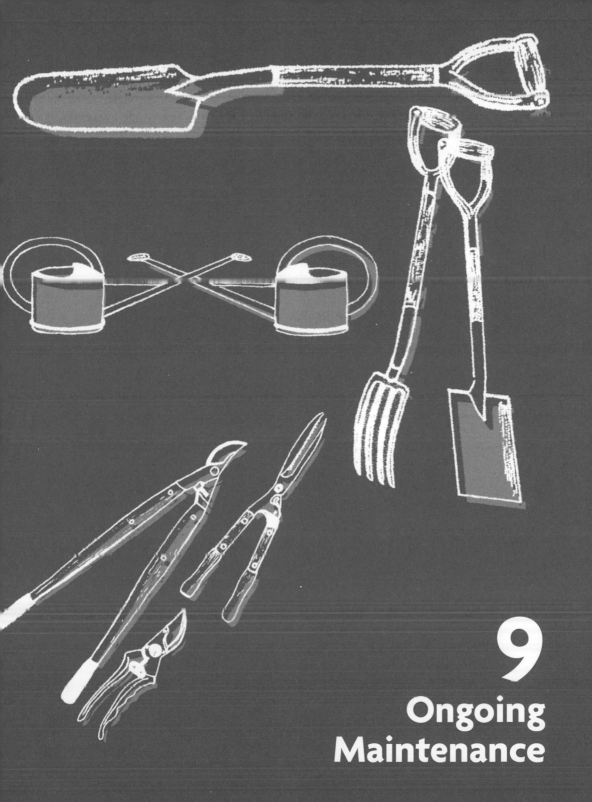

9
Ongoing
Maintenance

Ongoing Maintenance

More than any other art form, a garden is subject to change — through varying patterns of light each day, from season-to-season and from year-to-year. Unlike the architect's building, the artist's painting or the poet's words, a garden designer's best efforts exist in a state of evolution. Left untended, gardens die. Under the best of circumstances, garden designers don't live to see their work at full maturity. The sapling I plant today will not become the venerable oak I envision for another seventy years. From the moment it is installed, a garden will either be improving or deteriorating. This is where proper maintenance comes into the picture.

Good Bugs

Managing Pests & Diseases

Those of us who came of age shortly after World War II were promised Nirvana by chemical companies. Garden pests would be eliminated. Now, proponents of organic gardening, who were voices in the wilderness 30 years ago, have made us see the error of our ways. I've always opposed hiring a "service" that sprays on a regular, whether-it-needs-it-or-not basis, but I'm now advising my clients to only use organic products, and to use even these more judiciously. This is a complex subject, and it demands utmost common sense.

A few years ago I received a flyer from a "news service" directed toward garden writers. Under the heading, "A New Image for Pesticides," I found the following proposal: "The term 'pesticides' should be rethought. Indeed it seems, changing the name pesticide to 'a medicine for plants and turf' might go a long way for placing those products in a new light." My first reaction was to laugh, but the subject was far too serious to dismiss lightly. I do not have all the facts to argue the industry's assertion that pesticides "have given people safe and dependable food, clean and sanitary homes and hospitals." But, I cannot agree with the statement: "A *parts per trillion* measurement of pesticide residue is not a cause for alarm." Frankly, I am alarmed!

Pesticide residue in our soil and water supplies *is* a legitimate concern. Much higher concentrations than mere "parts per trillion" of numerous toxic compounds have been measured in streams throughout the country. The truth is that we don't know all of the long-term hazards to humans. What we do know is that because there are so many of us, what we use in our gardens quickly mounts up. I no longer see any need to resort to synthetic pesticides. What poisons "bad" insects also kills the good guys!

While I'm not a certified organic gardener, I've always freely admitted that I'm a lazy gardener. Having no time for hauling out the old sprayer and mixing chemicals when I was rearing my children, I figured that ignoring a problem would make it go away. This turned out to be a stroke of genius. What I inadvertently discovered is that birds, spiders, toads, wasps, flies, earthworms and beneficial insects would do my work for me. The latter compare to tigers as the world's most efficient predators, and nature strikes a balance in a garden that's friendly to these unsung heroes.

The only time I've ever lost a plant to critters was when snails devoured the hostas I never should have planted in Austin in the first place. I've come to believe that pesticides generally worsen our problems. Even naturally derived insecticides such as pyrethrum can be lethal to beneficial insects, so I recommend to my clients that they determine the number of pests they can tolerate and their plants can withstand. Any responsible gardener should accept the fact that a certain amount of damage is normal.

Bad Bugs

SENSIBLE SOLUTIONS FOR DEALING WITH PESTS

Good cultural practices are the first step toward keeping pests at acceptable levels. It has been wryly observed that the worst plant pest may be the species *Homo sapiens*! Without question, we humans leave our plants susceptible to disease and insect infestation when we fail to maintain healthy soil, prune improperly or inappropriately water the garden.

Malcolm Beck, who began farming without toxic chemicals when I was still in high school, has this to say: "Organic growers have the philosophy that plants growing in their preferred environment and soil balanced to suit their needs will be healthy, and healthy plants do not attract destructive insects." He notes that destructive insects act as censors to cut out the unfit and unhealthy plants. His philosophy has now influenced three generations of gardeners. His advice is to identify what's "bugging" your garden — it may be a bug, but then again it may be a plant disease, or it may be stress due to climate or poor maintenance. The book he wrote with Howard Garrett, *Texas Bug Book*, helps gardeners identify problems and offers simple, natural solutions.

Really Bad Bugs

Why haul out big guns to attack little problems, or worse yet, "scattershoot?" The first line of defense should be mechanical control. These solutions include removing the offenders by hand, pruning out infested leaves or branches (taking care not to butcher the plant) and setting out sticky paper or physical barriers such as netting and row covers. Another promising avenue is biological control, which includes the release of predatory and parasitic insects such as lady beetles, trichogramma wasps and praying mantises. There are two problems associated with purchasing predator insects to patrol your property. First, they may benefit your neighbor's garden more than your own. Second, natural enemies can only be expected to reduce the number of pests. If they eliminated all of their natural meals, the predators themselves would starve to death! Researchers are also discovering biological agents that keep unwanted insects under control by causing disruption to their mating processes.

Other pest control methods include smothering insects and pathogens with horticultural oils when the plants are dormant or the insects are most vulnerable. Another popular method is the use of insecticidal soaps, which are effective for thinning populations of aphids, mealy bugs, mites, whiteflies and other soft-bodied insects. For these soaps to work, you must make contact with the pest, so it's important to spray the plant thoroughly, including the undersides of the leaves. Some gardeners drown snails in little bowls of beer (they die happy) or spread diatomaceous earth, which is made of the fossilized remains of hard-shelled algae. The product works as a razor-sharp abrasive to destroy soft-bodied crawling creatures.

Organic gardeners use a variety of non-toxic homemade remedies for controlling pests and diseases. They control fungal diseases with four tablespoons of baking soda and a teaspoon of vegetable oil mixed in a gallon of water. To control sucking insects, they make an effective soap with a tablespoon of vegetable oil and a tablespoon of non-phosphate dishwashing detergent in a gallon of water. (Be sure to test it on a leaf or two before widespread spraying; some detergents damage plant foliage.) Chewing bugs are discouraged with a garlic-hot pepper mix. Liquefy two bulbs of garlic and two hot peppers in two cups of water in your blender. Strain out the solids and add enough water to make a gallon of concentrate. Add ¼ cup of this mixture to a gallon of water in a sprayer. I like inexpensive remedies.

EVEN A NON-TOXIC SOLUTION FOR FIRE ANTS

One type of critter I'm not willing to tolerate is fire ants. Since the 1930s, red imported fire ants have infested 260 million acres in nine southern states, including Texas, where they now have a $1.2 billion negative impact. They invade gardens, compost piles, electrical equipment and even homes. The large nests they make in turf make mowing difficult, and their sting is miserable.

Thankfully, Texas A&M University has developed an organic method to eliminate this common pest. Affectionately called the "Texas Two-Step," the method recommends spinosad as the active ingredient for the first step, and a citrus oil extract for step two. Spinosad (pronounced spin OH sid) is a relatively new organic insecticide that quickly and safely controls a variety of caterpillar, beetle and thrips pests, as well. It's derived from the fermentation juices of a lowly soil bacterium called *Saccharopolyspora spinosa*.

A number of companies are producing a wide range of non-toxic pest and disease controls. U.S. Department of Agriculture and The Texas Department of Agriculture have Organic Standards and Certification programs. To be certain you are buying an approved product, look for a USDA or a TDA label on the packaging.
Moneysaving Tip: Buy the smallest possible quantity of any new product until you see whether it works.

And, be sure you are using the right product for the particular pest or disease. Take time to read the label before you buy any product; even "natural" products should be handled with caution. Mix up only what you need.
Safety Tip: After applying the product, clean out your spray equipment. Fill the sprayer half-full with water, shake and pour the rinse water onto the area where you originally applied the product.

Watering Wisely

There's an old story about a cotton farmer in West Texas whose irrigated fields stretched as far as the eye could see. Right in the middle of the green landscape, visible from the front porch of his comfortable house, was a barren patch of bone-dry soil. Surprised visitors always asked why. "Well, once it was all like that," he replied," and I didn't want to forget."

After getting "spoiled" by abundant rain in 2007, the summer of 2008 reminded all of us, *again*, that sustained periods of low rainfall are a way of life in Texas. Folks who were around during the Great Drought of the 1950s saw how devastating a major drought can be. Even in a "normal" year, the gully-washing, frog-choking rains of spring are inevitably followed by long weeks of drought and intense heat.

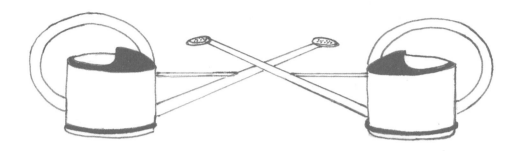

There are only two sources of water in Texas — lakes and underground aquifers. Both are fed by rain. For years most Texans designed their landscapes to look like England and simply turned up the volume on the sprinkler systems in summer. No problem. Twenty-five years ago water was cheap. I was living in Austin in the early 1980s when the sewer department (unwilling to build additional treatment facilities) began tying its rates to home water consumption. Never mind that water used on the lawn does not go down the drain: the higher our water use, the higher our sewer bill. By the time it began costing $250 a month in sewer service to water my average-suburban-lot grass, I got the point. Austin launched a highly successful program to promote low-water-use landscape methods, and my clients and I learned to cope.

New dams and treatment plants do not come cheap. Today a $250 water bill in Wimberley is considered normal, and we're making every effort to conserve! As the population grows, demand for water is increasing dramatically. If we don't learn to conserve, we'll pay dearly. Just as we're turning from gas-guzzling cars, expect to abandon water-guzzling landscapes throughout Texas in the coming years, drought or no drought.

STRATEGIES FOR REDUCING DEMAND

Lawns require about four times as much water as planting beds. The single most effective way to reduce water use is to reduce the size of our lawns. Until the early nineteenth century, only the very wealthy could afford great swaths of lawn grass, because mowing had to be performed with a scythe, and watering was done by hand. In the twenty-first century, lawns may once again become too expensive to maintain. Already, wise gardeners are questioning the sensibility of pouring not only water, but also fertilizers, herbicides and pesticides into great expanses of lawn.

Grass can be replaced with decking, paved terraces, water features, ground covers and wildflowers. Now, I'm not suggesting that you should plow under all of your grass. You may need a section of turf for children to play or for a grown-up game of croquet. You may simply love the texture of a soft green lawn. In the areas where you need mown grass, consider substituting one of the newer, more drought-tolerant varieties. Contact your county agent or a nearby botanical garden for recommendations on the grass best suited for your area, soil-type and sun conditions. Keep turf areas well-aerated to absorb maximum rainwater and free of weeds that compete for the available moisture.

The second strategy for creating a more drought-enduring garden is to select drought-tolerant shrubs and flowers for your planting beds. Texans have led the nation in converting to water-wise landscapes. Landscape architects and designers have adopted a more naturalistic standard of beauty. County extension services and water districts are busily researching plants that thrive with little supplementary irrigation. Homeowners are buying into the concept and actively seeking nurseries that specialize in native and drought-tolerant plants.

The choices in drought-tolerant plants are wider than anyone imagined when the word "Xeriscape" was coined a few years ago. My clients didn't want any part of those "zeroscapes," and even I resisted a conversion to dryland gardening, fearing that my design repertoire would be limited to yucca. What I discovered was that a number of lush-looking plants make "the list."

Most drought-tolerant plants are native to dry climates. Some evolved in the southwestern United States, and others come to us from wherever in the world climatic conditions have favored adaptation to periods of drought. Researchers are looking closely at plants from South Africa, Australia, the Mediterranean region and portions of South America.

Nature has devised numerous ways for plants to cope with long periods of drought, including a felt-like coat of hair or a varnish-like substance on the leaf surface. Silvery leaves reflect rather than absorb sunlight, and small leaves lessen the area of evaporation (pine needles are the ultimate example). You'll find handsome succulents that store moisture in thick stems and leaves and a number of plants that have deep taproots. Another ploy for survival is to simply go dormant in hot, dry weather.

A visit to regional botanical gardens and nature trails mentioned in Chapter Two will introduce you to a wealth of plants that thrive in dry climates. The particular plants displayed will vary dramatically from region to region. One can't simply drop desert plants into East Texas, where up to 50 inches of rain each year would rot the roots.

A third strategy is to group together plants with similar watering needs, even if that requires some transplanting. For example, mountain laurels are far less thirsty than hydrangeas or roses. If all three shrubs are planted in the same bed, you end up overwatering the drought-tolerant plant to keep the others happy. I would suggest moving thirsty plants to an area that's convenient to water, well-protected from afternoon sun and shielded from drying summer winds.

A fourth design strategy is to add more trees to your landscape. A plant growing in partial shade requires less water than a plant grown in full sun. As the tree canopies spread, fewer sections of your garden will need frequent irrigation. If you're starting a new garden in a sunny, open environment, select your plants from a list of native and other hardy, drought-tolerant species.

Good maintenance is another key component in conserving water. Chapter Five is all about the importance of good soil. It bears repeating here that well-aerated soil absorbs more water than hard, compacted earth. Organic matter mixed into the soil helps retain the moisture. Spreading an organic mulch on top conserves water by further reducing evaporation and helping to inhibit weeds. When weeds do pop up, remove them before they consume precious water. There are hundreds of little ways to conserve. Use bath water for watering container plants and houseplants. Wash the dog on the lawn. Don't overwater anything.

RAINWATER COLLECTION

More and more homeowners are collecting the rainwater that falls on roofs and washes into storm sewers. It's the ultimate in efficient watering. It's good for the environment, good for the pocketbook and — best of all — very, very good for plants! Rainwater is sodium-free, chlorine-free and pH neutral. Rainwater harvesting is just another of those old-fashioned methods modern gardeners are rediscovering in the 21ˢᵗ century. Storing water in cisterns dates back about 4,000 years. My own grand-mother had one, but by the time I was born, she was on a city water system and the cistern had been covered over. As a child, I was warned not to get near it because it might collapse and I would surely fall in it and drown! The word "cistern" still strikes terror in my heart.

Now that it's called a "water storage tank," I desperately want one for my home in Wimberley. A 2,000-square-foot roof will produce more than 1,000 gallons of water from one good rain. I know two couples here who have large tanks that supply all their water needs. Every time I pay a water bill, I'm green with envy. However, their homes are on acreage, and our home is in a subdivision that will not allow big and admittedly unattractive tanks. Digging into solid limestone to put the tank underground is not economically feasible, so rain barrels at each downspout seem to be my only choice. (These I could hide with plantings.)

For anyone building a new house in Texas, rainwater collection is the way of the future. The tank can be put underground or designed into the exterior of the structure in a way that it appears to be just another wall. It can even be attached to an automatic drip system, using a timer or a series of moisture sensors that auto-matically cut off the water via solenoid valves. The emitters on the drip system should be configured for maximum water conservation.

One way to estimate the tank size is to look at your winter and summer water bill difference in gallons. Typically you will double consumption because of outdoor needs. This amount difference should be multiplied by the number of growing season months to give you your outdoor water baseline. The cost of a tank becomes less expensive as the size goes up. A 10,000-gallon tank will run about $8,000, while a 20,000-gallon tank is about $13,000.

Safety Tip: Check with your local health department before installing a collection system that will be used for drinking water.

There are several other ways to make efficient use of your downspouts. A simple way is to connect the downspouts to rain barrels and use low-pressure drip lines to evenly distribute the water. Do-it-yourself types can find 55-gallon drums and all the necessary plumbing parts at hardware stores. Because open water sources pose a danger to children and breed mosquitoes, it's imperative to cover the rain barrels.

Another way to use the roof's runoff is to connect perforated pipe to the bottom of the downspouts to water the plants under the eaves of your house. A fan-shaped section of concrete or brick could also be used beneath each of the downspouts to divert water evenly throughout a planting area.

WATERING MORE EFFICIENTLY

When to Water

The question most beginning gardeners ask is, "How often should I water?" The answer is, "Only when the plant needs it." Water requirements vary with the age of the plantings, soil conditions and the weather. The first few weeks after installation, plants need lots of moisture. It's common practice to build a soil ring just outside the root ball of each new tree and large shrub. The ring acts as a reservoir, allowing you to provide extra water for the new plants without overwatering an entire planting bed. The soil ring should be removed after about three months or at the end of summer.

Once your garden is well-established, you will be able to determine precisely how much water it needs. One inch of water (including rainwater) per week was the old rule of thumb, but that may be too much. Different areas of the garden will have different needs, depending upon sun or shade and slope of the land.

Water only when the top four inches of the soil are dry (a bamboo chopstick makes a dandy soil probe). Chrysanthemums are good "indicator plants" — when they wilt, you know the planting bed needs water. The mums bounce right back. You can test the amount of water your sprinklers are putting out by placing cans in several areas (tuna cans, which are about an inch deep, work well). Run the water for thirty minutes and measure how much water accumulates in each can. Keep records. Pretty soon you'll know how often and how long you must water to keep your plants perky.

The best time to water is very early in the morning. From midmorning on, too much water is lost to evaporation. Watering at night encourages fungi and other pathogens. One long watering is generally better than several short ones. The idea is to encourage deep roots. But, long soakings may exceed the soil's infiltration rate, so keep a watchful eye and shut off the tap if you begin to see any standing water or runoff.

Moneysaving Tip: Learn to water without wasting a drop.

How to Water

Watering with hoses and portable lawn sprinklers is less efficient than a well-designed underground system because the spread is generally uneven and the spray is thrown high in the air where it evaporates quickly in hot weather. Also, there's a chance of forgetting to turn the water off when you leave to run an errand. (It has happened to me. About the third time I returned to find water running down the street, I solved the problem with a $15 timer.) There are several different kinds of portable sprinklers — impulse, rotary, oscillating and traveling. Look for one that delivers large water drops close to the ground rather than shooting fine streams of water high into the air where the moisture will quickly evaporate.

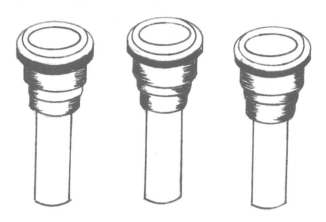

High Tech Irrigation for the 21st Century

Drip Irrigation

Drip irrigation has never been very satisfactory for watering grass in most soils, but I've had great results with my trees, shrubs, flower beds and container plants on a drip system operated with an irrigation system timer. Drip systems deliver water to the plant's root system with minimal evaporation. This can also help promote plant health by keeping the foliage dry, preventing erosion and lessening the leaching of nutrients.

I was advised against installing a drip system for my garden in Wimberley because the water here is so hard that emitters will clog within a year. But, if you live in an area where drip irrigation is feasible, the investment cost can be quite low compared to the savings you'll reap. A drip system I installed at a previous residence cut my water bills in half!

Some drip systems use simple tubing with small, regularly spaced holes. Others contain drip emitters (small plastic devices) installed in solid-wall tubing. A third kind is made of double-walled flexible tubing that regulates the drip rate and adjusts to a wider range of water pressure. Drip emitters allow you to place the water flow exactly where you want it.

Safety Tip: If the system you buy does not contain an anti-siphoning device, be sure to get one. This inexpensive item prevents garden water from backing into your home water supply, fouling the taste and possibly introducing algae and bacteria.

Maintaining an Irrigation System

If you install a new irrigation system, learn everything possible about its proper operation. For future reference, keep an as-built drawing of the system that shows the layout of the lines and the location of each of the heads and valves. Every spring and fall, check its physical condition zone-by-zone. Make sure the heads are not too low in the ground and not cockeyed, damaged or dirty. Add extenders to your shrub heads when your plants have grown significantly. Watch for mist over the sprinkler head, which indicates excessive water pressure. Make sure all of the valves open and close properly and are not clogged with dirt. Check for line breaks caused by construction or freezes. Run a test of the controller to be sure each station actually runs the length of time for which it is set. Program the system for maximum efficiency. Consider retrofitting old systems with drip lines and "micro sprinkler" heads to avoid overwatering.

Summary of Water Conservation Practices
1. **Develop a Good Design Plan**
   - Appreciate a less manicured, more natural aesthetic.
   - Replace unused portions of lawns with ground covers and wildflowers.
   - Replace lawn with more decks and terraces.
   - Add more trees.
   - Create wind barriers.
   - Group plants with similar water needs.
   - Use mulch or rock as a design feature for color and texture.
   - Control all rainwater falling on the site by carefully grading the slopes.
2. **Amend the Soil**
   - Add organic matter to maximize its water-holding capacity.
   - Cultivate to improve penetration and aeration.
   - Add polymer wetting agents to the soil in container plantings.
3. **Pick the Right Plants**
   - Select the least water-demanding turf grass available for your region.
   - Consider slope, exposure and soil type in your choice of plants.
   - Prefer drought-tolerant species to more thirsty plants.
4. **Plant Correctly**
   - Plant in early spring or mid-fall to take advantage of normal rainy seasons.
   - Make a soil ring around newly planted trees and shrubs.
5. **Mulch, Mulch, Mulch**
6. **Water Efficiently**
   - Water only when the top four inches are dry; use a soil probe.
   - Establish watering priorities.
   - Irrigate with the lowest possible volume to minimize runoff.
   - Water in early morning to minimize evaporation.
   - Collect water in covered storage tanks connected to downspouts.
   - Convert to drip irrigation wherever possible.
7. **Maintain the Garden**
   - Aerate the lawn
   - Raise the height of the lawn mower.
   - Judiciously prune trees and shrubs to reduce transpiration.
   - Fertilize only to keep plants healthy, not to encourage rapid growth.
   - Minimize competition for water by removing weeds immediately.

The Proper Way to Prune

Pruning is both an art and a science. Unfortunately, few people know how to do it correctly. A drive through any older neighborhood will provide examples of trees topped and shrubs sheared into balls and boxes and mangled beyond recognition. It makes me heartsick to see what *Southern Living* calls "crepe murder." I cannot imagine whose bad advice made people think they should cut crepe myrtles back to the nubbins every year? Such pruning not only leaves crepe myrtles ugly beyond redemption, but also it makes them more prone to disease.

I do all of my own garden pruning, unless the pruning requires a tall ladder. Even then, I will not let anyone (including my sweet husband) prune anything at our house unless I'm standing there to approve every cut that is made. In fact, I've warned the mowing crew that they will be fired if they ever come on the property with pruning shears or clippers in hand! *The Southern Living Garden Book* explains (with graphic, comprehensible illustrations) the basics of proper pruning. It's a good place to start learning the terminology and accepted techniques.

MINIMIZE PRUNING BY DESIGN

When designing a new landscape plan, I promise my clients they'll never have to do much pruning beyond occasional, judicious cuts to thin plants, remove unsafe or unattractive growth and repair damage. How can I make such a promise? By knowing the ultimate size of each plant and choosing the right variety for each situation!

For example, I use dwarf plants beneath windows, select small trees for small gardens, use low-growing plants at the front of a bed and graduate plant heights upward toward the back. I allow just enough space between the plants so that they'll ultimately grow together, but not crowd one another. And, I rarely design clipped hedges except when formal architecture demands a formal boxwood edging as a design element. (I often substitute native dwarf yaupon for the boxwood.) Anything more complicated than an occasional clipped edging is simply too labor-intensive for today's lifestyle. Besides, I basically prefer a loose, natural look for most landscapes.

Moneysaving Tip: The least expensive pruning is no pruning at all.

PRUNING TO REDEEM A PLANT

Before redesigning the planting plan for an older garden, I decide which plants can be salvaged and which should be removed. Hopelessly overgrown shrubs cannot simply be cut in half, and shrubs that have been pruned incorrectly for years will probably never become attractive again. It's better to take them out and start over, choosing a plant that will not grow too large for its location. I did manage to redeem a pair of large yaupon trees that flank a client's entry walk in Dallas. They had been pruned by her maintenance company into "lollipops." By removing some of the interior branches to open up the canopy and allowing the outer branches to grow naturally, we returned them to handsome trees.

Some large old shrubs can be pruned into attractive small trees. If the plant has multiple stems, select a few heavy upright branches to serve as trunks and cut the rest to the ground. Then start at the bottom, exposing each trunk carefully by cutting off lower branches, making the cuts close to the trunk. Stand back and look, then continue limbing-up the lower branches until the overall shape is pleasing. To "finish" the landscape, plant a ground cover under the tree.

Moneysaving Tip: Selective pruning can be used to salvage an overgrown plant you might be tempted to remove.

RENEWAL PRUNING

Another way to rejuvenate plants in an overgrown landscape is to cut the entire plant to the ground. This method works well on fountain shaped shrubs that tend to put on all their growth at the top. I've been known to cut leggy old specimens of oleander, abelia, nandina and spiraea all the way to the ground, allowing the entire plant to regenerate from the roots. Thereafter, the homeowner is instructed to remove a third of the growth each year, cutting out the oldest, woodiest canes. Such pruning forces plants to continually put out new growth from the bottom, keeping the plants fuller and more naturally shaped.

Thinning a tree or large shrub is acceptable if it is to provide good air circulation, let more light through the canopy or promote evenly spaced branching patterns. Sometimes it becomes necessary to prune to avoid excess dampness around the house foundation or to improve the tree's chance of survival in a time of extreme drought since removing excess foliage reduces water consumption. It's also appropriate to remove rubbing and crossing branches, suckers, weak branches and any broken or diseased limbs. In the latter case, always cut back to healthy wood and disinfect the tool with a solution made of one cup of bleach in a gallon of water before making the next cut.

Moneysaving Tip: You can add years of life to your tree or shrub with good pruning practices.

PRUNING TECHNIQUES

The best pruning removes branches back to the origin of growth. Make the cut almost flush with the branch from which it sprang, cutting just outside the ring that separates the branch from the trunk (called the branch collar). If you're removing a large branch, three cuts are needed to ensure that the bark won't tear. The first cut should be from the bottom, just beyond the place where the final cut will be made. The second should be made from the top to remove the branch. The third and final cut is made to remove the stump just beyond the branch collar.

To head-back growth, make the pruning cut so that the outermost bud left on the branch is pointing in the direction you want the branch to grow. Always cut quickly and cleanly. It's better to perform small annual cuts than to wait until a plant is out of hand and take a chance on hopelessly ruining its shape.

Timing is a critical factor in pruning. Some plants must be pruned during dormancy; others should not be pruned until after flowering. Some plants may be susceptible to fungus if they are pruned during the rainy season. If you are unsure, check with a professional arborist, qualified nurseryman or extension agent before beginning a pruning project.

Most people don't have the proper tools and ladders to safely prune large trees. If a tree must be removed, the International Society of Arboriculture recommends that you negotiate a written contract that specifies how the tree is to be removed, where the wood will be taken and who is liable in case of damage.

Safety Tip: A professional arborist may not only prolong the life of your trees, but also save you from a stay in the hospital.

Never top a tree. Instead of topping, thin the tree to a network of even, regularly spaced branches. If you must reduce the height of a tree, do it over a period of time. There is some disagreement about painting pruning cuts/wounds on trees. I don't ordinarily advocate it, but if there is any possibility of oak wilt in your area, the immediate use of wound paint when pruning both the branches and roots of oak trees is definitely recommended.

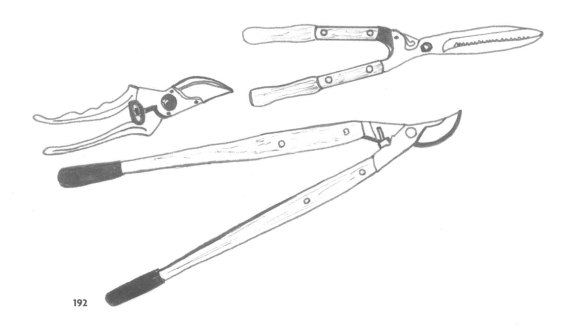

Live oaks and members of the red oak family (including Shumard oaks, Spanish oaks, water oaks and black jack oaks) are subject to oak wilt in some 60 counties in Texas. This fungal disease, which occurs mainly between Dallas/Ft. Worth and San Antonio has devastated vast areas of the Hill Country. Over the past 30 years, researchers, foresters and Extension workers at Texas A&M University have been working to eliminate the problem. Drs. Jerral Johnson and David Appel developed an *Eight-Step Program to Oak Wilt Management* that includes early detection, sanitation, creating buffer zones and replanting oak wilt-resistant species.

Dr. Appel recommends, "All wounding of oaks (including pruning) should be avoided from February through June. This is the time of year when fungal mats are formed and attractive to insects, which could vector the oak wilt spores to fresh wounds. The least hazardous periods for pruning are during the coldest days in midwinter and extended hot periods in mid- to late-summer. Regardless of season, all pruning cuts greater than ½ inch, including freshly cut stumps and damaged surface roots, should be treated immediately with a wound paint."

A second way oak wilt spreads is underground, via interconnecting root systems. So, in areas where oak wilt is rampant, many homeowners have had root graft barriers installed to further protect their trees. This is an expensive project, and it must be done by a trained professional. Your local Extension Service or Urban Forestry Office can help you find a qualified contractor.

Dead or unhealthy trees are a liability. It's probably time to consult a professional arborist if (1) the tree is leaning, (2) there's evidence of root rot and/or the trunk has hollows or deep open cracks, (3) there has been improper pruning in the past, or (4) there has been storm damage or construction injury. He or she is the person most qualified to determine if the tree can be saved. Should the tree pose a danger to a house, power lines, cars or people, let it go and plant a replacement.

Moneysaving Tip: Remove a dead or damaged tree *before* it can do damage.

Finding the Best Tools

A beginning gardener need invest in only a few basic tools. The five I use most are a medium-width pointed shovel, a spading fork, weeding hoe, garden rake and trowel. Over the years I've also acquired a flat shovel, leaf rake, edging tool and assorted other devices that promised to make gardening easier. For pruning, I have top-quality hand shears, loppers, pruning saw and a pole saw.

The more you use a tool, the better it should be. I look for tools that will last a lifetime. Several garden center managers told us that they've quit stocking garden tools because they cannot compete with the large home improvement stores. This is a pity. In their choice of tools, beginning gardeners need the kind of expert advice that's only available from experienced nursery personnel.

Serious gardeners appreciate the difference between an English spading fork that sells for $60 and the Taiwanese-made fork you'll find selling for $15 at the discount stores. The former is made in one piece of solid forged steel. Its tines will not rust or break, and it will penetrate clay soil with ease. For my money, it's worth seeking out the best and paying the difference.

Perhaps it's just my advancing age, but it seems to me that the biggest improvement in tools in the last ten years has been in new lines of ergonomically engineered shovels, rakes and hoes. Gracefully curved and long-handled, the tools are designed to reduce bending and stooping. Most are made with extra-long cushioned foam grips to lessen hand fatigue. Hand tools have also been drastically improved. A Google search for ergonomic garden tools today yielded 18,000 citations. I don't have time to pursue them all, but I was attracted like a deer to a veggie garden by a Radius Garden® trowel I bought recently at my local Ace Hardware. I've lost or discarded a few dozen trowels over the years, but this one is a keeper!

Moneysaving Tip: High-quality tools are the most economical in the long run, and the most satisfying to use.

The May 2008 issue of *Consumer Reports* had a section on lawn care that rates lawn mowers and trimmers. You'll find the lowest prices on mowers and power tools at the big hardware chains and home improvement centers, but if you're not the "fix-it" type, don't base your buying decision on price alone. When you shop at an independent dealer for lawn mowers and other mechanical garden tools, you're also buying service. Get to know the owner and ask a lot of questions before you invest in garden equipment.

Because I have minimal storage space, I rent the large tools I use only occasionally. There are a number of companies that offer such items as aerators, chippers, sod cutters and tillers listed in the yellow pages under "Rental."

Moneysaving Tip: Split the cost of rental tools with a neighbor.

Fine tools are expensive to replace, and sharp, clean tools make gardening easier. Clean off the soil and/or sap after each use and store your tools in a dry place. Periodically rub linseed oil on wooden handles and sharpen the blades of spades, hoes and pruning tools.

Moneysaving Tip: Take good care of your tools.

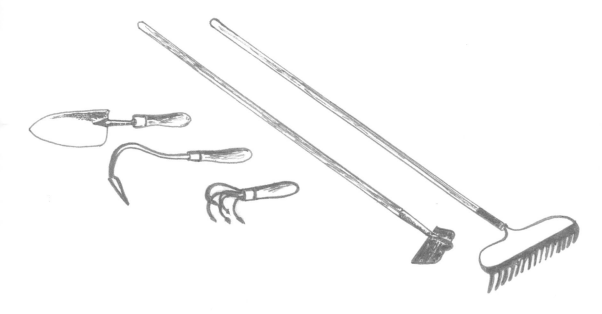

Dressing for the Sport

Now that health and fitness gurus have finally admitted that gardening is good exercise, it's time we gardeners get serious about our gear. Every well-dressed gardener will need gloves, hat and garden boots. If you are really into making a fashion statement, you'll have elbow-high goatskin gloves and organically grown cotton shirts that say "Save the Earth." But, if you are like me, you've always done your gardening in ratty jeans and paint-spattered T-shirts. Lately, I've noticed that my jeans are uncomfortable (not enough room to bend and squat). My cloth gloves have developed holes, I've ruined yet another pair of $60 athletic shoes, and I've misplaced my straw hat.

This year, I've vowed to get some decent garden apparel. My husband gave me knee-high rubber boots for mucking around in the winter, and for warm weather gardening, I'm planning to get plastic garden clogs. I'm also going to start the season with two new straw hats, a pair of goatskin gloves, kneepads, shatterproof sunglasses and sunscreen, and an apron that holds tools and seed packets!

Online Resources for Garden Maintenance in Texas

Disease Testing

Texas Plant Disease Diagnostic Laboratory
Texas A&M University, Department of Plant Disease
College Station, Texas 77843
979.845.8282
http://plantpathology.tamu.edu/extension/tpddl.asp

This lab offers soil testing for nematodes and plant diagnosis of fungal, bacterial and viral diseases. There are very specific instructions for gathering and submitting samples, which you can access off the web or by writing to the lab. The lab routinely works with County Extension Agents and specialists, homeowners, farmers, arborists and landscape contractors to provide recommendations for effective plant disease management. See the website for services, fees and forms.

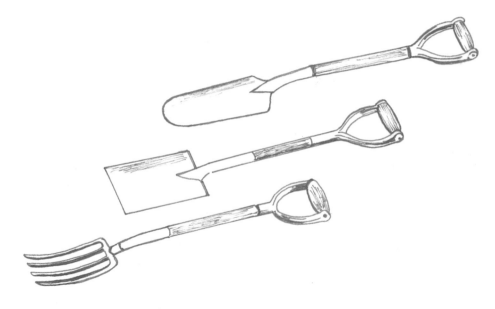

Pest Management Products

Biofac Crop Care, Inc.
P.O. Box 87
Mathis, Texas 78368
800.233.4914
www.biofac.com

This company's beneficial insects come in a *BioPac*™ kit for $26.95 that contains ladybugs, trichogrammas, lacewings and praying mantis. The owner, M. A. Maedgen, Jr., suggests serial releases throughout the year because many insects attack only at a certain stage in a pest life cycle. "These friendly critters are harmless to people, pets, wildlife, etc. Pesticides inoculate bad bugs over time, which make them immune to poisons in the plants they eat. Beneficial insects, which previously controlled these pests, are wiped out by the same poisons since they don't eat the plants and are not vaccinated. These poisons create a 'toxic mess' of pest problems in ever-growing proportions. It's fun and interesting for future science buffs and elegant in its simplicity and health benefits," he says. One kit will cover up to a quarter-acre.

Easy Gardener
3022 Franklin Avenue
Waco, Texas 76710
254.753.5353 or 800.327.9462
www.easygardener.com

This Texas-based company makes a wide variety of products designed for, well, making gardening easier! On its website, you'll find a good vinyl fencing material for keeping deer out of the garden, vinyl hardware cloth, pond netting, a weed-block material made from recycled bottles, tree stakes, sun screening fabrics and a host of other helpful products. Besides this company's well-known Jobe's Tree Spikes®, there are now organic fertilizer spikes for trees, vegetables, container and bedding plants, and roses and flowering shrubs. These products are sold exclusively through garden centers and hardware stores. You can call the company to find a nearby dealer.

Green Light Co.
P.O. Box 17985
San Antonio, Texas 78217-0985
210.494.3481
www.greenlightco.com

Founded in 1947, this Texas-based company manufactures a broad range of products for the lawn and garden. Its "SafetyPlus" packaging is designed to prevent leaks, odors or accidental ingestion by children, which is a good thing because the majority of its products are toxic. But like many companies of its kind, it is embracing the organic approach. Among the products now in the company's line are Spinosad® (step one of the Texas Two Step fire ant control), Organic Rose & Flower Spray, Organic Spot Weeder and Biorganic® products for lawn care and pest control. The company does not sell directly to the public, but its products are available in garden centers and nurseries throughout the state.

Indeco Products, Inc.
P.O. Box 865
San Marcos, Texas 78667
888.246.3326 or 512.396.5814
www.indecoproducts.com

Covering plants with Grow-web is an excellent way to protect seedlings from birds and varmints and to protect vegetable crops from leaf-eating caterpillars and virus-carrying thrips and aphids. TAMU has recommended this product as part of its Earth Kind program. It can be used as a row cover on seedlings or around cages. Unlike plastic covers, the translucent, fabric-like material of Gro-web allows the plant to remain covered throughout the growing season. (It does need to be firmly anchored into the ground.) The product can be found in some nurseries or ordered directly from the manufacturer by e-mail (gailsprings@indecoproducts.com).

Kunafin Trichogramma
Route 1, Box 39
Quemado, Texas 78877
800.832.1113
www.kunafin.com

Frank and Adele Junfin mass-rear tiny wasps (*Trichogramma spp.*), which arrive at your home packaged in breathable pouches, ready to rid your orchard or garden of such undesirables as pecan casebearers and 250 other kinds of moth eggs. The company also supplies fly parasites and lacewings. "We believe in an all-around beneficial program custom-built for your specific needs. Beneficial insects alone are not the complete answer to pest insect control; however, it's a most effective tool when used in association with other natural methods. Any sound pest management program requires continuous attention to detail and good professional advice."

Pied Piper Traps
445 Garner Adell Road
Weatherford, Texas 76086
800.287.2748
www.piedpipertraps.com

After 24 years in the business, this company can provide a trap to catch everything from a rat to a mountain lion! The brochure tells you how to bait and set the traps (skunks like peanut butter, while armadillos prefer carrots and potatoes), as well as how to handle the critter afterwards (very carefully). There's even a trap designed for turtles and another for catching catfish. There are traps in many different styles and sizes, plus carrying cages, rabbit cages, hay racks and saddle racks available from these folks. Why didn't I know about this company when a family of armadillos destroyed my lawn?

Voluntary Purchasing Groups, Inc.
P.O. Box 460
Bonham, Texas 75418
903.583.5501
www.fertilome.com

Begun in 1957 as a co-op (hence the odd name), this Texas-based company markets gardening products through retail stores throughout the country. It holds trademarks on many familiar chemical products, including ferti·lome® and Hi-Yield®. The company's Natural Guard® line is promoted to help gardeners work with nature. Among other products, it offers copper soap to be used as a fungicide, Crawling Insect Control with diatomaceous earth, Plant and Pet Insect Spray and Neem Py, which combines neem oil and pyrethrins. The catalog for Natural Guard® is online, and you can enter your zip code for the name of a local dealer.

Tools and Environmentally Friendly Products

Clean Air Gardening
2266 Monitor Street
Dallas, Texas 75207
214.819.9500
www.cleanairgardening.com

"Here at Clean Air Gardening, we don't just sell eco-friendly stuff, we live eco-friendly stuff!" said Lars Hundley when we called. "Clean Air Gardening might never have come into existence if I hadn't been too cheap and environmentally conscious to buy a gasoline-powered lawnmower." The website and online catalog offer a wealth of ideas and products. Besides the push-reel lawn mower, which he insists his 5'2" wife can handle, there are electric trimmers and blowers and other lawn care tools. There are rain barrels and an incredible range of composters from ceramic countertop pails for kitchen waste to sophisticated 71-gallon tumblers. The site also features outdoor furniture and accessories, gifts for serious gardeners and an assortment of interesting eco-friendly gifts and items for the home.

Marshall Grain Company
2224 East Lancaster
Fort Worth, Texas 76103
800.361.1286 or 817.536.5653
www.marshallgrain.com

Billing itself as "nature's merchant," Marshall Grain has been serving Texas farmers and gardeners since 1946. Its 21st-century online catalog offers 200 to 300 natural gardening products, including liquid and dry fertilizers and soil conditioners, composts, mulches, potting soils, natural herbicides and insecticides and insect traps. You'll also find a wide array of garden tools, weathervanes, rain gauges, rain barrels, decorative garden accessories, seeds (including heirloom flower varieties), bat and bird houses, organic pet products and helpful garden books. "We turn away products the company is not sure about. People come from all over the DFW Metroplex to the retail store, and we hope that folks from other parts of the state will order from us," says owner Jim Connelly. The website updates availability every night. When we looked, the company had a fresh supply of Turffalo brand turfgrass varieties and grass plugging tools to install it.

Organigro
206 Harrington Road
Waxahachie, Texas 75165
972.938.0929
www.organigro.net

In business since 2004, this company's mission is to provide the best organic selection for home, garden, farm and ranch at an affordable price. It's a small, locally owned business with its warehouse located on Helen and Dewan Hinsley's family farm. Ellis County residents are encouraged to come and browse

(LISTING CONTINUED ON THE NEXT PAGE)

(CONTINUED)

(Wed-Sat 10-6 and Sun noon-6). Organigro ships its wares by FedEx to gardeners in the four corners of the state and beyond. There is real depth in their organic soil amendments and pest control products, and they stock lots of other gardening essentials from books to beneficial organisms. They have good wild bird supplies and natural home products, as well. If you want something special that they don't have, they'll try to find it for you.

Spray-N-Grow, Inc.
P.O. Box 2137
Rockport, Texas 78381
800.323.2363
www.spray-n-grow.com

This company's online catalog is quite extensive. It features a number of labor-saving gardening tools and gadgets, including plant stakes, a moisture, light and pH meter, insect attractants, organic mosquito repellants, a variety of sprayers, seed starting trays, grow lights and water timers. It also markets products developed by company owner/chemist Bill Muskopf: micro-nutrient rich Spray-N-Grow, Coco-Wet (a coconut oil-based wetting agent which helps foliar applications adhere to leaves) and Bill's Perfect Fertilizer. All of the soil and plant products are organic.

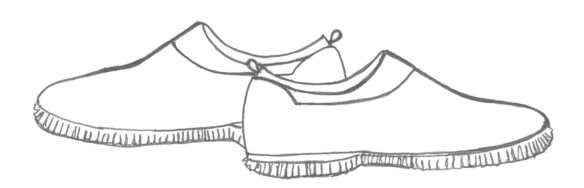

Index

Notes

Notes